Hitler's Face

MATERIAL TEXTS

Series Editors

Roger Chartier   Anthony Grafton
Joan DeJean   Janice Radway
Joseph Farrell   Peter Stallybrass

A complete list of books in the series is available from the publisher.

Hitler's Face

The Biography of an Image

CLAUDIA SCHMÖLDERS

Translated by Adrian Daub

PENN

University of Pennsylvania Press

Philadelphia

Publication of this volume was supported by a grant from the Goethe-Institut.

Originally published as *Hitlers Gesicht: eine physiognomische Biographie* by Verlag C. H. Beck oHG, Munich

10   9   8   7   6   5   4   3   2   1

Published by
University of Pennsylvania Press
Philadelphia, Pennsylvania 19104-4112

Library of Congress Cataloging-in-Publication Data

Schmölders, Claudia.
   [Hitlers Gesicht. English]
   Hitler's face : the biography of an image / Claudia Schmölders ; translated by Adrian Daub.
      p.   cm. — (Material texts)
   Includes bibliographical references and index.
   ISBN-13: 978-0-8122-3902-7 (alk. paper)
   ISBN-10: 0-8122-3902-4 (alk. paper)
   1. Physiognomy—Germany—History.   2. Hitler, Adolf,
1889–1945—Portraits.   I. Title.   II. Series.
DD247.H5S29313   2006
943.086′092—dc22   2005042323

Contents

Introduction

In 1973, Walter Kempowski published the results of a limited survey conducted on about two hundred West German citizens: "Did you ever see Hitler?" As might be expected, the responses were mixed. Some still recalled the excitement, some the hatred, some also the complete apathy with which they had perceived Hitler. In many cases, the encounter was a childhood memory, not critical as such, but rather part of recollections of ritual splendor, of propagandistic clamor. Very few responses made immediate reference to Hitler's physical appearance. Those older than thirty-five at the time of the survey seemed to react to it as a physical imposition: "He had really big, deep blue eyes, eyes like Frederick the Great must have had," some observed: Another wrote, "The women turned out the whites of their eyes and fell down like wet rags. They lay there like slaughtered calves, sighing heavily. Joy and fulfillment." Yet another person wrote, "I was shaken in a negative way. I had never seen such a characterless face. I still don't understand it. . . . Sometimes I think that it was a void that other people filled up."

Should one even remember Hitler's physical appearance? A recent wave of movies seems to suggest that there is indeed demand for this. The great biographies of the last decades—from Joachim Fest's to Ian Kershaw's—appeared in German without the dictator's picture on the dust jacket; that taboo seems to have been broken, not least by U.S. motion pictures. Hitler's face is once again used in everyday politics: be it as a bugbear, be it as a caricature, the latter being actually more frequent. Fest's criticism of these new tendencies applies much more to visual recall than to recent biographies: they take insufficient account of the evil in this figure, ultimately underestimating it. But can the evil in Hitler actually be visualized?* Is there such a recognizable "face of evil"—if not of *the* evildoer, then at least of *this* evildoer? Hitler's hate-

*Joachim Fest has also guided the development of the recent movie *Downfall.* In it, Bruno Ganz plays Hitler as a wreck, as a deranged dictator haunting a spectral underworld with the inferno of the last days of the war far above. What does his face communicate to us other than derangement? Neither "good" nor "evil," even if Bruno Ganz is still much too good looking when compared to the pictures of the real dictator, with his narrow mouth and, toward the end of his life, his dead and bloated eyes. C.S. [Notes that are new to this English edition appear as footnotes.]

filled contemporaries seemed to believe there was. They spoke of his "excremental visage," of the "brute mask," of the "mask of the Gorgon," of a "panoptic basilisk gaze," and finally of the empty "nothingness."

Today, at a time when not only entertainment, but above all science, are obsessed with visuality, we would have to agree with such formulations. They arrest evil in obviousness. Once again, scientific studies purport to demonstrate that one quarter of a second of visual exposure [*Anschauung*] is sufficient for the apprehension of a person's character. However, we don't know only of hate-filled descriptions of Hitler's face, but also, much to the contrary, of downright entranced ones. There is a symbolic trap here. If Hitler's face were, in accordance with the above testimonials, in fact an index of the evil in Hitler's heart, what would we say was shown by the brutal abjection of the Jewish face in film, photography, and caricature from 1918 to 1945? Would we not run the risk of sanctioning that visual demonization? Recent movies and television series about "Hitler's willing executioners" skirt that trap by a set of devices. Usually, they borrow from the toolkit of television news: eyewitness interviews supplement historic depictions of the actors and the places of action, which are in turn commented on by a narrator. No biography could deliver such immediate object lessons of suffering and catastrophe.

The "silent image" that biography mostly relies on, that is, photography, seems by contrast completely detached, almost unobtrusive, however dramatic its content. The recent exhibition on the Wehrmacht* has once again shown that in order to be documents, "silent images" depend on individual translation by their consumer. The consumer has to learn and know how the pictures came about, what their context is, how they were used. Without language, the picture is incomprehensible. For example, none of the known photos of Hitler shows him in any kind of indicative context, say, next to a corpse or in a concentration camp, or in the commission of an act of sadism. The pictures do not as much as show him rifle in hand, only sometimes with a dog whip or, over and over, of course as public speaker in frenetic pose. Contemporary caricatures rather than these photographs speak directly to the calamitous thoughts, projects, and actions of this man. All references to these by

*This exhibition opened in 1995 under the name "War of Annihilation: Crimes of the Wehrmacht," and was reissued in 2001 as "Crimes of the Wehrmacht: The Dimensions of the War of Annihilation, 1941–1944," but became known simply as the "Wehrmacht Exhibition." Put together by the Hamburg Institute for Social Research, it disposed of the persistent myth that the German army had been largely uninvolved in, and indeed largely ignorant of, the atrocities committed during World War II. It became a hot-button issue in the late 1990s in a debate ostensibly about matters of historical accuracy. Trans.

Hitler's photobiographers and interpreters are projection; virtually every picture adduced to prove beyond a doubt Hitler's "schizophrenia" or "lupine nature" can, without knowledge of the relevant historical facts, be interpreted entirely differently. No face bears more eloquent witness to the desire for and the impotence of physiognomic interpretation than this face, in which half a nation between 1919 and 1938 wanted to recognize pure, undiluted futurity, among them the most educated Germans. "How could someone so uneducated rule Germany?" the philosopher Jaspers asked Heidegger in 1933. "Education is unimportant; just look at his marvelous hands," Heidegger reportedly replied.

* * *

This emphasis on visuality marks the point of departure for the present investigation. Instead of using elements of visuality as illustrations, this book reverses the relations of biography by making visuality the starting point. It tells the story of Hitler from his march on Munich to his end in Berlin from the perspective of the contemporary, who confronted Hitler as living spectacle before having any real idea of the history unfolding before his or her eyes; it tells the story from the viewpoint of the "spellbound" spectator, who venerated Hitler in his photographic, filmic, later even painterly mise-en-scènes as a national icon [*Inbild*]; finally, this book tells the story from the perspective of the parascience that dominated the theory of bodily cognition in Germany between 1918 and 1945: physiognomy. Physiognomic biography is always also the biography of physiognomy. Our subject will be the theoretical conditions of physical perception, also the acoustic kind, which set in motion a history of fascination, which in turn eventually gave way to a history of hatred. The preconditions for this undertaking are auspicious. After all, no epoch devoted itself so fully to questions of physical appearance and effect as did the period between 1918 and 1945; no epoch, lacking orientation, was so obsessed with its own mirror image. And no dictator thrust himself upon his voters with the sheer corporeality of Hitler, with his increasingly virtuoso visual propaganda, with his voice, with his stare eye to eye. "From the first moment on his eyes fascinated me. They were clear and big, calm and confidently fixed on me. But his gaze did not come from his eyeball, it came from much further in, I thought perhaps from infinity. One couldn't read those eyes. But they spoke, they wanted to speak. They didn't ask, they talked." Thus comments Otto Wagener, one of many who succumbed to Hitler's gaze.

As is well known, the shift in politics to immediate corporeality, inaugurated by the declaration of war of August 1 and followed by the most dire consequences, was pushed ahead rabidly by the ideologues of *Volk* in the Weimar Republic. Disagreements during gatherings were resolved through brawls, personal thugs and paramilitary units (SA) were created, and enemies were murdered without much thought. Beside this crude corporeality, with which Hitler used to style himself as "a man of action not of ink," there was a more refined strand of corporeality, which itself began to sublimate physical cognition philosophically. It provided the intellectual backdrop for the technological revolution of the media, photography, film, pictorials, and radio. Phenomenology and the theory of forms, profound acoustics, but in particular what Peter Sloterdijk has called "physiognomy as weltanschauung" accompanied Hitler's rise and the increasing sophistication of his propaganda. As such, the interpreters of this persuasion are as fitting an example as there will ever be for what Hitler biographer Ian Kershaw has termed German society's "working toward the Führer." Since the eighteenth century there prevailed in Germany a tradition of reading physiques, in science and in art, in literature and in politics—a tradition that existed so emphatically only in Germany. Around the same time that Hitler came to Munich, this tradition was modernized for the beginning of the "short century" (as Eric Hobsbawm has called it): as the physiognomic gaze on the "great man" and the "German *Volk*" with the deranged goal of understanding these two as one and the same.

Looked at from this angle, Hitler's undeniable charisma appears in a new light. Moreover, however, so do anti-Semitic hermeneutics of the physique. Although the racial theories of the nineteenth century had done painstaking spadework, although Nazi biology and propaganda conditioned the population ceaselessly, the hateful contemplation of the Jewish physiognomy in the press and on postcards, in films, and on posters between 1922 and 1945 took its format from the contemplation of the idealized *German* face in all its various aspects. It was the fanatical devotion engendered here that gave the hateful glance on the Semitic "counter-type" (Erich Jaensch) its edge. Thus the latter cannot be thought without the former. Nonetheless research has in recent years focused on the ostracism of the Jewish face rather than on the senseless adulation of the German face—or Hitler's face, for that matter, certainly less hateful [*hässlich*] than deserving hate [*hassenswert*]. Both constructions, however, have their proper places in the canon of our memory.

Chapter 1

Models 1913–1918

Of Merit and Ancestral Pride: The Project of a National Portrait Gallery

Adolf Hitler left Vienna on May 25, 1913 in order to relocate to Munich.[1] He had just received his inheritance from his father (819 crowns, 98 hellers), and thus managed a change of wardrobe, landed a job with master tailor Popp, and moved into a room at Schleißheimer Strasse 34. Hitler came with his friend Rudolf Häusler in tow. Four years Hitler's junior, Häusler was a druggist glad to be educated by Hitler when he was not in too doctrinaire a mode. The friends' beginning in Munich failed to go off without a hitch, however; both ran out of money. Hitler had to paint postcards and have Häusler sell them, just like in Vienna. But while doing so, Hitler read voraciously and lectured day and night. It is probably in this year that he read Bernhard Kellermann's new novel *Der Tunnel* [The Tunnel], in which he later recalled having discovered the role model of the popular speaker for himself. Young Häusler's life soon became intolerable as the sole audience member of Hitler's all-night monologues. Häusler moved out. In 1914, Hitler was discovered by the Austrian authorities in Munich and called in for a draft physical in Linz; he was found unfit for service. On August 3, he volunteered for the German army instead, "ready at any time to die for my (!) people and for the Empire that embodied it."[2]

One of the earliest photos we have of Hitler, to be exact the third one after the one baby picture and the one class picture of him that are known, shows him on the Odeonsplatz in Munich in the crowds gathered on August 1, 1914 for the reading of the declaration of war. The photo is by Heinrich Hoffmann, later Hitler's "personal photographer" and so-called *Reichsbildberichterstatter* (visual reporter of the reich), according to whom the picture became in time "one of the most popular" images of Hitler. [Fig. 1].[3] The photos actually from the war were taken at Fournes (April 1915); one shows Hitler with two dispatch runners, Schmidt and Bachmann, and his dog Foxl. A second picture, dated May of 1916 from the same region, has him seated at the very right edge

Figure 1. The first photograph of Hitler by Heinrich Hoffmann, later his "court photographer," was taken in August of 1914 on the occasion of the declaration of war. It shows Hitler in the enraptured crowd on Munich's Odeonsplatz. The only thing we can read in his face is this excitement.

of a throng of soldiers, wearing a serious expression, his mustache untrimmed. Lastly, we have the relatively famous picture from the field hospital in Pasewalk, where Hitler was being treated for mustard gas poisoning in 1918 and where he received the news of Germany's ignominious defeat, which triggered his resolution "to become a politician" [Fig. 2]. Other photos from the same time are either useless from a technical standpoint or depict very similar scenes.

Nothing about this face strikes the observer as in any way especially unpleasant or remarkably beautiful. From the ruddy-cheeked ten-year-old with jug ears, to the already skinny adolescent from the student magazine, to the even more emaciated lance corporal with dark eyes, nothing in these pictures points to memorable actions, special intelligence, or drastic physical misfortune. According to his passport, his eye color is blue; he first wears the notorious mustache in the August 1, 1914 picture. His boyhood friend August Kubizek describes him as slight, pale,

ICH ABER BESCHLOSS,
POLITIKER ZU WERDEN

Figure 2. Hitler as a soldier, and the honorary bust by Ferdinand Liebermann, later erected at Pasewalk, the field hospital in which Hitler witnessed Germany's defeat. The tender gesture with which he here puts his arm around another adult is not found in any other known pictures of him. Perhaps it owes its existence to the photographer's instructions.

and serious, always correctly attired and behaved. Kubizek knows too how Hitler's face can liven up in the heat of speech, which Häusler later learned in Munich. But neither of them knows what audience this speaker's face will have in the coming years and what that audience will read in it.

In 1913, the year Hitler came to Munich, Ludwig Justi, general director of the national gallery in Berlin, handed the German emperor a small pamphlet entitled "Mission and Scale of the German Collection of Paintings," written as a call for a national portrait gallery modeled on the one in England. Ever since the London National Portrait Gallery opened its doors in 1856, but certainly since the foundation of the Second Empire, the collection of busts of outstanding German men housed in the "Valhalla" near Regensburg since 1842 [Fig. 3] had been deemed insufficient by the German government, consisting as it did of merely one hundred heads. In 1872, the emperor called on his minister of culture to create a portrait gallery, "in order to keep great men fresh in the memory of this nation";[4] the crown prince had advocated it since 1878. Nonetheless it was not until 1913 that the emperor could attend the inauguration of the collection, housed in nine rooms of Schinkel's Bauakademie building. Its intellectual ground was of course transformed after 1918 by the war. The gallery reopened in 1929, featuring a revised canon of Germans worthy of memorialization, this time in the spirit of democracy and thus much heavier on the men of the arts and sciences than on military heroes. In general, new admissions were to be administered along the guidelines of the order Pour le mérite.

What is perhaps more interesting than the gallery's institutional history is Justi's original justification for the project in 1913. Following the "old principles of portrait collecting," he claimed, a traditional distinction was made between "series of images inspired by ancestral pride" and "series of images inspired by merit." Especially the latter, Justi claimed, had to be followed up on in the new gallery in the interest of the bourgeoisie. The new gallery had to differ in two ways from traditional practice: Neither could it erect gigantic monuments in the style of the nineteenth century, such as for Bismarck, on which no face was discernible, nor should it take the shape of a mere agglomeration of portraits made possible by the (then) new media, as had been done so far. According to Justi, owing to the revolution in graphic technology, his time faced a "veritable deluge of photographic portraiture" without actually having a "public national picture gallery of appropriate significance."[5] It was now important to bring together "ancestral pride" and "honoring merit," that is to say, to bring together the great family galleries of the princely houses of Germany on the one hand with the portraits

Figure 3. The pantheon of model Germans, the so-called Valhalla, built by Leo von Klenze, opened its doors in 1842. It got its painted counterpart in 1913 in the shape of the National Portrait Collection, housed in the Berlin Bauakademie. Among the reasons the then director of the national galleries, Ludwig Justi, gave for the project was the observation that the highly placed sculptures of the Valhalla prohibited direct gazing upon the faces.

of so-called "great Germans" on the other. This was to be accomplished in a collection expressedly of paintings.

It is obvious that banishing the specter of ever more present photography was one of Justi's main motivations, even though its triumphal march since the mid nineteenth century was in fact unstoppable. Not only could everybody soon let themselves be portrayed, but picture books, family albums, and photo collections, many small portrait galleries in book form, gained widespread acceptance.[6] Clearly, before the war, Justi looked upon this development with horror. The rise of the bourgeoisie, the development of lithography and photography, he claimed, had led to a flood of portrait collections, but the largest of these were in possession of the police and the print media. "Just as the noble disposition of the ancien régime relates to the sober calculus of the present moment, thusly relates the old princely gallery of honor to the modern state's delinquent album."[7]

But ultimately it wasn't the sober "present moment" that saw the realization of the project. Instead, it was the nationalist fervor of the year before World War I, which Hitler too imbibed in Munich. "The nation honors in gratitude its great men and at the same time it erects itself a monument of its age, its continuity, and its greatness."[8] In its thrall Justi presents an estimated thirty representations each of rulers and of military notables, but one hundred each of scientists and high servants of the state, one hundred of architects, sculptors, and painters, fifty of poets (!), twenty each of musicians and people associated with the theater, and a hundred others. His dossier concludes: "There will be few images of exceptional women to be added, for, as long as they did not establish themselves in the artistic professions, their role, so important for this nation, has hitherto been limited to the quiet of the domestic sphere."[9] Twelve hundred images in total—this was the extent of the English gallery, a scope that exceeded the reach of the new German gallery. According to Paul Ortwin Rave, who became the director of the national galleries after 1945, the emperor saw at the gallery's opening in 1913 no more than 150 images, in other words about as many men and women "of merit" as had been eternalized in bust and engraving in the Valhalla. This number seems to have stayed constant in the gallery's democratic reincarnation in 1929.[10] It was merely appended by further images of Dorothea Schlegel (née Mendelssohn), David Friedländer, Schadow and Herder, Goethe, Caspar David Friedrich, Fritz Reuter, and others.[11] Rather than nationalist pathos, it was supposed timelessness that informed these choices: "Concrete features are more interesting to most people than abstract concepts; the latter stay in memory much more easily when mixed with concrete features."[12]

Photographing the *Volk:* Portrait Galleries from Below

In a subtle way the idea of a national portrait gallery, by 1913 still insufficiently accomplished, became a driving force in the construction of the Führer's image. Not only did Hitler seek a place in this honored line of ancestors, but new portraits of Hitler were featured each year from 1937 on at the *Munich Grand German Art Exhibit.* The National Socialist cult of heroes, starting with the ceremony honoring the fallen of Langemarck on November 11, 1919, gave rise in consciousness to a new *ordre pour le mérite* based on the patriotic readiness for self-sacrifice and a desire for death, irrespective of personal accomplishment.[13] At the same time, the conceptual tool of the line of ancestry became between 1918 and 1933 a tool of nationalist-inflected class warfare, a core tenet of racism.

*   *   *

While Justi (socially speaking "from above") pulled together his few images in order to create a gallery comparable to that of the English, different forces altogether were at work to create the same in the manner of a portrait gallery "from below," with different technology and with different conceptions of "merit and ancestral pride." The photographic image now played a key role. Beginning in 1910, photographers created their own nationally conceived exhibitions. One such photographer was August Sander from Cologne, the first images of whose famous sociography of German society date from around 1910. Sander's work *Menschen des 20. Jahrhunderts* [People of the 20th Century] was, according to his plans, to comprise twelve portfolios with forty-five images each, thus more than five hundred pictures in all. The imposing project, in essence a photographic atlas of contemporary Germans, was not to be published, with the exception of one famous selection in 1929 titled *Antlitz der Zeit* [The Face of the Times]; the National Socialists prevented the publication of the others.[14] The images showed Jews as well as farmers and craftsmen, professors and artists, gypsies, and old men and women. Although posture, clothing, and environment indicate their social standing and lend their own sort of dignity, the subjects of the portraits are robbed of their names [Fig. 4]. Beginning in about 1925, Sander subtitled each image with a professional moniker—shepherd, farmer, professor, musician, writer, sculptress—and thus transformed the subjects into types; this was a problematic transformation, however, because it is the linguistic negation of photography's main formal achievement, namely, the possibility for explicit identification. And why were these particular professors, musicians, seamstresses, farmers, and sculptors of "merit"? Only someone who knew the subjects' identities

Figure 4. The photographer August Sander aimed at representing not individual exponents but rather the entirety of German society in his works conceived beginning in 1910. Each estate received its own "portfolio" with photographs of people who remain anonymous. Close-ups reminiscent of silent movies remain an exception.

could judge their individual merit as professor, musician, seamstress, farmer, and sculptor; Sander instead dwelled on the "merit" of the visual appearance, and the subject's profession remained a sociographic surface.

* * *

Photographers contemporary with Sanders similarly classified and typified people and eventually, motivated by nationalism, moved away from the image as a historical source altogether. Erna Lendvai-Dircksen, for instance, began her preliminary studies for *Das deutsche Volksgesicht* [The

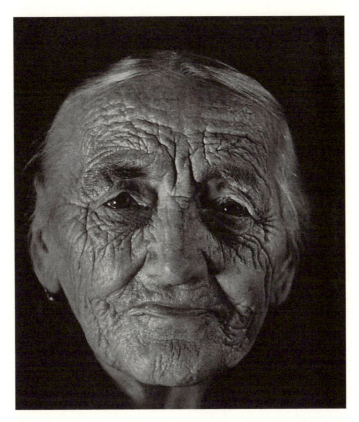

Figure 5. Like August Sander, Erna Lendvai-Dircksen labored at creating a group picture of the German people; she specialized in producing the silent-movie-style close-up such as this one. She later came to be regarded as a representative of nationalist photography.

face of the German People] in 1910; it became available first as a book in 1932, then in a whole series of photo books arranged by region. Her myopic portraits drew inspiration not only from the film close-up but from painting as well [Fig. 5]. Face and body are marked by geography and the region much more than by socially indicative apparel or posture. "There is no such thing as a face [that is] too close for me to read in its landscape," she wrote in a self-profile in 1937.[15] The picture of the nameless face (which was not restricted to Lendvai-Dircksen[16]), or, rather, the long series of images of nameless faces, nonetheless added to the bourgeois imaginary a definite notion of ancestral pride, which saw reflected in a face homeland and age, work and woes rather than a particular accomplishment or the owner of the land. The farmer in particular became representative in this way: "the monumental simple-mindedness of the man of the *Volk*,"[17] Lendvai-Dircksen remarked, allowed the photographer to avoid the many faces of city folk, which had similarly irritated Rilke around 1910.[18]

* * *

It was in any case the petit bourgeois turn to the "nobility" of the physique, to the natural countenance of the *Volk*, the ur-image of the racial countenance, that led to the closing of the Berlin *Bauakademie* in 1933 and thus finally to the end of the national portrait collection, which, as is widely known, still does not exist in Germany, except possibly in the storerooms of various museums.[19] Only once after did the NS body cult and bourgeois pride of ancestry enter into one of their strange entanglements. I am referring to the great exhibition on the occasion of the Olympic Games in the Berlin Kronprinzenpalais. With 460 paintings and bronzes, the exhibition vastly exceeded the old holdings in the collections. But the given occasion, namely the performance of the athletic body, nonetheless called into question (if it did not deny outright) the dignity and merit of the individual German ancestors presented there, all of them past exponents of German high culture specifically named. And of course no Jewish Germans were featured. Rather, in the Hitler bust by Ferdinand Liebermann, which adorns the frontispiece of the exhibition's catalogue [Fig. 6], the master of dishonoring entered the picture. One year later, in his secret speech of November 23, 1937 in Sonthofen, Hitler sketched his own conception of "merit and pride in ancestry" and German greatness quite succinctly: "In our Valhalla every single German can find a place, who in our past labored to shape the preconditions on which we now build today. When we understand our history in so very large terms, from our darkest prehistory until today, then we are the richest people in Europe. And when we then allow in great tolerance all our German heroes to march up, all our past leaders, all our great Germanic and German emperors—without exception, as they were—"[20] then German self-confidence will bend the world to its will. But is Hitler really making reference to merits in deed? What kind of wealth is evoked here? Hitler caused the idea of a Valhalla to be pursued consistently, though it gained its characteristic outline only with the onset of war, once every idea of merit had transformed into military-economic forms. In 1942, once again in a secret speech before new officers of the Wehrmacht, the great leaders were transformed into pure capital, a spectral Valhalla of the *Volk*'s wealth: "When we look at the national assets of a people as a whole, then there can be no doubt that the greatest national asset of a people is the sum

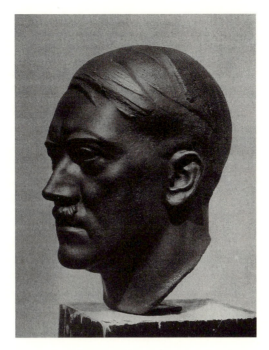

Figure 6. Another bust by Ferdinand Liebermann, whom Hitler liked especially.
It stood at the entrance of the exhibition *Great Germans in the Depictions of Their
Time,* put on in the Berlin Kronprinzenpalais in 1936 on the occasion of the
Olympic Games—an exhibition that could be seen as the final version of the
"national portrait gallery."

of its most important minds. For the true national capital are the innumerable inventors and thinkers, the poets as well as the great statesmen
and generals. Everything else is, in final analysis, fungible."[21] There was
of course some distance to be traversed in order to get to this pure quan-
tification of the idea of greatness.

The project, as of 1914 still inexplicit, of a national "portrait gallery
from below," orienting itself by build and facial expression rather than
social status or history, was really the result of a long-standing traditional
mode of perception of bodies and faces: perception, that is, under the
spell of so-called physiognomics, an early version of what is today
dubbed physical anthropology. For example, at the same time that Sanders pursued his photography, the doctor Willy Hellpach—who ran for
president of the Reichstag for the social democrats in 1924—worked on
a German physiognomy, which, however, appeared only in 1942. But, he
wrote, as early as 1901 the idea had "flared up" to investigate whether

the different appearance of Germans "was mostly a *facial* difference, and whether it was caused by differences in tribal descent." Just as the Italian founder of criminal anthropology, Cesare Lombroso, had done as early as 1860, Hellpach later took advantage of the war and his own position as a military doctor to "constantly inspect and compare soldiers from the most varied troop detachments."[22] The insights Hellpach gleaned from his comparisons stay close to the details and eschew nationalist pathos; he thought little of Werner Sombart's dictum that physiognomy had to be intuited, not just seen and prised apart. The physiological inventory of a people from east to west and north to south culminated in the 1920s at first in the racial doctrines of Hans F. K. Günther, the author of a book on the "heroic thought" (1920) and eventually an influential race theorist in the Third Reich.[23] Here, the pride of ancestry was pursued based exclusively on blood and bodily features; the profession and habitus of the person were completely eliminated from the list of values.

Physiognomy took part in this deletion or devaluation from its inception. Its most frequently cited modern prophet, Johann Caspar Lavater (1741–1801), a minister from Zurich, sought to identify by his interpretations of faces God's chosen, if not the son of God himself.[24] In his four-volume work *Physiognomic Fragments* he had indeed done the spadework for the "portrait gallery from below" to an astonishing degree, in terms of both media and psychology. Lavater's insistent interrogation of face and body became in his works the ideational precursor to photography in several respects. For one thing, the physiognomic gaze could take in all that which traditional production of artistic likenesses had had to avoid, if it was to fulfill its mission of commemoration and veneration; Lavater could, even had the obligation to, study madmen as well as criminals, monstrous births as much as animals, hoary doters as much as hideous witches. Naturally this study did not proceed without prejudice—but it refused censored perception. In addition, Lavater paid obsessive attention to details, much like the close-up was to do in films and in the photography of the New Objectivity later on: isolated eyes, noses, foreheads, legs, toes, and so on. Above all else, however, physiognomy handed down to photography the claim to the status of evidence. It is precisely the naïve, short-circuit diagnosis of the physiognomist, who regards the undetached earlobe as proof—as *evidence*—of a criminal predisposition, that can count as the precursor to medical as well as criminal photography, as is the case with Lavater's use of description as a means of verbal identification or "portrait parlé," as it was referred to around 1890 in Paris police precincts under Bertillon.[25]

The physiognomist's hope, by which the exterior speaks of the merit (or crime) of the interior, had a remarkable career between 1780 and

1914. Lavater's pan-European success incensed his opponents, almost all of whom hailed from the Enlightenment camp: in France, Diderot and D'Alembert; in Germany, Kant, Hegel, and Lichtenberg, even Goethe, who, in concert with Lavater, had originally done preliminary work in similar directions. But in the blind spot of the philosophical Enlightenment, physiognomy took the natural sciences and its juridical periphery by storm, at first in the name of anthropology and phrenology,[26] then psychiatry,[27] eventually in the guise of police science, and since the turn of the century increasingly under a mandate from race studies. Paralleling this career was the growing acceptance of physiognomic perception in the literary field, embodied above all in Oscar Wilde's novel *The Picture of Dorian Gray*, but also in numerous novels of the nineteenth century, in which it functions as a compositional tool rather than a narrative end in itself. When Marcel Proust began his defining work *Remembrance of Things Past*, there existed already a virtual philosophy of the countenance, which was only later understood as a philosophy of love[28] *and not at all as* the technique for identification deployed by the investigators and anthropologists of the period.

Greatness in View: Wilhelm II, Stefan George, Ernst Haeckel

Around 1914, the physiognomic perspective reigned supreme among wide circles of the educated classes, and where it did not reign it at least made forays. In 1913, the same year Hitler came to Munich, and the year in which Ludwig Justi could finally open the national picture collection in Schinkel's Bauakademie with the emperor in attendance, the European film industry made a gift to the sovereign: a richly illustrated volume entitled *Der Deutsche Kaiser im Film* [The German Emperor in Films]. It was a gift commemorating the twenty-fifth year under the kaiser, and it functioned as a reminder that this emperor was not against the new media, neither against film nor against photography; much to the contrary. Much like his royal cousins in England, Wilhelm II gained an early appreciation for the photographic medium and assembled over time a gallery of himself.[29] Most recent research indicates that he employed as many as thirty court photographers: They were allowed to follow along on his travels and photograph everything; only the eventual selection and control of the images resided with the court. Beginning in 1893, picture postcards became available; the Neue Photographische Presse dealt in group photos of the imperial family in editions of hundreds of thousands, not to mention pirate copies. In the 1890s, these pictures made it into illustrated newspapers. Soon, reproduction became possible on all kinds of trinkets, making the imperial face more famous but also slightly ridiculous. In World War I, the imperial house

Figure 7. Wilhelm II, here in a photograph before his accession to the throne, was a great proponent of the new visual media. He had himself photographed copiously and was the star of the early Wochenschauen news reels.

gave out photos to the soldiers, who carried them with religious devotion. Just like his grandmother, Queen Victoria, the emperor Wilhelm turned the giving of photographs into a virtual knighting gesture.

One of the photographs thus signed and distributed would eventually come back to haunt the emperor. Toward the end of the 1880s, the historian Ludwig Quidde found a picture of then-prince Wilhelm with the personalization "oderint dum metuant"—let them hate me, as long as they fear me [Fig. 7]. "This was, as everyone knows, the favorite saying of Caligula. Years later I learned that Prince Wilhelm gave away photographs with this personalization in great numbers."[30] This was great news for Quidde, who had been working since 1889 on a satire aimed at the emperor, which took the shape of a historical portrait of the Roman emperor Caligula. In both Quidde found disturbing traces of mental abnormality. When the book was published in 1894, it created quite a stir, leading to several reprints.[31] It is almost certain that Hitler knew it.

Even though Quidde had sketched the physiognomic portrait of Caligula in but few words, his pamphlet stirred others in the scientific community into action. In 1914, the psychiatrist Ernst Müller published the first of three volumes on the "Cäsarenportrait," the emperors' countenances as depicted on the coins and statues of ancient Rome. The somewhat awkward book, entirely amateurish from an art history perspective, contains many bad illustrations and comes straight from the world of physiognomic pathology. We get a good indication of the state of that "science," at least in the provinces, in the simple-minded preface. Here, the author, deputy medical director in a sanatorium near Cologne, declared his intention to treat the Caesars much like the patients whom he routinely subjected to physiognomic evaluation. He read Caligula's degeneracy from the emperor's images on coins: "His sickly body, which bore the mark of degeneracy, was reminiscent of the Julian [dynasty] and his uncle Claudius; he had much body hair, a large stomach, thin legs, epilepsy, and suffered from insomnia. The emperor was mentally inferior."[32] None of these features was present in the kaiser, thus no mental illness. Nonetheless, after the emperor's abdication, Müller wrote a psychiatric report in which he called him an "overbred degenerate," endangered by "psychopathy and weak nerves." Müller's book was published in 1927 and was thus already under the spell of F. K. Günther's racial doctrines.[33]

Obviously, before 1918 the degeneracy thesis stayed for the most part out of public consciousness. The emperor's image was much more determined by the publicity policies of the imperial court, through the mass dissemination of photographs, by numerous paintings, and not least of all through the medium of film. Wilhelm II is considered today the first real German star, present as he is in more than one a hundred *Wochenschauen* [weekly news reels]. The editors of the 1913 volume *Der Deutsche Kaiser im Film* [The German Emperor in Films] went so far as to declare him the "most interesting personality ever to appear before the cinematographer's lens."[34] He has been called omnipresent, constantly occupied with his own charisma, which made him the national symbol for all Germans. It may have been a tragic characteristic of his regime that this image policy dissolved his charisma by its very reliance on mass-media dissemination. The more familiar the Kaiser became to his subjects, the more militaristic he behaved politically.[35]

In spite of the persistent visualization of the Kaiser, there seems to have been hardly any "close-up" of him, nor even a sympathetic description of his person or physiognomy. Apart from early and always concerned descriptions by and to his parents, when his congenitally malformed arm kept the court on its toes, no one, not the popular biographer Emil Ludwig, not the great journalistic physiognomist Theodor Wolff, seems to have deemed the emperor a suitable subject for analysis.[36] Possibly the imperial court's image policy had something to do with this. Count Harry Kessler, the emperor's bitter enemy, confided to his diary that the emperor was a mixture of "bestiality," "brutality," and "coiffed" hairdo—as though he was describing Hitler.[37] The emperor received an entirely different treatment from young Alfred Kerr, who in 1897 saw the Kaiser up close for about half an hour:

If one wanted to describe his exterior in a true Berliner manner, one would have to say: "There's something inside." Despite all the good humor frequently evidenced when his head is tilted in conversation, his countenance most eloquently displays a certain self-reliant decisiveness. He looks like someone who, if need be, doesn't beat around the bush. He will strike no one as insignificant. Very endearing is an expression of care, almost of paternal feelings. One understands, all in all, the enthusiastic reactions he elicited from foreigners who met him. Fate, they said, had granted him good advisors. . . ."[38]

All the motifs, which the emperor purposefully or involuntarily combined in public perception, will later repeat themselves in public perceptions of Hitler: the tremendous number of photographs and photo books, the ever more highly stylized filmic depictions, the countless paintings. The increasingly perfected mise-en-scène of this media propaganda "following the body" (Nietzsche) utilized the tension between proximity and distance, intimacy and out-of-reach power. In the late 1920s, the first purely physiognomic diagnoses of Hitler began appearing, first as race portraits, later as actual medical studies. How closely tied to this the Kaiser's image remained is evidenced in Hitler's secret speech in 1937 before the Führer's new recruits. Here, he invoked the idol of the *Volk* with the exact same words of Caligula with which the young kaiser had shocked his peers. "We want to lead our people to the very forefront. Whether they would love us for it doesn't concern us, as long as they respect us! Whether they would hate us doesn't concern us, as long as they fear us!"[39]

*   *   *

What fundamentally distinguished popular perceptions of Hitler from those of the emperor lay in a different direction and had less to do with the visual arts and more to do with language, less with the imperial pose and more with the gaze face-to-face. Importantly, Lavater's magnum opus, the *Physiognomische Fragmente* [Physiognomic Fragments], didn't just contain images. After all, it was dedicated to "knowledge of mankind" as well as "love of mankind." Inspired by a religious passion for the human body insofar as it was a divine creation and enraptured by the countenances of his friends, Lavater commented for pages on those faces he loved, verbal close-ups *avant la lettre*. Today, they strike us as clunky prose, aconceptual and high-strung. Take, for example, the description of Goethe: "... notice the eye, with a fleeing, darting, loving glance that pierces—a soft, cambered eye, not very low-lying, bright, motile,—the eyebrow draped gently over it,—this nose, in itself already so poetic; and that so authentically poetic segue to the [*lippichten*] mouth, quivering from vibrant sensation, [yet] containing this suspended tremble,—this masculine chin—this open, defined ear. . . ."[40] Descriptions of this kind subsequently became common throughout Europe: from Honoré de Balzac to Marcel Proust, Edgar Allan Poe to Oscar Wilde, Nathaniel Hawthorne to Melville, Heinrich Heine and Theodor Fontane to Thomas and Heinrich Mann. While Lavater's *visual* physiognomy gave rise to a tradition of "portraiture from below," that is to say one paying particular attention to the sickly and the criminal, *linguistic* physiognomics created a tradition of permanent attention to "those above," the immersion into the face of the other, the question whether the other was worthy. This corresponded to traditions of rhetoric; in antiquity reference to physical characteristics was an indispensable component of the *laudatio* of a person "of merit and ancestral pride."

The *Physiognomic Fragments* was thus dominated linguistically not by scientific discourse, but rather by an everyday discourse of the life world, even when the description concerned types, even entire peoples. That there should be series of pictures not simply of individuals of "merit and ancestral pride" but of entire peoples as well was beyond question; contemporary anthropology made itself felt. Strangely enough, the Germans did not always cut a good figure: Goethe, for example, found their features "criss-crossing lawlessly, often without so much as intimating a character."[41] In contrast, the romantic exponent of physiognomics, Carl Gustav Carus, in 1853 wanted "to insist that that great skull, which, by its high and wide brow on the whole and around the forehead in particular, permits a strong development of the brain, and, insofar as it finds itself in a certain congruence with the body's other development, provides the material for a rich mental life, is at home WITH THE GERMANS, apparently more so than among the other cultivated tribes of Europe (and that means really in the cultivated world as a whole). . . ."[42]

This phrenological self-certainty must have taken a dent sometime after, however; in any case, Hugo von Hofmannsthal complains in the *Briefe des Zurückgekehrten* [Letters upon Return] in 1908, much like Goethe, that the same German countenances showed merely "an eternal coming and going as in a pigeon coop, of strong and weak, of next-best and far-out, of the common and the high, an unquiet of possibilities."[43] Among these possibilities was of course ugliness. Even before the First World War, George Grosz is reputed to have planned a three-volume work on the "ugliness of the Germans": the project of a dandy.

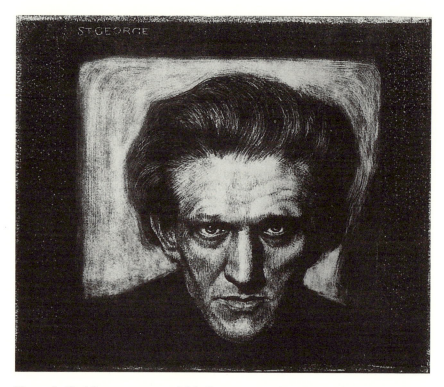

ST GEORGE

Figure 8. Karl Bauer, creator of this George portrait, portrayed many great Germans. George appears in the photographs of his time as a charismatic visualized head even into the 1950s.

Stefan Zweig wrote a tragic drama about ugly Thersites of antiquity: a project against heroism.

Sublating German disquiet and insecurity and turning them into outright adulation in certain circles was the feat of none other than Stefan George, the "secret emperor" [Fig. 8] of literary production. The center of something of an art-religious sect since the turn of the century, George carried physiognomic valuations into the literary scene with an unprecedented intensity. No German poet of the time was described and photographed as often as George, and no German poet devoted himself so intimately and passionately to photography, nor tied his poetry as religiously to the human voice. One of his first disciples, Robert Boehringer, assembled a collection of more than two hundred portraits after World War II, and provided it with emphatic commentary.[44] The following, clearly infatuated, almost "homofacial" word portrait by Edgar Salin from 1913 can count as representative:[45]

From the low-lying eyes the gaze wandered to the nose, which was at once deli-cate and pronounced—to the lips, tightly pressed together; the lower lip thrust forward ever so slightly and gave his mouth an air of austere decisiveness; it led downward to his chin, on whose mighty precipice the majesty of this ruler seemed collected. How beautiful and pronounced was the ear—it seemed to us farther from eye and nose than in other people, as though this part of his head were for itself and as a whole complete. The gaze then followed the hair to the brow, hard and sublime, crowning his head—it was almost unfurrowed, the spiri-tual brow of a thinker, and was at once slightly hunched and bulged above the eyes; the will-charged forehead of a man of action, it was of stone and as if chis-eled by a hard chisel, and, in consonance with the rich, wavy hair, in whose brown the first strands of gray were woven, was suffused with that graceful dig-nity, for which the term Charis-like forced itself on the viewer.[46]

Stefan Breuer dedicated a sociopsychological study to George's circle a few years ago. In his analysis, the circle is dominated by a "high priest" or "seer" who encourages the "grandiose self," a narcissistic identifica-tion with an ego-ideal. Without the rigor of literary pretensions, without the broad and worldly education, which meant that George attracted a circle of unusually intelligent young men, he may have easily played a much more ominous role. It is contested whether he didn't perhaps in fact play such a role—after all, he cultivated the idea of a "secret Ger-many," of the "empire of ideas," and it was its demise that he feared in the First World War.[47] After the war, he hoped for its revival, even though he eventually came to reject it. It was hard for any real state to match the national enthusiasm of his "state" of poets and thinkers; but he was not militant enough, or not versed enough in realpolitik, as Salin's phys-iognomic "emperor's portrait" showed us. Here, George is a man of "merit and ancestral pride" at once. No picture, rather his physical appearance itself, the flesh made word, is meant to convey this to us: the nose, the mouth, the chin, all in the eyes of a reverent observer. This linguistic picture, taking the body as its guide, is ultimately close up and seducible. Thus, the chiseled brow—a topos of the period's facial description—which is "suffused" with "graceful dignity," doesn't give us a real picture of political rulership, but rather of an androgynous god-head, of a mélange of masculine dignity and feminine grace; it is a skull that combines without mediation the features of an ascetic demon and even more fatally those of a transgressor. Neither the series of pictures of "Goethe's external features" (Ernst Beutler 1914), which had been circulating for decades, nor the much-discussed skull of Gerhart Haupt-mann measured up to this attractiveness, both carnal and shocking. Nonetheless, these three idols constituted fortifications against the loss of face discovered and lamented everywhere by the educated at the time: with the rise of the fourth estate, the mushrooming of the metropolises, and especially the new developments in photographic imaging. It was a

Figure 9. Ernst Haeckel, the world-famous founder of so-called monism, received an entire picture volume on his own person from his son Walther: *Ernst Haeckel in Pictures: A Physiognomic Study.*

fear of these new developments that seems to have inspired the cult of the "Charakterkopf" [a striking head] at least subconsciously: the quest for the "face of greatness" heated up with the beginning of the war proportionally to the greatness of the face in film and photography, that is to say to the technique of the close-up, which had been available in textual form much earlier.

* * *

Since Lavater, secular devotion to faces was not limited to the literary sphere, but spilled into the scientific sector as well. Since the middle of the nineteenth century, the uncontested "emperor" in this domain was Ernst Haeckel, the German representative of Darwinism and founder of monistic religion [Fig. 9]. When, in 1914, the natural scientist and dedicated Haeckelian Wilhelm Bölsche congratulated his world-famous teacher on his eightieth birthday, he delivered a head-based bodily hagiography of the man of merit:

When one's gaze climbs down Haeckel's countenance, from the proud keep with its snowy clouds, which today crowns the highest "vertebrae" [*Wirbel*] of this ever-erect spine, down to the eyes, fine and always somewhat discreetly cooped up, questioning in a friendly manner, to the fine wrinkles that surround them like a gentle, almost childlike, but so telling rune script; when the always youthful and friendly smile illuminates every angle down there once more and finally even flashes up to the rosy temples, under the snow of old age—then one feels the magic of the mind, the heart, which has welded together all the crevices and lava streams of this old Faustus into one titanic essence and cooled it off into the shape of a genuine form of art, an art of effortlessly aristocratic humanity in that peaceful struggle of life—in the struggle for peace.[48]

The overflowing facial prose testifies to a remarkable change in the perception of images "from above." Kerr on the emperor, Salin on George, and now here Bölsche on Haeckel, the prince of the intellect—speaking art historically, they all create "ruler portraits," even if verbal ones. But the restriction to the face, as though in a filmic close-up, eclipses the stature, the torso, the garments, and the poise of this "ruler portrait." What is thus missing is the distance of the representation, or perhaps the representation of distance; what is missing is the actual height of the depiction "from above," to which, for example, the kaiser's photographers had always adhered. Notwithstanding the obvious admiration apparent in Bölsche's words (no matter how exaggerated), in them do we not hear the tone of the increasingly familiar colleague, of the student or scientific politician? Thus in Lavater's wake, there arose explicit devotion to great faces, reminiscent of religious professions of piety, but with one remarkable psychological consequence. Because these "ruler portraits" weren't painted, but rather intoned like hymns, they were by their very manner of appearance always verbal expressions of the spirit of the observer and the spiritual expressions of the eye of the admirer. Thus the verbal "ruler portrait" approaches a self-portrait; more precisely perhaps, it becomes a portrait of the "grandiose self."[49]

It had yet to become obvious that such analyses were heading for the dark side of physiognomic perception. Of course there existed aggressive caricature in word and image, but much more in image than in word. Nonetheless facial hagiographies such as Bölsche's had their antipodes, for instance from the pen of the passionate satirist Oskar Panizza. His story *Der operierte Jud'* [The Operated Jew]—written already in 1893 and reprinted in 1914—painted the portrait of a Jew long before the foundation of *Der Stürmer* by Julius Streicher, the cruelest anti-Semitic propagandist between 1923 and 1945:

Itzel Faitel's countenance was highly interesting. A pity Lavater never saw it. A gazelle's eyes, dim and dark like a cherry, floated in the wide expanses of a velvety-slick, slightly yellowed skin over brow and jowls. Itzig's nose had that high priestly form Kaulbach gave to his most prominent figure in his picture of the "Destruction of Jerusalem." His eyebrows had united, but Faitel Stern assured me that this was quite popular. He also knew that people with such eyebrows were to drown one day; but he paralyzed this possibility by assuring me that he never ventured into water. The lips were fleshy, the teeth pure crystal; between them a fat, bluish-red tongue made inopportune appearances. Chin and upper lip were fully without hair, for Faitel Stern was still very young. Let me mention of the rest of my friend's body that he had bow legs, but whose swath was not excessive, and now I will have at least sketched Itzig's silhouette. I will later speak of the countless black locks in his hair.[50]

Faitel Itzig is the main character in one of the most vitriolic satires on Jewish assimilation attempts around the turn of the last century. In order to make it in the Christian world, the Ostjude (eastern Jew) not only changes his name like many others; he also submits to surgical alterations to his entire body. His efforts are to no avail; at the decisive moment (he is marrying a gentile woman) his old physique reasserts itself and brings about his downfall.

Panizza's satire combined a number of motifs that were to accompany the physiognomic obsession's path into inhumanity. Not only the image of the "foreigner," but also his desperate attempts at assimilation along with their eventual failure all break into a German national delirium and disturb the self-referential idyll. That both—the idyll as well as the hell outside it—can be depicted on the same biopsychological level demonstrates the remarkable and ever deeper integuments of both aspects.

"Wallenstein's Face": A Führer Story

One of the key texts in the dialectic and tradition of the physiognomic "grandiose self"-portrait comes from the author Walter Flex, who became famous for his 1916 novel *Der Wanderer zwischen beiden Welten* [The Wanderer between Both Worlds] and remained famous even after the Second World War. In 1918, a posthumous collection of his stories appeared under the title *Wallenstein's Antlitz: Gesichte und Geschichten aus der Zeit des Dreissigjährigen Krieges* [Wallenstein's Face: Sights and Stories of the Time of the Thirty Years' War]. The title story of the volume, which saw reprints well into the 1960s,[51] deals with a young boy who assists his war-injured father in a life of crime, but then suddenly happens to meet Wallenstein. Here, the narrator implies, he sees for the first time a human face—and blushes with shame over his existence so far. Wallenstein himself is touched and takes the boy along with him; eventually the boy saves Wallenstein's life, at the cost of his own. Hitler himself had spoken of Wallenstein the generalissimus with great admiration at the dinner table in 1942.[52] Whether he knew Flex's story or not, its motifs were central to the history of ideas in Germany as it became increasingly entangled in the ideological preconditions of National Socialism.

Walter Flex, born in 1887, was an author of the youth movement, which had held its founding assembly on the Hoher Meissner mountain in 1913. He enlisted as a volunteer in the war effort; he died as an officer in 1917 on a reconnaissance mission. In the *Wanderer* he had memorialized his friend Ernst Wuche as a born leader. Wallenstein makes a similar appearance in the 1918 story, this time however in physiognomic close-up:

What so shook the boy was nothing other than the sight of a human face, which he had foregone for weeks and months. He felt—I am using his own words—like Adam upon seeing the face of the Lord after the fall. He had the full foretaste of the shame that runs through the soul when it stands naked before God on the day of reckoning. He felt as though he sensed his soul for the first time after so many deaf and dead centuries, and at the same time the dreadful necessity of its irrecoverable loss. Rebirth and judgment in one shattering moment. What was life and death before this shame, which ate life and soul, and which doused him, who knew blushing from his childhood days, with all his blood over neck and face?[53]

This gaze is not directed at a *ruler's* face but at a *leader's*, half paternal, half divine. Such a gaze would not have been possible without Lavater, but nonetheless it goes beyond him as well.

The motif of the overpowering feeling of shame of a human being before God finds its counterweight in the narrator's second "reading" of the face. The officer with the telling name Mohr vom Wald [Moor of the Forest] has an altogether different experience of the leader:

At this hour, Mohr vom Wald thought he saw Wallenstein's face for the first time. . . . He had never seen it like this: this battle-raked, stiffly alive countenance was like the many-shaped earth, the clear forehead rising over the strong brows with a noble swath in a sublime line was like the clear sky above the earth. And forehead and countenance, heaven and earth, all greatness and audacity of earthly and heavenly powers were molded into one in the deep embers of his lordly black eyes.[54]

The two glances Flex has cast on Wallenstein's face illuminate, as though with a concave mirror, the conflict of mentalities when it comes to the maintenance of right and custom or else their overthrow by natural forces. While the boy still moves within the field of shame and piety, to the point of immolation, the grown-up Mohr moves in the open fields of nature. Without God, without a moral law, he sees Wallenstein's brow clearly "like the clear sky above the earth" and is transfixed by the "deep embers of his lordly black eyes." It was similarly in terms of cosmology that Wilhelm Bölsche saw his Haeckel:

We know the mighty words of old Kant: of the two highest wonders in the entirety of our world of sense: the sky above, which stretches, gradually sparkling, over this earth; and the moral law in our bosom. But there is a third—and this third is at once the most complete shape the art of nature can take on earth: this is the human countenance in its beautiful form, in its spiritually and psychically transfigured ennobling formation. If you recall that each moral act has once glinted in the gaze of a human eye, and that those stars up there in all their grandeur of milky ways and nebulae have only been thinkingly grasped by such eyes, then one might wonder whether this is not perhaps the highest of these three marvels. And it is certain that this countenance is also at once the final and decisive object of all real art—that it always has been and always will be—so that nowhere are the dark beauty of nature and the bright ideal actions of human consciousness so at one in a thing as here.[55]

The way in which Bölsche here integrates Kant's moral law—the starry skies above me and the moral law within me—into one symbol, the human face and its brow, points to a fatal fugitive point Lavater's facial devotion developed once in the hands of "scientists." Inspired by the romantic cult around skulls, for example in Carl Gustav Carus, Bölsche can see in "starry heavens" nothing but a literally transposed human forehead:

It would be hard to find a more glorious example for the perfect form of beauty of this human skull at the normal height of one's powers and without crossing boundaries, for this "secret vessel, giving out oracles," as Goethe called it, than the image presented to us when we inspect Haeckel's imposing brow. While for the aesthetic sense it integrates itself harmoniously into the rest of his profile, itself exceptionally strong, it appears nonetheless to be the unmistakable source of lighting, the true sun of the entire face, from which even the eyes recede noticeably. Always when I saw Haeckel again after so many years, when he emerged from the forest twilights before me, or from the half-dark of his study in Jena, suddenly into the light, [I had] that experience that has become for me inseparable from his person: [the experience] of that lonely brow proceeding toward me as though by itself.[56]

Certainly the apparent naturalism of such statements has a double, if not a triple bottom. A late echo of the astrological link between human brow and planetary significance reverberates in these statements—the pagan aura of Lavater's physiognomics. The brow is to be seen as a heavenly body because stars write our fates on our foreheads, not symbolically after all, but perfectly concretely. At the same time, the metaphor of the face as landscape is one of the most popular *topoi* of facial prose in general—and not just prose, but facial painting as well. Landscapes have been painted as landscapes since the Renaissance, according to a mannerist codex, which inspires both visual and linguistic satire. As such, landscapes constituted the naturalistic, really pagan counterpart to iconic contemplation before the countenance of Christ, as Max Picard would write at the end of the 1930s.

The Wallenstein story also deals with the collapse of symbolic functions. It deals with being overcome by charisma, with the entry of the moral subject into an amoral space of strange intersubjective closeness. This entry is staged as a mimic drama; what begins as blood-red shame ends as a bloodied face, as though the mimic allusion led to purely surface semantics alone. The narrator has the boy die for this leader.

The "leader," the Führer, was, as a figure and as a name, at that time already a core element of the German youth movement. Also and especially as an aspect of progressive pedagogy, with the homoerotic undertones always suspected and later rejected by the Hitler Youth, this Führer was also always a seducer [Ver-Führer] into a new, more human existence, away from the fathers' generation. A breathless Goebbels (surely a reader of Flex's story and at the time still a writer) noted in his diary in 1924: "The modern battle for the face of Germany is the age-old struggle between father and son. Despair! Despair!"[57] It was from this despair that the shock of the leader Hitler was to release him; and Goebbels remained one of his most fanatical believers.

The story "Wallenstein's Face" advertises this idea of the Führer years before there is a political "Führer" named Adolf Hitler and establishes the motif of facially inspired loyalty to the death long before the arrival of its object. For not only does Walter Flex's story date from the time before the First World War, it is also patterned on a much older original, stemming from classical German literature. The seductive face was introduced by none other than Schiller in his *Wallenstein* as a centrally significant, if disenchanted motif; Schiller was no friend of Lavater's. Wallenstein's favorite, Max Piccolomini—the model for the boy in Flex's story—attempts to wean himself of his leader: "No, do not turn your countenance toward me! / To me it was always a godlike face," he says in *Death of Wallenstein*. And the military leader himself has a premonition that this power is beginning to slip away from him with regard to the troops as well: ". . . they shall / Now look upon my countenance and hear my voice. / Are they not *my* own troops? Am I / Not their commander and their awesome lord? / We'll see if they can recognize this face / That was a sun to them in darkest battle." The sun doesn't shine for him himself, but Walter Flex reverses that relationship. His Max, the wild child, dies for a leader of almost cosmically exaggerated power of countenance.

Wallenstein's prominence as a figure between 1913 and 1920 is not limited to Flex's story. Ricarda Huch dedicated a character study to the great general (1915), and Alfred Döblin wrote a great novel about him (1920). Schiller had set the lines of demarcation; for Wallenstein's outburst: "Could this be true? Can I no longer act / as I would choose?"[58] inaugurates the tragedy that develops between the hypothetical game and the real execution, when the hypothesizer is no longer playing. The use of metaphors around the popular movement in Germany was to prove a special case of this tragedy, even if not yet recognizable as such. For not least by brutally driving out the hypothetical, Hitler managed to declare something a weakness of the *Bildungsbürgertum* that Schiller's Wallenstein, seeking his own downfall, had wanted to lose.

On Physiognomics and Shame

The story "Wallenstein's Face" shows a physiognomic line of reasoning in the hands of a writer. It is not an accident that it concentrates on that aspect of facial conditioning that deals with the mimic qualities in a situation of *mutual* regard. Physiognomics, conceived as gaze and countergaze, is always also linguistically constituted and always remains in dialogue. It is no accident that the topic of shame should be so prominent. Even before 1914, Georg Simmel, the cultural sociologist, wrote about the dialogical ground of human shame:

It is impossible to take through the eye, without giving at the same time. The eye unveils the other's soul, which in turn seeks to undress him. However, since this becomes visible only in the immediate gaze eye-to-eye, we are here at a most complete mutuality of human relations. Only thus can we understand entirely why self-consciousness forces us to look down, to avoid the other's gaze. Certainly it is not only because it saves us at least from noticing that [the other looks at us] and how the other looks at us in so embarrassing and confusing a situation; rather, the deeper reason is that the lowering of my gaze takes from the other some of the power to read me. The gaze into the other's eye doesn't simply help me recognize him; on the line connecting both pairs of eyes, he carries his own personality, his own sentiment, his own impulse, to *his* other.[59]

This thought, that the frontal gaze on another living face as a rule solicits a countergaze and thus submits to the setting of shame, runs counter to the ruling physiognomic rage of the natural sciences. Since and including Lavater, there developed a psychology of naturalistic abolition of shame diametrically opposed to the literary valorization of and devotion to the face. It developed particularly in the sciences and was helped along by the advances in photographic technology. The peculiar stare into a foreign or a naked face, or on a foreign or a naked body became one of the most noticeable attitudes of anthropological interest, half scientific, half voyeuristic, increasingly warding off the countergaze; this created the ideal point of departure for caricature and propaganda. The physiognomic gaze, conceived from the *image*, remains untouched even where it is combined with curiosity or empathy: be it in psychiatry with its burgeoning collections of pictures of the faces of psychopaths or hysterics,[60], in movie making with its close-ups, or even in the excessive "face eulogies" in Lavater's throng, which left no pore unmentioned.

It was this scientific perspective that transformed the physiognomic field fundamentally in the course of the nineteenth century. Traditionally encompassing the living ensemble of face and body, voice and smell, movement and clothing, it now limited its analysis to one fraction of this field, even if perhaps the most important one. The objectifying gaze fundamentally calls for the "naked face" or "the true," even when expressive. Nietzsche's well-known dictum from *Beyond Good and Evil*— "Whatever is profound loves masks; what is most profound even hates image and parable"—was untimely.[61] What *was* "timely" were passionate efforts to tear the mask off man's face, the wish to look upon a "true face," to expunge life lies, and on the whole abolish with a grand gesture the theatrical constitution of society, newly objective and supposedly humane at once. Edward Timms has emphasized this point in his great biography of Karl Kraus,[62] as well as Kraus's proximity to art critics of the period such as Adolf Loos, who considered ornament in art as much a crime as Lombroso once had a broad chin.

The reorganization of the physiognomic field, which began at the end of the First World War and whose effects are still noticeable today, thus occurred within an odd tension between the scientifically artificial and the living face. At a time when all masks have disappeared, all lies have been exposed, all truth been made accessible to science, the sociolinguistic construction of the face as sketched by Georg Simmel has been abandoned. This construction had not only relied on the dialogical rhythm of gaze and countergaze; the semantic field of the face itself, its horizon of meaning, appeals to a unique sensitivity, made use of in particular in verbal composition. It is essentially a sensitivity to so-called "primary" or immediate community, for example when we speak "face to face," when someone "lies to my face," when someone wants to "save face," or on the contrary when someone "loses face." However, all these highly affectively charged bits of face-based communication—candor, intimacy, aggression, shame—disappear from consciousness once the "face" refers simply to univalent positivity of the object. In the language of sociology, the face is transplanted from a "community" into the social formation of a "society,"[63] with the flâneur, the moviegoer, and the scientist as protagonists of the new interest in faces, and with a clear shift away from language and to the image.

The extent of this transplantation is at every point visible in the political field. The phrase "saving face" or "losing face" entered the everyday

European vocabulary only at the beginning of the twentieth century. According to linguists, it emerged during the Boxer Rebellion in the 1890s and was thus of Chinese origin. The first usage in German occurred in a newspaper that certified that a drunk city official had nonetheless saved face. The word became highly political in the so-called "*Daily Telegraph* Affair," in which the emperor made a few careless remarks on Anglo-German relations to a newspaper. Only a subsequent public explanation saved Germany from "losing face," as the newspapers put it. The linguist Storfer, recapitulating the word's origin in 1935, described the ostensibly Chinese usage of the word: "The son of the Middle Empire esteems reality less than appearance. As long as appearances are maintained, all is well. If someone surrenders face however, it is tantamount to cultural suicide, often leading to quite actual suicide. . . . When appearances are maintained, all parties involved, even those which knowingly let these appearances deceive them, consider the matter fully dispensed with."[64]

Nothing of course could be more un-German than this concept of honor, especially read vis-à-vis the motifs of "Wallenstein's Face" or the face-crazed coven around Stefan George. Both Flex's story and the George circle denied vehemently the element of simulation, that whiff of performance. Nonetheless, it was precisely this "lost face" of Germany that Hitler wanted to regain, when after 1918 "the flush of indignation and shame burned in my cheek,"[65] and which he was to come to represent, or at least wanted to represent. The project of the "national collection of images," to represent a nation of merit and ancestral pride, accidentally helped as much as the intense devotion to faces by which Stefan George could bind his transcendentalist disciples to himself. These themes further intertwined with the development of the media, with the "losses of face" feared since the advent of photography for the "age of mechanical reproducibility." The eulogy for the lost aura of the human face sounded long before the early 1930s.

"The more I tried to come to a clear realization of the monstrous event, the more the flush of indignation and shame burned in my cheek": recent sociopsychological research knows of the extraordinary role played by feelings of shame after the twin traums of defeat and the Versailles treaty.[66] We hear of a replacement of the old culture of guilt by a culture of humiliation, allied to the visual sphere. The essential elements of this "culture of shame," the worry about outward appearance, about the loss of honor and a fear of becoming a laughingstock, are carried over from feudal societies and aristocratic centuries much older than the Protestant "culture of guilt." The literary historian Helmut Lethen traces the passing of the old culture of guilt to the new culture of self-consciousness in the Weimar Republic in a study that has attracted much attention. This transition is perhaps more complicated than Lethen makes it seem. It is certainly true that society after 1918, and perhaps more so than before, judged itself by its outward appearance. It was at that time a scientifically and technologically effected turn to the outside, owing to medicine and racial studies on the one hand, and to film and photography on the other. According to the American sociologist David Riesmann, it was simply the transition from an "inner-" to an "outside-directed" society. But it was merely a transition. How under these conditions the idea of shame as a loss of face articulates itself and how the physiognomic obsession of the period provides compensation remains to be seen.

In any case, we need to reconsider from this perspective all those theories that confronted Hitler with the problem of shame. The thought that there may be a reason for the dictator's entire career to be found in his individual biography or perhaps even in his childhood alone has not been supported by most research.[67] Nonetheless, the psychoanalytic hypotheses of Helm Stierlin remain worthy of consideration.[68] It is impossible to confirm that Hitler never quite got over his mother's death from breast cancer, that he subconsciously blamed her Jewish doctor for it. Much points to the contrary: Hitler treated the doctor in question quite well, even if he didn't actually protect him. What weighs much more importantly are the traceable moments of degradation in his life: his rejection by the art academy, his dependency on other men who had to sell his paintings and postcards, the situation in the Vienna Men's Home in general, and the intransparent humiliations suffered from the other sex. These triple or quadruple sources of feelings of inferiority constituted a reservoir of shame to be tapped into; and it is worth investigating the hypothesis that Hitler at a moment of national "loss of face" found an inner link to a society that had discussed physiognomic questions for more than a hundred years on all levels. It was a society that, under Lavater's spell, looked at the face less and less with the eyes of honor and more and more with those of science, thus robbing itself of the symbolic basis that might have prevented a literalization of the metaphor. It was precisely this tendency toward literalness that had made biological racism as acceptable as it had become: as a reclamation of the supposedly "lost face" in a concrete biological sense.[69]

Chapter 2
Warrants and Projections 1918–1923

The Invisible Orator

The years 1917 and 1918, the time immediately before Hitler was brought to the field hospital in Pasewalk for mustard gas poisoning, are today regarded as the formative stage of his ideological development.[1] The experience of the war, the news of revolution, the end of the German monarchies, but above all the Treaty of Versailles provided the supposedly blind lance corporal with his (to him) visionary calling: "I, however, decided to now become a politician." All the information he later provided in accounts of this phase, whether oral or in writing, such as in *Mein Kampf*, whether before the courts or before friends, seems to agree on the one point that he had at this moment, traumatized and angry, found his counterimage, the enemy, back then as yet in twin guises: the Marxist and the Jew.

On November 19, 1918, eight days after the armistice had been signed by the centrist deputy Erzberger, Hitler returned to Munich; owing to limited employment prospects, he remained on the army payroll until March of 1920. What he actually did between November of 1918 and May of 1919 is not clear. All that we know is that he, along with fourteen other soldiers from his regiment, did guard duties at the POW camp in Traunstein, especially gate duty.[2] The camp was run by the soldiers' councils, and Kershaw confirms the contested theory that Hitler was not only trusted by his company, but also passed information to the socialist councils' government and eventually became deputy battalion representative. Later, he of course was silent on this "leftist" phase. His partisanship for the social democrats and demonstrably against the Bolsheviks, however, made it possible for him to enter into the anti-Marxist courses given by Captain Mayr in early June of 1919, Mayr having taken command over the reconnaissance and propaganda operations. Here, during a week-long seminar on political education, Hitler first garnered notice as a public speaker while lambasting the audience of the historian Karl Alexander von Müller. Müller described that audience later: "entranced by a man in their midst, who addressed them with a

strangely guttural voice, inexorably and with growing passion: I had this strange feeling, as if their excitement was his work, but was simultaneously giving him his voice. I saw a pale, meager face under a strand of hair which hung down a bit unsoldierly, with a trimmed mustache and remarkably big, bright blue eyes, which glowed fanatically and cold."[3]
In any case it was Mayr who dispatched Hitler to a course at the Reichswehr's Camp Lechfeld near Augsburg, where he was to return the troops, demoralized and bolshevized by the war, to the nationalist fold. It was here that Hitler found his element: "I began my task with delight. Here all at once I had an opportunity to speak before large audiences; and what I had always assumed, simply as a matter of feeling, without knowing it to be so, now proved true: I could 'speak.' [. . .] I 'nationalized' the troops. [. . .]"[4]

The stages of his further career are well known. In September of 1919 he became a member of the German Workers' Party, the head of which, Drexler, took him under his wing as much as Mayr had previously done. In 1921, he took over as chairman himself, and until the putsch in November of 1923, he became increasingly adroit at mobilizing the masses, in particular by pointing at sacrificial lambs and appealing to a national pride severely wounded by the "disgraceful treaties" [*Schandvertraege*] of Versailles. Obviously this orator knew of a road out of this misery; clearly, he had a vision for the future.

This vision was the subject of a caricature in *Simplicissimus*, which appeared on May 28, 1923, ten years almost to the day after Hitler had arrived in Munich. The drawing by Theodor Heine, the magazine's editor, is entitled "Wie sieht Hitler aus?" [What does Hitler look like?] [Fig. 10.] It shows twelve small pictures captioned with rhetorical questions such as: Does he wear a mask? Is he thin or fat? Beautiful or ugly? They are questions straight out of physiognomic discourse, some on the skull, some on the profile, some on the whole body, some only on expressions or a possible mask. The central, the most action-oriented physiognomic consideration, however, is: How should one represent this man? What will he do? Picture No. 12 shows the caricature of an abstract, but somehow highly dynamic painting with the caption: "These questions must remain unanswered. Hitler isn't an individual at all. He is a condition. Only the futurist can portray him." In other words, he is allied with the future, he is and has himself a "future," just as Mussolini has had one since November 3, 1922, in league with Italian futurism.

In purely physical terms, as is well known, Hitler for now "talked for" and even "screamed for" his future, thrusting himself onto his audience with his voice rather than (as later) with his whole figure. Just as he had practiced in the Vienna Men's Home and on unsuspecting young Häusler, Hitler understood rhetorical overpowering as his true calling—

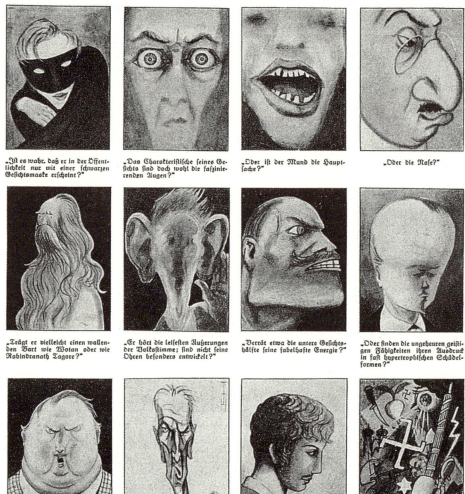

Figure 10. This caricature from the May 28, 1923 issue of *Simplicissimus* provides an introductory lesson in physiognomic education, although of course laced with a highly uncharacteristic hermeneutic insecurity. Allegedly, it was this caricature that inspired Heinrich Hoffmann's interest in photographing Hitler.

overpowering if possible of masses. Two experiences are supposed to have influenced him in this direction: hearing Wagner's opera *Rienzi* in 1905 in Linz, whose titular tribune sent Hitler into fits of rapture according to his friend Kubizek,[5] and reading Bernhard Kellermann's *Der Tunnel* [The Tunnel][6] in Munich in 1913, which also prominently features a public speaker—even if the novel's fulcrum is a man of quiet and wordless decisiveness, an architect and engineer. According to Albert Speer's memoirs, Hitler often named the novel as one of the "major reading experiences of his youth."[7] This may have been a projection of Speer, the architect, and perhaps Hitler was much more interested in the grand technological vision of the novel, and later the movie, than in the story of a small unionist.

From 1919 on, Hitler appeared in fact as a political orator. Ernst Hanfstaengl, who first heard him in 1922, spoke later of the "many-registered and full-bodied instrument of his natural voice, during the first years when it wasn't artificially amplified"; this verdict from an exceedingly musical man is confirmed by other ear-witnesses, as by the few surviving recordings in which Hitler is not screaming.[8] A recent study went so far as to call Hitler the very embodiment of the orator because he fulfilled the "mass-psychological arrangement" with full complementarity of tone, rhythm, and scansion, ranging over two and a half octaves.[9] Many records[10] from the years between 1919 and 1923 document in any case how impressively Hitler performed as a speaker even with a somewhat doughy voice and how impressively he must have perorated on Germany's humiliation. They further document that he himself grasped how the relative invisibility of the public speaker could be turned into a successful effect. In an extensively quoted remark he made during the National Socialist Party's eleventh annual rally in 1936, he reminded his faithful of the following scene: "Long ago you heard the voice of a man, and it struck your hearts, it awakened you, and you followed this voice. You followed it for years, without so much as having seen him whose voice it was; you heard only a voice and you followed."[11]

As so often, Hitler was here alluding to an older scene. The Georgian poet Grigol Robakidse reminds us of it later:

Like millions of others, I hear this voice inside. From time to time I don't listen to the words, I listen for the inner language, and I cannot turn away from a strange vision. Two million dead men lie on an exhausted soil, seven and one-half million are still bleeding, the great German army lowers its weapons. A silence drapes itself over a heavy moonless night as though not of this world. All of a sudden a voice sounds from far away, lamenting, but pulsing with life as well. You hear this voice in the silence as something strange—is it the voice of the unknown soldier turned myth? You apprehend it in the silence as something strange, but at the same time everybody feels it in his very depths—as though he was speaking himself.[12]

The mythic incense, which draped itself over Hitler's voice in such speeches, may have owed its existence to a legend from the war's first year. On November 11, 1914, shortly after the battle of Ypres—or Langemarck—the military spread a blazing communiqué: "West of Langemarck, young regiments, singing "Deutschland, Deutschland, über alles," broke through the first line of enemy fortifications and took them. About two thousand French infantrymen and six machine guns were captured."[13] None of this was true, according to recent historical insights; the German soldiers had sacrificed themselves in defeat and there was little reason to sing. Nonetheless the report of the sacrificial song of the soldiers became a national myth, debunked as a myth after the Second World War, but still very much an article of faith in 1919 when the returning soldiers heard the voice of the selfless lance corporal, who was in fact an ear-witness to the myth, his Bavarian regiment having in fact been deployed in that very battle. "From afar, the songs drifted to our ears," he wrote in *Mein Kampf* about the famous scene, "coming closer and closer, leaping from company to company; and just as Death was busy in our ranks the song reached us too, and we in turn passed it on: 'Deutschland, Deutschland über alles, über alles in der Welt.'"[14]

With this voice of German nationalism, Hitler attracted many to his party with almost somnambulant assurance, in particular since at the time he still spoke in uniform and thus solicited identification with the soldiers' plight.[15] The number of party members jumped from 190 in 1920 to 3,300 in August of 1921, to 6,000 in 1922, and to 55,000 by the end of 1923.[16] During this time, Hitler had no loudspeakers at his disposal; furthermore, he saw himself so much in the role of the orator that even after the machines had been introduced he didn't want to be depicted on posters with a microphone; nor, incidentally, with glasses.

Phonetic Conditioning among the Elites

Very early on, this acoustic agitation encountered a clearly developed physiognomic attunement and receptivity, in particular among the educated classes. The sense for acoustics was surprisingly sharp. As early as 1916, a museum publicly suggested recording the war phonographically: "the terrific drumming noise of battle, in particular during a world war, is after all an acoustic event that leaves a deep impression."[17]

In 1918–19, Karl Krauss's magnum opus *Die letzten Tage der Menschheit* [The Last Days of Mankind] was published. The book was a gigantic montage of acoustic citations from the chorus of warmongers and war profiteers, of its victims and its hangers-on, which, in Karl Krauss's own readings from the work, encroached disturbingly upon his audience. As though an antidote to this apocalyptic *Dies Irae*, a much more popular, lyrical counterpart appeared in 1919. *Menschheitsdämmerung* [Twilight of Man], one of the most influential anthologies of German modernism,[18] reached a printing of twenty thousand in three years—immense for a book of poetry. Very noticeably the introduction holds on to the poem as a "voice" and the collection as a "symphony." "Listen to the poetry of our time," the editor wrote as though all the poets had submitted records rather than pieces of writing, "listen deeply, look all around [. . .], listen [. . .] in concert, all at once. Hear the harmony of poetizing voices: hear symphonically. The music of our time resounds, the booming unison of hearts and minds."[19]

Of course, this phonetic orientation of poetry even before the war owed much to the central poet of "secret Germany," Stefan George, who selected disciples into his elite circle based on their ability to recite to his satisfaction. Furthermore, in the *Jahrbuch für die geistige Bewegung* [Yearbook for the Movement of Spirit] of 1911 , one of George's most devoted pupils, Robert Boehringer, formulated explicitly the ground rules for "saying poems"[20] out loud, as opposed to the modish declamations of the period's actors. George's plangent singsong, however, went even more against the rage of the expressionists. Friedrich Gundolf, who was passionately attached to sonorous classicism, criticized it cuttingly: Expressionism, that was merely the hole the war had torn, and the scream that went along with it:

a venting wail, sobbing, groaning, cries for help or cries of encouragement of the drowning and crazy laughter, [. . .] [but] even the scream, the outburst, the expression in general is of our time and the shattering of formal structure itself does not give rise to a single new sound. [. . .] The scream is at once animal motion, politico-social program, and mental tension. You scream for that which will never come true, for Utopia, because the scream itself is already abreaction, salvation, no matter what you scream for. You shatter language into its illogical, eyeless fragments, into its childish babble, because this shattering itself expresses something.[21]

This was of course satirical and exaggerated and aimed mainly at the dadaists' phonetic experiments. Nonetheless, the observation that the young authors of the *Menschheitsdämmerung* perhaps called for a new form more than they brought it about is correct. And perhaps they didn't call for a new form as much as for a form giver beyond George. The poet Ludwig Rubiner, in any case, exalted even back then the "voice of the leader," without thinking of Hitler of course:

Leader, you stand there looking small, a quivering pillar of blood on
    the narrow platform,

Your mouth is an arched crossbow, you are shot off whirring.
Your eyes cast in horizontal flight luminous wings into the
  green[. . .].[22]

How deeply embedded the association of voice and leader were in particular in the context of the youth movement becomes evident in one of the oddest best-sellers of these years, a book not at all expressionist, whose title, *Die schöpferische Pause* [The Productive Pause], entered the German vocabulary as a standard phrase. It has the following to say about the rhythm of the dialogue between the leader and the led: "If the leader speaks from the heart, it will go to the heart, and those who hear him won't think of speaking after him, but [will] speak for themselves. And [they will] first be silent. Words coming from the depths will not give rise to opposing words in the hearer. Silence is a worthy answer in a growing human being. Silence says: I have listened. Silence is the productive pause between hearing and saying, the respite from which alone man's own words may well up."[23] This esoteric line was continued and deepened more and more. It continued in 1926 with the publication of *Das heilige Schweigen* [Holy Silence].[24] In 1930, *Der hörende Mensch: Elemente eines akustischen Weltbildes* [Man Listening: Elements of an Acoustic Image of the World] provided a veritable anthropology of listening. It was a dense critique not of vision but rather of the supposedly dominant sense of touch.[25] Even a pious theory of the origin of language[26] made the rounds after the end of the First World War: "At the beginning of language was the 'I' that emerged from a cry of woe," it noted about the dialogue of the first man with God. This may sound expressionistic, and of course Hitler himself with his passionate manner of speaking was much closer to expressionist screaming than to the contemplative and formal acoustics of the conservative elites. And if he seemed to embody anything in his screaming, then it was the German "I" emerging "from a cry of woe."

How much even elite thinkers allowed themselves to be guided by the paradigm of sonorous language is evident not least of all in the philosophy of Martin Heidegger, in which the concepts of "hearkening," of silence, of speaking, of "idle chatter" and of "the call" play a central role.[27] The idea of a "conscience as a call of care" evokes the experience of an inner voice, even if in somewhat hollow form, since Heidegger's call of conscience says nothing other than itself.[28] The association of "hearing and obeying," prefigured as the correspondence between God-given "reason" and human "receptivity" [*Vernehmen*] as early as the eighteenth century, now appears in its modernized form, without divine speaker. Eventually, the notion of order became supreme among the linguistic building blocks of the conservatives. Carl Schmitt, the philosopher of law and later crown jurist of National Socialism, was behind this. "What are the original forms of speech?" asked his contemporary Oswald Spengler rhetorically in 1931 while presenting an ostensibly dialogical philosophy of language: "These are sentences, originally quite brief, which are *invariably* addressed to others, such as: Do this! Done? Yes! Go ahead!"[29] And one year later, Ernst Jünger got even more precise: "Obedience, that is the art of hearing, and order is readiness for a word, readiness for an order, which strikes like lightning from the peak to the roots."[30]

This acoustic education ran parallel to the *technological* formation of broadcast and loudspeaker technology and of course to the *economic* career of the medium as well. For example, the stocks of the Radio Corporation of America climbed tenfold between 1919 and 1929, only then to trigger the stock market crash in October of that year.[31] In 1923, the first broadcasts began in Berlin; in 1926, one year after the formation of the Nazi Party, loudspeakers were first used. Soon the party made use of the new technologies; Goebbels later developed absolute virtuosity in their utilization, going so far as creating a sort of church via the radio, at least an institution with literal "receptivity," exactly like the party itself. With instinctive clarity, then, Hitler bridged the party and the mystificatory currents of the era when he conjured the clarion call of his own voice at the party rally on September 11, 1936.

In coping with the misery of the post-war years, the depression over the defeat and all that resulted from it, the "voice" and its philosophical-poetic hypostatization became a first-rate factor. It incorporated what recent social psychology knows as "interiorization" and links to the so-called "culture of guilt." The "inner voice" is always also the "voice of conscience" or of "the fathers" (never the mothers, incidentally). The stunning successes of the orator Hitler with his audiences may have their reasons not least of all in the fact that he appealed to the Allies' bad and the Germans' good consciences when he attacked the peace settlement. No topic of the years 1919–21, not even the question of the Jews, was touched on as frequently as the Versailles treaty. To demand back the "face" lost there was one of the conditions of Hitler's success as a speaker, even if, by all appearances, there was no real possibility of revenge and satisfaction, even if the grim spectacle of the war cripples that populated the streets was irreparable.

"What Does Hitler Look Like?"

Hitler's performances as public speaker in the years between 1919 and 1923 were received differently from his later ones, precisely because it was only possible to hear him, not really to see or to photograph him.

According to his first biographer, Konrad Heiden, Hitler had forbidden anyone to take pictures of him. "During rallies, he knew how to stay half-invisible by way of clever lighting tricks. When he entered a hall, he quickly walked through an alley formed by his SA and remained for most visitors a hushing, instantly fading impression."[32]

It was thus with some justification that *Simplicissimus* asked in May of 1923 "What does Hitler look like?" with the cartoonist's commentary "Adolf Hitler won't let himself be depicted. During my stay in Berlin I was beseeched to reveal what he looks like"—even if he pretended not to know the answer or rather made Hitler even more mysterious as a futurist figure. This fully physiognomic caricature was much more than a compendium with punch line. In its form it may have been reminiscent of a warrant, such as may have been produced for law enforcement in the case of a gang of robbers, and as it appears in the books of Cesare Lombroso for the purposes of physical identification of criminals. But even here another in-joke of *Simplicissimus*'s educated editor lay hidden: On the one hand, the last picture-within-the-picture made unambiguous reference to Mussolini's association with Futurism. On the other hand, the picture's caption referenced a figure of German social history who had committed a similarly crazy albeit much more innocuous assault on the powers-that-be, creating hilarity throughout the empire: the Captain of Köpenick.* In 1906, the *Kladderadatsch* had dedicated a warrant caricature to him with the caption: "Description: Indescribable." For Hitler we now read in the last *Simplicissimus* caption something along the same lines: "The questions [concerning his appearance] must remain unanswered."

This warrant with its series of small portraits was of course a citational satire with predecessors. In 1834, a similar multifaced gallery of a single important man appeared in the satirical *Charivari* about the French king Louis Philippe[33] [Fig. 11]. Here we find not only numerous variations on the royal head on the wall (the famous pear shape), but even in the spectators themselves, who display the same shape. Ludwig Justi's strange observation on the proximity of the modern state's "delinquent album" (the Hitler warrant) and the portrait gallery (the caricature of the king) had thus been clearly confirmed by *Simplicissimus*, even if it

---

*Wilhelm Voigt (1849–1922), the "captain of Köpenick," became a cause célèbre of the Wilhelmine empire with his 1906 confidence scheme, in which he impersonated a captain (in a uniform assembled from various second-hand purchases), commandeered a small group of soldiers, and used them to take control of the town hall of Köpenick, near Berlin. He had the mayor arrested and confiscated municipal funds before escaping by train. Captured a few weeks later, he was sent to jail but pardoned by the emperor. Carl Zuckmayer's famous play based on the captain's exploits was first performed in 1930. Trans.

wasn't in the medium of photography where Justi had alone thought it possible in 1913.[34]

Hitler's initial reticence before and rejection of cameras has most recently been discussed in depth by Rudolf Herz. In his biography of Heinrich Hoffmann, Hitler's so-called court photographer, he cites a range of different opinions on the subject. For example, Hitler's followers (Baldur von Schirach, for instance) respected his mystification as a personal idiosyncrasy; the press tended to view it as a propagandistic legerdemain and reported that at public appearances two or three of Hitler's deputies were always charged with keeping the press from taking pictures.[35] There is no real proof of a stratagem; rather to the contrary. Herz mentions the fact that Hitler was wanted by warrant in Prussia and other northern German states where the Nazi Party was outlawed. He thus had to remain incognito when traveling in those states.[36] But this was of course impossible to keep up in the long run. The first photo from those years comes from the press photographer Georg Pahl, who recognized Hitler during a visit in Berlin's Luna Park in April of 1923 and photographed him. According to Pahl's testimony, Hitler jumped on him and unsuccessfully attempted to wrest the camera from his hands. Hitler eventually persuaded Pahl to destroy the negative. But a few months later, on September 2, 1923, Pahl landed another snapshot of Hitler in Nuremberg, leading the latter henceforth to trust only the strategic portraits by Heinrich Hoffmann. His first portrait session with Hitler took place in early September of 1923. Hoffmann immediately began selling the pictures in a number of reproductions: as a wall poster, a postcard, a press picture, and in a photo-based drawing by Otto von Kursell, the most important artist of Hitler portraits for popular pamphlets. Hoffman had vast success with his sales, all the more because Hitler attained unforeseen notoriety following his November coup attempt and subsequent imprisonment in Landsberg Fortress.

* * *

Between the caricature in *Simplicissimus* in May and the coup attempt in November, there was one more opportunity to answer the question "What does Hitler look like?" At the end of September, after a speech on the occasion of "Germany Day" at the Bayreuth Reithalle, Hitler was granted an audience with the old and decrepit Houston Steward Chamberlain: the Englishman, Cosima Wagner's son-in-law, one of the most notorious nationalists and anti-Semites on the German scene, was the author of a racist best-seller called *The Foundations of the Nineteenth Century*. Chamberlain was influential owing to his liaison with Bayreuth. This well-known man wrote Hitler a highly memorable letter about two

Figure 11. With the famous caricature of Louis Philippe from the *Charivari* from 1834, the illustrator Daumier had created a much-referenced model of "the pear" as a portrait gallery all by itself. Hitler too was ridiculed in similar galleries from 1933 onward.

weeks after the meeting. With freakish hymns of praise, he thanked Hitler as the "rouser of souls from sleep and rut," for granting "me so long and so refreshing a sleep recently," "the sort of which I had not had since that fateful August day of 1914, when that vile suffering attacked me [the multiple sclerosis from which Chamberlain suffered]. Now I believe I see that this precisely marks your essence and as it were contains it: the true rouser is at once a granter of peace." And Chamberlain continues, prophetically wrong with every word: "You are not as you had been reported to me, a fanatic, rather I would call you the immediate opposite of a fanatic, . . . yes, I would also call you the very opposite of a politician—taking this word in its usual meaning—since the central axis in all politics is party business, while with you all parties disappear, devoured by the fire of your patriotism. . . . In spite of your will-force, I do not think you are a violent man. You know Goethe's distinction between violence and violence!" And Chamberlain closed his letter with a physiognomic sketch: "That you gave me peace has much to do with your eye and your hand gestures. Your eye is as it were good with its hands, it touches a person and holds it, and it is peculiar to you that at every moment you address your speech to one particular one among your listeners—that I noticed as something quite characteristic. And as regards your hands, they are so expressive in their motions that they compete with the eyes in this aspect. Such a man can give peace to a poor, beset spirit."[37] In general the story of this letter is well documented. Chamberlain had it reprinted in pamphlet form for New Year's 1924,[38] and on April 10, 1932 the *Völkische Beobachter* printed it once more. It is possible that Heidegger read the letter then; his colleague Karl Jaspers, when he asked Heidegger over lunch in 1933 whether so uneducated a man as Hitler could rule Germany received the response: "Education is irrelevant, just look at his wonderful hands!"[39] The noose of physiognomic fascination, the motif of "Wallenstein's Face," was thus tightened. Briefly before Hitler's accession to power, even Rudolf Kassner wondered whether "true fitness to rule [*Herrscherbegabung*] should not be expressed in the hand" and whether one could not tell a race fated to dominate by its hands rather than by its faces.[40]

Indeed, Chamberlain tapped into a physiognomic repertoire when remarking that Hitler's eyes were "good with their hands." Since Carl Gustav Carus, the hagiographer of the German skull and the author of a treatise entitled *Die Symbolik der menschlichen Gestalt* [The Symbolism of Human Figure], the gaze of the educated observer of human nature had been directed at the hands as well, not unjustifiably, since apparel and coiffure may be bought, while the hands reveal the work that lies behind them. Carus distinguished the motor from the sensible hand, and the elementary from the spiritual hand, all terms modeled on the

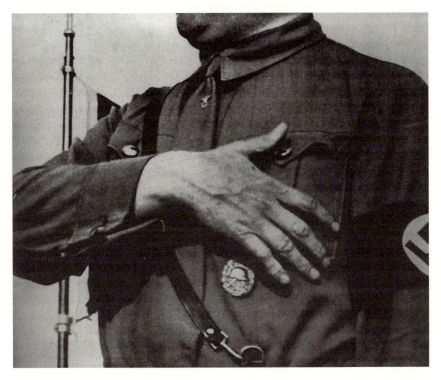

Figure 12. Hitler's hands have often inspired adulation across the board, unlike the rest of his appearance, which was always highly controversial. This snapshot from 1932 is probably another of Heinrich Hoffmann's.

doctrine of the four temperaments. Inspired by this analysis, Reichssen-deleiter [chief of broadcasting] Eugen Hadamovsky resolved to adore Hitler's hand as sensitive and artistic: "This infinitely fine-jointed hand with the strong lumps above the joints, the wonderful contour of the veins, and the lines on the insides of the hands were more intricate and variegated than I ever saw in the hand of another human being. This hand then is the tool of a similarly thousand-faceted spirit and a similarly intricate and rich soul. It is the hand of a great artist, of a great shaper."[41] Whether Hadamovsky ever had the opportunity to inspect the inside of the Führer's hand may reasonably be doubted; if at all one could imagine his devotion to have progressed to the point at which he fantasized of inspecting the Führer's hand while eating out of it. The case is different with the hand's front: the picture from the 1930s [Fig. 12] suggests Carus's hermeneutic, by which "strong articular eminence [. . .] always indicates the predominance of the motor element, giving

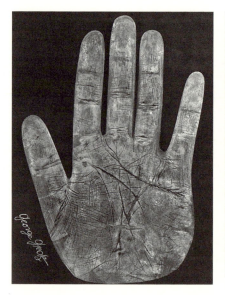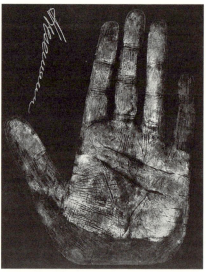

Figure 13. Two hand prints—one from George Grosz and one from Gustav Stresemann—from the collection of Marianne Raschig. Her *Introduction to the System of the Study of Hands* appeared in 1931 from the Gebrüder Enoch Verlag in Hamburg. The number of handprints bespeaks the *Introduction*'s popularity: the volume contains more than four hundred, of almost all of the famous people of the epoch, oftentimes accompanied by a signature—a national portrait gallery all its own.

the hand a grasping character. Such development usually points to the preponderance of will and understanding over disposition."[42]

Chamberlain's association of an "eye-hand" points beyond the physiognomic tradition, almost citing a topos of saint worship by something like hand icons: the eye of God drawn or painted onto the palm of a hand for the purposes of contemplative devotion. It was a displaced devotion to faces invented by the Counter Reformation.[43] But the hand figured prominently among other authors of the 1920s. The Institute for Cultural Research commissioned a film on "productive hands," with pictures of artists' hands; entire volumes of handprints appeared, continuing the project of a photo gallery to memorialize men "of merit," as it were, "from the margins" [Fig. 13]. This happened by way of geometric traces, which of course didn't really invite pious contemplation but esoteric vatecinations.[44]

The hand was inextricably linked to handwriting and its analysis, one of the best cultivated physiognomic subdisciplines of the period, proving profitable for economic exploitation, as in the case of Ludwig Klages, for philosophical cogitation, as in the case of Walter Benjamin, and for charlatan schemes, for example those of the famous Rafael Schermann, who claimed to be able not only to tell a person's character from his or her handwriting, but in the reverse to guess someone's handwriting as well. Hitler's handwriting was certainly analyzed more often than hitherto presumed.[45] Since he largely eschewed expressing himself in writing, there wasn't much material to go on. One of the first reports, if not *the* first, dates from 1924. The graphologist Wenzel wrote to Ludolf Haase, the leader of the Nationalist Party's Göttingen chapter, who at the time opposed the party's entrance into Parliament and apparently discussed this with Wenzel. In concluding his letter of June 21, Wenzel writes:

On the other hand, as a graphologist I don't like the look of our friend's signature at all. Even before, the downward tilt in his signature worried me. This [tilt] has now intensified, and is visible in both the first name, in which moreover the "l" before the final "f" drops out (!), and especially in the last name. This characteristic points to a type of person whose energies may be as great as they want, but will at the decisive moment fail him. If you take the crossbars in the "f," which dip off to the right (far below the line!) and in the "t" as well, then the sad expression of this broken former warrior becomes obvious. What is very noticeable and deeply saddening is finally the formation of the m's and n's, which are given highly unnatural corners[. . .].[46]

Graphologists reiterated this interpretation of Hitler's signature [Fig. 14] well into the 1940s. In hindsight, its plausibility is striking, but what does this mean for graphology? Haase didn't have his way back then; the Nationalists merged with the Nazi groups and ran candidates for the national election. Hitler, from his prison in Landsberg Fortress, had given his approval.

Even if not evident in his writing, the enormous charisma Hitler seems to have exuded at close quarters (provided that he wanted to) has been widely reported. Even during the war years, experienced generals came to him with set plans only to change their minds after a few hours under his persuasion, not because of his hands or his voice, but because of the "large scale of nuances at his disposal."[47] His early confidant Otto Wagener believed that his eyes' suggestiveness could fully absorb his actual speech: "Hitler was no longer sitting, but he was no longer standing either, he was simply 'word' with glowing eyes and radiant gaze." He allowed the listener "a glimpse into the dark depths of what's coming, which he penetrated for brief moments like a spotlight, casting light on things that otherwise remain hidden to the human eye."[48]

The fact that Hitler managed to impress himself upon the Germans as a *speaker,* that he was able to overwhelm them rhetorically and win them over even in close contact, surely contradicts the supposition

Figure 14. Hitler's handwriting—in particular his signature, which later developed a dramatic downward tilt toward the end—has been frequently observed and probably always interpreted negatively. This photo is dedicated to Carin Göring.

that Hitler was merely the product of photography and film, a rationally designed "trademark."[49] The power of Hitler's transfixing gaze—universally reported—demanded to be *experienced*, even if by eyewitness account or through propagandistic lore. No photograph, no film managed to capture it; nonetheless, Hans F. K. Jünger could ascribe its passionate fire officially to the eye of the Aryan race: "Nordic eyes often have something radiant about them; also in certain states of mind what the Romans called a 'terrible gaze' among the predominantly Nordic Germanic tribes."[50] At the beginning of the 1930s, we even find a philosophical version of this thought in Oswald Spengler's work. Spengler, who otherwise didn't think highly of Hitler at all, provided a biography of Hitler's gaze in the full sense of the word, translating the gaze into living, evil nature: "The eye of the preying animal gives a *target*. The very fact that [. . .] the two eyes can be fixed on one point in their environment enables the animal to bind its prey." Chamberlain had experienced Hitler's "talent" similarly for grabbing the individual listener as though with a paw; other eyewitnesses tended to register what Spengler thought of as philosophical about the predator: "The eye of the animal of prey determines things according to positioned distance. It apprehends the horizon. It measures up in this *battlefield* the objects and conditions of attack."[51]

Five years later, this predator had become a dangerous statue, a Big Brother: "His temples tell of an iron distance," the boss of the so-called Reichschrifttumskammer, Hans Johst, noted in 1936. "Like sensible membranes they rest between ear and eye. They are the loneliest temples I ever saw. They mandate inapproachability. Only in the crowns of great German minds do we find this remarkable concave form. Here, perceptions are filtered mercilessly. One looks into the eyes, is welcomed by them, but at the same time cross-examined by the temples, perceived and weighed."[52]

Another forty years later Joachim Fest reports the contemporary observation that "his [Hitler's] eyes [. . .] never stood still and wandered about unquietly even in moments of statuesque petrification."[53] As is known, this was the image Hans Jürgen Syberberg took recourse to in his Hitler film of 1977, where he showed the dictator over and over as a wooden doll with an insanely flickering gaze. Had he been inspired by the Georgian poet Robakidse? He after all had thought in 1939 that no painter could "exhaustively portray Hitler's inner image; perhaps a woodcutter might succeed." But the woodcut would lack "his densely blue and yet clear eyes, which contain his true essence. Before the severe regard of these eyes, all inauthenticity and all mendacity must scatter in confusion."[54] Syberberg, however, shows the wooden doll not only with the insanely flickering gaze, but places him right into the hands of a puppeteer: Ludwig II, the fairy-tale king and the author of German history, at least in the eyes of the post-1945 generation.

Face and Space: Facial Literature

The pictorial avenues available in 1923, caricature, photography, and eyewitness account, would accompany Hitler's rise to power in the following years. Much like his speeches or, perhaps better, like his acoustic intrusiveness, his visual intrusiveness was met at the time by a multiply conditioned and highly expectant audience. The time between 1918

Figure 15. The portrait collection entitled *The Face of the Ruling Class* by George Grosz, which appeared in 1921, created quite a stir and controversy at the time. Count Brockdorff-Rantzau (the subject of this portrait) had militated against the Versailles treaty. He embodied the German resentment of the Allied conditions for peace; in Grosz's picture, however, he embodied the left's resentments of German militarism.

and 1923 had already seen a high point of physiognomic speculation and hermeneutics of "merit." In particular since the defeat, the old project of a "national portrait gallery" oscillated increasingly between considerations of biological and mental "merit." The starting gun, perhaps the most realistic but certainly the most satirical and challenging, was sounded by George Grosz in 1921 in the shape of *Das Gesicht der herrschenden Klasse* [The Face of the Ruling Class], which struck a central nerve of the German quest for physiognomic national identity [Fig. 15].

One reason for this may lie in the change of state form itself. The Weimar Republic went through twenty governments. Among all its leaders, only General Field Marshal Hindenburg, president of the Reich since 1925, was permitted to bridge the span between empire and Third Reich; Stresemann, in power since 1924, died in 1929, while other faces appeared only to disappear again, if they were not violently dispatched. The jump from a dynastic government like the house of Hohenzollern, which was obtrusive, but at least orderly in its self-presentation, to the revolving door of constantly changing democratic ensembles must have stirred up a physiognomic confusion all its own. Some authors reacted to it with a yearning for a single face of leadership, a ruler portrait, even if only in the form of a satire. Lavater's facial prose had blossomed into a distinct kind of text, into an attitude of expectation at the time, on which the hatred later projected onto Hitler's face clearly feeds. For example, in a high-expressionist prose volume of 1923, Robert Müller, an Austrian eccentric and friend of the writer Robert Musil's, sketches almost yearningly and ecstatically the leader type of yore, the head of General Falkenhayn, author of the catastrophe of Verdun, based on a—lost—caricature by the French illustrator Faber from Buenos Aires:

Within him lies the explanation for a world war; but perhaps only then, when this head is viciously depicted by the finest Gallic mischief and mounted in the room of a German connoisseur. This head, a bestial caricature, actually appears quite noble, in any case of good breeding [*rassig*]; what was intended as sneer and mockery comes across as nefarious greatness. The caricature is not linear, but spatial; it is precisely the stereometric that is exaggerated, the head just stands in space coldly, the gaze virtually knocks against this empty squareness, in which numbers, principles, prejudices, dry forces of the will are reposited. The head IS space, a common, *the* most common, kind of imperialism, that imperialism which simply demands space, a lot of space. The elliptical, cylindrical, conical, and prismatic elements of which this head is made are not the means of a kind of popular cubism; they do not reside in the apperceiving subject, they lie, if we follow the artist, entirely within the object. The artist's distant memory conjures up the public perception of the German as the *tête carée* [square head], which he then bends and flattens a bit. The geometry of it all lies in the object. It is without imagination par excellence. The head is firstly that of the Junker, the reserved person, the "caste." "Caste" is also a special term.* Then [it is of] the man who is fully concentrated, brief, parsimonious, even though he rules in space; who doesn't consist of anything but little tiles of alignment and disposition [*Gesinnungsziegel*], without grace or creativity; who is infinitely hard and strong, but no organism, rather a crystalline force. How the band collar stiffens underneath his chin, warding off any accidental humanity like a turret! How the crown of his skull, no, no skull, a skullcap, cambers against the arousal of humanity! It is a $2\text{-}\pi\text{-}r$ skull, a manifest relation of numbers; you notice how he bristles with logarithms of supply and deployment into life. In his crinkles run the projections of sensuous physical forces; the graphic expression of beastly mechanisms combines into his facial expression. Through the monocle, a circle, a flat pane, he sees the world like a Ludolfian number,† which gives him a posture, becomes a character trait, designating the mathematical correctness

*A pun: in German, "Kaste" (caste) is very similar to "Kasten" (box). Trans.

†"Ludolfian number" is an old German designation for the number π, and the sixteenth-century mathematician Ludolf van Ceulen, who calculated π to thirty-five decimal places. Trans.

of his outlook. . . . The Frenchman has shown him without frills, boxed him in, penetrating, brusque; now he is a diamond of presentation, a reflecting, newly shined leather of expression.[55]

Theodor Wolff, editor of the *Berliner Tageblatt* and fellow physiognomist of rank, also conjures up the image of a particular type among the old leaders of society—of all people the Russophile eccentric Count Brockdorff-Rantzau, whom George Grosz had depicted on the dust jacket of his 1921 portfolio:

. . . seemingly so similar to the original, and retouched with canny deceptiveness ever so slightly, the caricature was barely apparent as such. The illustrator seemed to want to say that there was little need here for exposing and mockery; that in this case nature itself showed humor (which is clearly at work in the creation of so many of its creatures) far superior to any artist, giving rise to the typical head of an epoch, leaving nothing in the dark and achieving, to all connoisseurs, a satirical masterpiece. Could one express that mixture of decadence and Junker arrogance better than through this head, through every feature and detail of this pale, nervous face—the brow bearing the traces of too long a past and yet commandingly wide, framed by the thin, straightened, and carefully parted hair, the narrow, straight nose, the tiny, rakish mustache, the protruding chin, the eyes, shrouded yet challenging the viewer, in which were visible both the blasé attitude of this fatigued and ending line and its enduring imperious self-confidence? Wasn't he the indisputable grandson of those aristocratic buccaneers who dueled over any small matter, who looked down on the city tradesfolk with contempt and who, when they could no longer plunder the burgher and work the peasant, sold themselves to foreign courts and didn't forget to bring back from each country some fashionable frills?[56]

This is how Wolff recapitulates the intentions of Grosz's drawings—only then to go into similar depth in providing a counterimage of the "true" Rantzau. Both characterizations, just like Falkenhayn's by Müller, bespeak how closely physiognomic interest was intertwined with genealogical interest. In all three portraits the viewer attempts to discern the "ancestral pride," in some sense the gallery behind the picture, be that a gallery of members of a caste or of those of a family. The individual is made to represent a character as well as a legacy, and this in the double sense of that word: in terms of dignity and merit, but also in terms of constituting biological inheritance.

But this is where disagreement starts. Whereas Theodor Wolff sees in the count's head nothing but history, Müller, under the guise of graphic requisites, wants the skull to anchor a spatial order. Müller's idea to transform punningly the notion of the "caste" into a spatial term is captured by the illustrator's *tête carée*. This transformation corresponds to that naturalization and physicalization apparent in the perception of Haeckel's head in 1914 and Wallenstein's face in 1918. The creeping transition from the portrait to the prototypical head of the New Objectivity, to the medical example, to the measured man of anthropometrics, which no longer triggers a countergaze, is thus clearly visible.

It is this borderline that is straddled by the numerous facially oriented books written (and by all appearances eaten up voraciously) in Germany between the end of the World War I and the end of inflation and onwards. They are books published on the left and on the right, by Jews and non-Jews; photo books, medical textbooks, literary physiognomy and physiognomic world analysis.[57] "Doing" physiognomy becomes a fashion, if it wasn't one in its previous guise, nineteenth-century racism, already. Physiognomy also becomes the battle cry of those unwilling to come to terms with psychoanalysis and more ready to pay service to "biopsychology," compatible with the arts as well as with medicine and natural science. Physiognomy, a colorful way of thought somewhere between what Martin Blankenburg has called "morphological idealism" and a zeitgeist-fed search for meaning, between banalities about human nature and dangerous dehumanization, gives a clear direction to the oft-discussed German *Sonderweg* (special national path). Inspired and fascinated by Dostoevsky, Stefan Zweig, a passionate collector of autographs and an advocate of a "typology of the creative spirit," described for pages and in clear opposition to the silent movie the gesture, mimic expression, build, and apparel of his protagonists. Journalists such as Theodor Wolff, poets such as Franz Kafka, cultural politicians such as Count Harry Kessler, as well as their perfectly average contemporaries experimented in their journals with physiognomic modes of evaluation.[58] Socially conscious authors such as Lion Feuchtwanger asked about the life chances of the ugly (*The Ugly Duchess Margarete Maultasch*, 1923, later made into a film). The psychiatrists of the period diagnosed children and the mentally ill from a physiognomic point of view; psychologists invented concepts such as eidetics in order to explain visual memory[59] or established selection criteria for professions or the military culled from mimic, posture, and build;[60] philosophers and essayists provided the accordingly inflated views on the world. Anti-Semitic propaganda, since 1923 unremitting and merciless in the hands of Julius Streicher and his paper *Der Stürmer*, was thus received by a German society that was visually highly sensitized and almost obsessively conditioned and with an ever growing tendency to evaluate itself and others in a mirror, rather than (as in psychoanalysis) in a conversation.

It was Oswald Spengler's monumental 1918 cultural history *Der Untergang des Abendlandes* [The Decline of the West][61] that inaugurated this physiognomic search for meaning. Spengler declared physiognomy the science of the future, at least within historiography and distinct from "systematics," which didn't know what to do with the phenomena of the individual. According to Spengler, cultures have "faces"; as a connoisseur of the world and of human nature, the art historian can give a diagnostic portrait of these faces. "Physiognomics is a true portrait in the sense of Rembrandt, which means history banished into a single moment. The row of self-portraits is nothing else than a—truly Goethian—autobiography compared to it. Thus, the biography of all cultures remains to be written."[62] In spite of this reference to art, Spengler was really performing a physiognomic diagnosis of sickness. His "international portrait gallery of all cultures" looked for cultural histories "of merit" in the sense of health; it sought to separate flowering cultures from unripe or withered ones, for example Spengler's own Western one.

Spengler was not the only one to peddle physiognomically inspired cultural histories quite successfully. Even the first book on physiognomy from one of the most difficult, mannered authors, *Zahl und Gesicht* (Number and Face) by Rudolf Kassner (1919), went through several printings. According to its subtitle, the book detailed the "Outlines of a Universal Physiognomy," but anyone looking to find any simple Lavater-inspired correlation of bodily features with mental or spiritual ones would have been disappointed. Kassner's book is in many respects comprehensible only from today's standpoint. It is true that, just like Spengler, Kassner subscribed to a sort of "morphological idealism" (Martin Blankenburg); but at the same time, he desperately engaged with Einstein's mathematics and physics. He suspected that the face was the final human configuration before the human body disappeared in quantitative thought.

The year 1920 saw the publication of the first German portrait collection hailing from Jewish quarters: *Das ostjüdische Antlitz* [The Face of East European Jewry], with texts by Arnold Zweig and fifty-two coal drawings by Hermann Struck. With its physiognomic turn the book clearly differed from the more Zionist undertaking of Samuel Meisel, who in Vienna in 1926 published a catalogue of Jews of cultural merit in the spirit of the "national portrait gallery" under the title *Judenköpfe* [Jewish Heads]—in words, sans pictures. Zweig's picture volume appeared in 1922 in a second edition. The pathetic, socially romantic evocation of the good, inward-looking, pious eastern Jew [Fig. 16]—a poignant if not kitsch-free portrait gallery "from below"—presented a thoughtful counterpart to Aryan self-exhibition. That exhibition was inaugurated by Hans F. K. Günther, a professor in Jena since 1930 who was called "Race Günther," and appeared first as *Rassenkunde des deutschen Volkes* [Racial Study of the German People] from 1922 to 1935 in sixteen editions with copious pictures; from 1928 onward, it was amended by a far more widely available popular edition. It was a completely racist portrait gallery "from above," propagating the aristocracy of physical build: "The

Figure 16. The portrait collection entitled *The Face of Eastern European Jewry* was published in 1920, with accompanying text by Arnold Zweig and fifty-two coal drawings by Hermann Struck. Zweig evoked the pious eastern Jew, who really does not belong in the world of pictures but in that of books.

Nordic race. It is tall, long-legged, slender, with an average height of 1.74 meters in the case of the male. The appendages appear strong and slender, the neck, the outlines of hand and feet. . . . The face is narrow with rather narrow brow, narrow high nose, and narrow lower jaw with pronounced chin."[63]

Günther was given a professorship in Berlin at the faculty for agriculture and veterinary medicine; the anthropologists had rejected him. In fact, the vocabulary of his racial discourse comes out of animal husbandry, in particular from horse breeding, where customary "doctrines of the exterior"[64] had been in use for more than a hundred years. That Germans submitted to this kind of self-reflection with such abandon is confirmed by Robert Musil's early diagnosis, according to which the epoch wore a "jockey face, all melted together." The nation was already going to the races.

But for now, physiognomic studies of humans were dominated by the medical side. In 1921, there appeared psychiatrist Ernst Kretschmer's *Körperbau und Charakter* [Build and Character], a highly successful book, read even by laypeople and available in German bookstores till this day. The "Investigations into the Problem of Constitution and the Doctrine of the Temperaments" (1921) gave physiognomy a greater air of seriousness by putting it on a statistical basis. With its doctrine of the two or three body types—asthenic (leptosomic), pycnic, athletic—which in turn were said to appear in conjunction with certain mental illnesses, the book fed a much larger addiction as well—of the classification of bodies, and of classification in general.

All of the concessions to the evolutionary principle of the natural sciences notwithstanding, a switch in mentality became apparent here. Since the emergence of anthropology and certainly since the victory of Darwinism, history had been conceived as progress, and the notion of development had led to a radical temporalization of phenomena. "Processualization and denaturalization of the notions of the time, development of techniques for the acceleration of and coping with progress,"[65] dominated throughout the nineteenth century. Since the turn of the century, even more since the end of World War I, a countermovement has been in existence: with Wilhelm Dilthey's and Karl Jaspers's taxonomy in the history of ideas (*Types of Weltanschauung*, 1911 and *Psychology of Weltanschauung*, 1919, respectively), but above all with the many more or less biologistic attempts at facial and body typing. However, the principle of classification is based on the presumption of the aboriginality of all phenomena, or at least of their simultaneity. It develops—at first—mental topographies. In fact, physiognomy and its normative systems are much closer to the study of regions than to a theory of development; the highly popular and age-old metaphor of the face as a landscape bespeaks this fact already. Even Lichtenberg, aloof to any notion of nationalism, called the face the "most entertaining area of the earth," and the notion of a "cultural physiognomy," such as developed by the Africanist Leo Frobenius in conjunction with Kretschmer and Spengler, segued quite naturally into a spatial way of thinking. For Spengler too thought spatially when he analogized cultures and plants, which after all do not wander, but are instead dependent on their environment; thinking territorially, however, was above all the domain of politics.

The Face of the East: Arnold Zweig

The appearance of space as a hadean dimension of desire in the discourse of the period has been frequently observed and variously interpreted. Kershaw thinks that this political tradition has its roots in imperialism under the kaiser before 1900;[66] only a little later we also find a specific cultural radius. The variations on this theme run the gamut from cubism in painting, which Carl Einstein promoted so exigently, to the *Literary History of German Tribes and Regions* (1912–28) put forward by the Austrian Germanist and later National Socialist Josef Nadler, from Spengler's lecture entitled "The Plan to a New *Atlas Antiquus*," given before an audience of Orientalists in 1924,[67] to the famous talk by Hugo von Hofmannsthal entitled "Literature [*Schrifttum*] as the Mental Space of the Nation" of 1927. They find their philosophical reflection in such nonhistorical disciplines as phenomenology, gestalt psychology, physiognomic morphology, and others. Most of these themes became preponderant among the German-speaking peoples, or at least were pushed to their fullest extent under German influence, as in the case of the "cubist graphology" of the Mendelssohns[68] or Nadler's *Literary History*, the second edition of which was riddled with *völkisch* slogans. In any case, only Germany saw this kind of national implosion of the idea of expanse and openness, which is after all always a correlate of the notion of space. There was a sense of lacking breathing space, perhaps even, as a consequence of the war, a veritable claustrophobia. One of the main authors of this implosion is probably Karl Haushofer, who had held a chair in geopolitics since 1921, met Hitler in 1922 through his student Rudolf Hess, and certainly influenced the former intellectually. In 1924, he founded the *Journal of Geopolitics*; in 1926, it was followed by the bestselling novel *Volk ohne Raum* (A People without Space) by Hans Grimm, a political scientist and former member of the foreign department of the army high command in World War I. Three years after the occupation of the Ruhr, this book was a firebrand and a signal; with the second volume of Hitler's *Mein Kampf*, just recently published, it became an exposé of that *Lebensraum* [living space] thesis, which for Hitler went along with the demand for the destruction of "Jewish Bolshevism" from then on.[69] For the war that he envisaged was not only to give Germany's wounded honor "revenge" over the Western powers, but was also to serve biological and imperialist ambitions in the East: to return the Germans living in once German lands into the fold and at the same time to bring the German people to the sources of raw materials and the wheat baskets of eastern Europe. This turn east had been briefly anticipated by the German military in the summer of 1918 with its (proposed) advance into Russia, but immediately abandoned at the time; nonetheless, in the words of Sebastian Haffner, it "made a deep impression on many Germans—among them Hitler."[70]

From a *physiognomic* point of view, the spatial projections of the time may have had very similar sources. Granted, it is apparent in the period's facial prose how customary moral [*sittlich*] traditions and spiritual history segue into purely body-based speculations and spatial configurations, perhaps even how one superseded the other. But at least since Bölsche's gaze on Haeckel these countenances have seemed Janus-faced, just like the Third Reich would later: they look forward and back-ward, out into the open space and back into the traditional community (as opposed to civil society), the facial attachment of which was always also linguistic and subject to the setting of shame as described by Sim-mel. The face as landscape or an open field is of course exempted from this setting. There is no more reciprocity here; no landscape could lower its gaze in shame or avoid that of the viewer. The face as landscape could however, if we stick with the image, fend off this gesture of shame. For looking into a face as though the gaze were scanning a terrain (one of the physiognomists of the period speaks categorically of a "mimic ter-rain")[71] would be in itself nothing other than looking "to the ground" and would thus thrust the gesture of shame on the viewer. "At once the glance sought the ground as though consumed by shame"—this sen-tence from "Wallenstein's Face," the 1918 story by Walter Flex could function as the motto for a whole canon of facial observations, which owe their existence neither to ahistorical (pseudo-)scientificity nor to mythical genealogy, but rather to the trauma of the defeat of 1918 and its peculiar physiognomic compensation. A military loss of "ground" is of course always a loss of face. And this loss is best compensated for as lost soil; with a military leader who knows no "as if," like Hitler, this soil will not be symbolic, but rather very concrete.

Perhaps there is no better diagnosis of this conspicuous mutual con-vertibility of "face" and soil, long before German photography of the period began depicting the human face as a face of "Blut und Boden" [blood and soil], than the pages-long portrait that Arnold Zweig gave of Erich Ludendorff, Hitler's idol from World War I (and his comrade-in-arms in the abortive 1923 coup attempt), in the novel *Der Streit um den Sergeanten Grischa* [The Case of Sergeant Grischa]. First drafts of the novel date back to 1917 when Zweig was part of the press corps with the chiefs of staff headquarters in Bialystok and thus was privy to German plans of annexation. Ludendorff appears in the middle of the novel under the name of Albert Schieffenzahn and under the title "Portrait of an Autocrat":

Major General Schieffenzahn sat at work in a blue civilian jacket, and his front view was most impressive: a straight tall forehead over a pair of small gray eyes, the manifest nose of an autocrat, beneath it a moustache trimmed in the English manner, a shrewd, subtle mouth, the whole face set squarely upon a majestic double chin above the red collar of the General Staff. Broad-shouldered and tall, he sat enthroned at his writing table, looking quickly through some newspa-pers and marking them in blue and red pencil. But seen in profile, his appear-ance was far less imposing: the whole magnificent effect was strangely and sadly marred. He had the sagging cheeks of an old woman, his shoulders were too round, and from the oval outline of the weak receding curves of chin and forehead the nose stood out sharply like the beak of a parrot, with two ominous wrinkles at the nostrils and the bridge deeply marked by the spectacles he wore for writing. And when he got up, as he did now—to put a sheet of paper covered with bluish writing on a pile of other such sheets—his appearance seemed to shrink. His legs in their black red-striped trousers were too short, and he had small hands and feet, so that although he could pass for a giant when seated, when standing he was revealed as no taller than a man of average height.

While the physiognomic portrait in a few lines stages a complete physical defeat—from the front, Schieffenzahn appears imposing, from the side limp, and standing up like a dwarf—this physical loss of honor is amply compensated, like a "loss of ground," by the brain behind the "wall-like brow": "It was, in fact, the truth that in that cropped skull was the directing brain of the whole area between the Baltic and the Carpathians. It was not, indeed, a mind that worked in darting flashes of inspiration; it was far more like a brightly-lit central exchange in which consciousness, judgment, and purpose were organized and controlled. Behind that brow was a vast system of ordered knowledge."[72] The novel follows this up with four pages about the completely preplanned and fully elaborated seizure of power and the colonization of eastern territories by the major general and the German people respectively.

Zweig's novel was not published until 1928. But his aforementioned earlier hagiography, *The Face of East European Jewry*, testifies to how self-evident he too deemed the connection of face and soil with a sense of honor, and thus in terms of the psychology of shame and the taking of its departure from the semantic field immediately after the war. In his attempt to defend the type of the eastern Jew against both its Christian enemies and its western-identified Zionist detractors, he set up bearings that strike us today more like the unhappily internalized judgments of others: "For it is out of the stern, modest, forward-turned face of the Jew—the witness to the indolence of our times and to the mightiness of a willfully chosen national substance—that the bloated, transparent, and flat face of the Jewish trader on Nordic terrain is made, destined to disappear in the muck of eternal 'newness' in all big cities. . . . *The old Jew of the East, however, maintained his face*"[73] because he stayed on his soil, in his homeland, rather than chasing money, the author concludes.

But even independently of the vision of the eastern Jew, the metaphor of the face as region is noticeably linked to this particular Cartesian direction. A constant evocation of the "face of the East" runs through the Weimar years. In 1919, Alexander von Gleichen-Rußwurm published a supposedly expository book entitled *Das wahre Gesicht: Eine Weltgeschichte der sozialistischen Idee* [The True Face: World History of the Socialist Idea]. René Fülöp-Miller responded in 1926 with *Geist und Gesicht des Bolschewismus* [Spirit and Face of Bolshevism], a richly illustrated, in-depth monograph on the cultural situation of Russia with a notably differentiated, almost enthused look on the new man of Communism and on the "collective" itself. In 1934, Fedor Stepun, a Russian émigré and philosopher in Dresden, offered his own critical rhapsody entitled *Das Antlitz Rußlands und das Gesicht der Revolution* [The Russian Countenance and the Face of the Revolution]. That the view to Russia was again and again conceived of as a glance into a face may have something to do with the Eastern Orthodox tradition of iconic worship; after all, even the abstract painter Jawlensky still rendered homage to this cult. And in 1920, already Stefan Zweig had built a bridge east in his great portrait of Dostoevsky by having his face emerge as though automatically from the earth itself—"loam-colored, almost dirty the cheeks fold, tilled by years of sorrow"—only to erect a cathedral with that earth—"from shadow and darkness the spiritual cathedral rises bright and chiseled." Of course, Zweig is referring once again to the brow, the skull, similarly to Bölsche's description of Haeckel, though in this case conceived in pious rather than pagan terms.[74]

But just as in the case of Major General Schieffenzahn, there is not simply adoration at work here, but first of all a concrete politics of population: where there were Germans outside of Germany, there was a German face. In 1937, the book *Das Gesicht des Deutschen Ostens* [The Face of the German East] appeared. It was a portrait collection filled with hope and anticipation by Erna Lendvai-Dircksen. And even Werner Peiner's 1937 book about Africa spoke of a "face" when it talked about the east of that continent—*Das Gesicht Ostafrikas: Eine Reise in 300 Bildern* [The Face of East Africa: A Voyage in 300 Photographs]. By now the originally awkward alloy of face and landscape, "countenance" and "soil," or, as the case may be, space for settlement or life had attained such currency[75] that as late as 1963 among German "displaced" circles [*Vertriebene*] speeches were given on "the german countenance of Upper Silesia."[76]

Another book going in a similar direction that went through several editions was *Das Gesicht des Jahrhunderts* [The Face of the Century] by Frank Thiess, a successful novelist born in Livonia who was a "physiognomist of weltanschauung" of the Weimar years. *Das Gesicht des Jahrhunderts*[77] was a collection of highly critical letters to individual representatives of the arts in Germany, decrying on the one hand the loss of face of western culture through mass-based Americanisms and on the other hand hoping for salvation by the face of the East. Even so late as his 1931 collection of essays, Thiess fantasizes—ominously or idealistically?—about a possible match between the socialist bridegroom Russia and the national bride Germany.[78] The frequently recurring image of the "burning" of old Germany in World War I and the hope for a "glowing rebirth" in the East turns the loss of face into a travesty, a mimic signal of the first order: as the burning redness of shame, which pours down the face of the boy in Walter Flex's story "Wallenstein's Face."

Shameful Appearances: Count Kessler on Matthias Erzberger

As chance would have it, it is precisely of the originator of this shame that we have one of the most haunting physiognomic portraits *tout court*, moreover one by a contemporary. Count Harry Kessler, the first German ambassador to Poland in 1918 and an early proponent of the idea of a League of Nations, describes in his memorable diary a meeting of the Weimar Parliament in the summer of 1919, in which Matthias Erzberger played the lead role. The centrist deputy with an often-referenced "*Ohrfeigengesicht*" (a face begging to be slapped) was one of the few Parliamentarians to plead from the get go for acceptance of the Allies' conditions for peace.[79] Furthermore, he was the one who signed the cease-fire treaty for the German delegation. Now he had to defend his position in the Weimar Parliament. German National Party deputy Graefe went so far as to accuse Erzberger of indiscretion and of having been bribed, perhaps by Austria or France. Kessler reports:

[Weimar, July 25, 1919]
Erzberger who had been grinning all over his plump face, went white, then red, and screamed, "Impudence! What do you mean by that?" Graefe remained imperturbable. He repeated the quotation [from Bismarck, which he had used to suggest Erzberger's treachery—Trans.]. From this moment forward the feeling of a life-and-death struggle, with two gigantic opposing forces having each other by the throat, prevailed.
As Graefe sat down, it seemed that no oratorical effort could screw the situation to a higher pitch. Indeed Erzberger, with his commonplace appearance, his boorish dialect and his grammatical errors, presented a sad contrast, although his opening phrase was dexterous and dramatic: "Is that all?"
I had a full view of his badly made, flat-soled boots, his comic trousers rising via corkscrew crinkles to his full-moon bottom, his broad and thick-set peasant shoulders, of the whole fat, sweaty, unattractive, utterly plebeian creature. I could see every clumsy move of his clumsy body, every change of color in his chubby cheeks, every drop of sweat on his greasy forehead. But gradually this comic, uncouth figure grew into a personality enunciating the most frightful indictments. The badly framed incoherent sentences piled fact on fact, formed themselves into ranks and battalions of accusation, and fell on the members of the right, sitting white, cowering, and ever more isolated in their corner. When he quoted [Cardinal] Pacelli's telegram, horror held us all in its grip.[80]

It would be hard to find a similarly developed and lively picture of any contemporary of the Weimar Republic. In particular, it would be hard to find one with the sympathetic "gaze from above," with which the count here looks down on the man of the people, who has happened to become a signatory to world history and continues making it rhetorically. The majority of the abundant facial prose of the period directed its gaze "upward" in devotion, describing ruler portraits, no matter whether in art or in politics—in the case of Müller's comments on Falkenhayn, subverting even the contemptuous and equalizing tendency of caricature. There are very few exceptions: for example, the art historian and film critic Béla Balász, who comments on close-ups of any class of people quite extensively; and of course the doctors with their diagnoses who relegated even emperors to the equalizing position of the patient, as the psychiatrist Ernst Müller did in the case of Caligula and later of Wilhelm II.

Even for those disinclined to believe in hidden forces of simultaneity, the date and content of Kessler's diary entry have a certain uncanniness to them. For one thing, this appearance of an ugly, sweaty little man with his "face begging to be slapped" [Fig. 17], *who nonetheless can speak thunderously*, takes place in that same summer of 1919 in which Hitler too is discovered as a public speaker. The paradigm of the negative ruler image, that of the small man on top, jumps as though out of nowhere here—for even Communist leaders such as Trotsky and Lenin, Eisner and later Stalin must have appeared to their contemporaries more impressive than these public figures of the petit bourgeois scene, to say nothing of the admired Roman skull of Mussolini.

What further makes for the uncanniness of Kessler's entry is that the breathless description of the Erzberger speech comes from a man for whom one would have had to invent the label of the aesthete had Beau Brummel not existed earlier. That same Kessler, who not only found the emperor disgustingly ugly, but who in 1897 expressed his surprise that "the world judgment [*Weltgericht*] over Caesar or Bismarck would be spoken in the last instance by so weazen, bandy-legged a manikin"[81] as Theodor Mommsen, now defended small, sweaty Erzberger. To accept that the man from the people, disagreeable to any aesthetic *sensus*, nonetheless appears to be doing the obviously right thing—politically, nationally, and in terms of world history—must have entailed unbridled embarrassment to the aesthete, and yet it was, at least at this point, conceded willingly and readily, almost enthusiastically. Even if it is correct that the erstwhile pro-war count had turned pacifist in the meantime, even if it is true that he later hated Erzberger and accused him of plagiarizing his outline for the League of Nations,[82] even and especially then we must look at the recognition of ugliness in the service of the just cause as a dandy's self-conquest. The recurrent critical dilemma, why more educated Germans were not offended by Hitler's origins and appearance, may have its potential explanation here. The painful humil-

Figure 17. Matthias Erzberger, often impugned for his "*Ohrfeigengesicht*" (face made for slapping), supported the Treaty of Versailles after having negotiated the cease-fire agreement in Compiègne Forest. Of the hand that signed the Versailles treaty, Governor Scheidemann said that "it ought to wither." In 1921, Erzberger was murdered by the ultra-right-wing Erhardt Brigade.

iation over the defeat was displaced onto a physiognomic level; nothing could be more ugly than the "lost face." Germans punished themselves by looking at Hitler and by accepting his "excremental visage" and suffered the further humiliation that it wasn't even the visage of a "radiant Antichrist," but rather that of a "middle-class Antichrist."[83] But there is no description of Hitler that would have engaged in such merciless physiognomic critique as Kessler's did in the case of Erzberger while simultaneously attributing to him the abilities of a great statesman. Whoever did the latter sought to embellish Hitler's face. It was a mark of the consistency of this kind of thinking that even years after Erzberger's 1922 murder, the most renowned graphologist of the time, Ludwig Klages, thought he had discovered in the handwriting of the man who signed the Compiègne cease-fire serious physical weaknesses in the shape of repressed sexuality.[84]

There is only *one* historical figure of the prewar era that may have had a bearing on the acceptance of shameful or embarrassing appearances such as that of Erzberger or Hitler, and that figure was once again none other than Wilhelm Voigt, the "Captain of Köpenick," with his not entirely lawful attack on the gargantuan state apparatus, lauded afterward even by the emperor. It is quite possible that Kessler unconsciously referred to the caricature from the *Kladderadatsch* [Fig. 18]—"badly made, flat boots," "broad, stocky peasant's shoulders"—or the *Berliner Tageblatt* report from 1906, which commented on the episode as follows: "that ten grenadiers would follow an improperly attired major with bow legs and . . . a bent nose just like that . . . is an object lesson on the wisdom of our military education, which no satirical rag could have invented better."

Excursus on Mien and Skull

Kessler's description of Erzberger is not just singular at its particular point in time. It also brings to the fore a little-discussed issue in the disciplinary history of physiognomy: the role of physiognomic judgment among the aristocracy. In fact, the social "view from above" is much older within the discipline than that "from below." One of the most influential anonymous writings to come out of the school of Aristotle is a letter to Alexander the Great, instructing the nobleman, much like a prince's primer, how to read the bodily signals of his most immediate subordinates, lest he choose them unwisely. The glance "from top down" is of course even older in the area of the slave trade; every slave needs to be evaluated physically—can he bear the required loads, is he pleasant to look at, does he have rough or fine hands. It is similarly prevalent in the area of animal husbandry, especially horse breeding. And if there was an aristocratic habitus the European bourgeoisie gladly picked up and codified into a science, it was physiognomic evaluation. Its application in gender relations was identical with biological, species-specific "selective breeding." In the mid-nineteenth century, Arthur Schopenhauer could still claim, all bourgeois individualism in matters of love notwithstanding, that small breasts, snub noses, and narrow pelvises were decisive obstacles to the choice of mate and thus to procreation in general. In Theodor Fontane's *Schach von Wuthenow*, the protagonist is a would-be bourgeois in this regard.

None of this means that there was not an equally sharp look "from below." But for reasons of power differentials it had to exhaust itself in caricature and satire. Or else, as can be gleaned from the famous *Hand*

Steckbrief

Gegen den obenstehend abgebildeten, unten beschriebenen
Hauptmann von Köpenick,
welcher flüchtig ist, ist die Untersuchungshaft verhängt. Der=
selbe hat einen Bürgermeister und einen Kassenrendanten
gestohlen. Es wird ersucht, ihn zu verhaften und an den
Unterzeichneten abzuliefern. Kladderadatsch.
Beschreibung: unbeschreiblich.

Figure 18. Caricature from the *Kladderadatsch* of 1906.

Oracle of World Intelligence of Baltasar Gracián, it could consist in the analysis of aristocratic facial expressions as a piece of life world. This meant that the prince could count on "dogged" attention to his expressions and communicate orders and whims by beck and call. This class distribution of a physiognomy of build and of mimic has maintained itself until today, even if its sociohistorical origins have been forgotten. Speaking schematically, one could say that the famous quarrel between the inventor of physiognomy, the pastor Lavater, and the physicist Georg Christoph Lichtenberg, who was himself highly interested in physiognomic questions, revolved around just that difference between an imitated aristocratic habitus, which really pays attention only to build—good "race," good "breeding"—and a submissive lackey's eye for the mimic qualities, which may communicate the disposition of the lord or lady. Lichtenberg thought physiognomy possible only as "pathognomy" because he realized that it was impossible to draw conclusions about character from bodily build alone. In fact, however, this is common practice when settling on a price at the horse market; and it is from there that the scientific physiognomy of the eighteenth century took its bearings.[85]

The same differential physiognomic habituation resurfaces in the twentieth century—this time around the area of film, as in the difference between the Hungarian Béla Balász and the Russian Sergey Eisenstein. The Janus-face of film—on the one hand a mode of entertainment for the little people, on the other hand an indispensable propaganda tool of the dominant class—leads automatically to someone taking each position. Béla Balász appears as the star witness of the silent movie, who points to the mimic expressions of desperate, crazy, in any case introverted little people—all the way to the murderer M in the movie of the same name by Fritz Lang. Eisenstein, in contrast, goes from the very beginning and certainly with *Battleship Potemkin*, into the direction of propagandization of the social idea, by having large crowds and entire peoples appear and intercutting between them. At least in that segment of the physiognomic field the medium is not the message, but may be utilized for very different kinds of messages. Among the borderline phenomena, which sublate these perspectival differences and force the view from "above" and "below" into one appearance, is the appearance of Adolf Hitler.

Chapter 3

Iconizations 1923–1929

Death Masks: A Weimar Cult

Following the coup attempt of November 9, 1923, Hitler stepped off the rostrum for the time being; he was arrested, sentenced, brought to Landsberg Fortress, and slapped with a prohibition of speech. The NSDAP [National Socialist German Workers Party, or Nazi] was outlawed. The Stresemann government overcame the crisis of the Allied occupation of the Ruhr, the rampant inflation, and revolutionary unrest, ushering in a period of relative calm. Beginning in 1924, Wilhelm Marx headed a minority government with Stresemann as foreign secretary; in 1925, Hindenburg was elected president and in the summer of the same year the Allies withdrew from the occupied Ruhr area. It is during this time that Hitler wrote and published his first book, volume 1 of *Mein Kampf*, with the help of, among others, Rudolf Hess, Max Amann, and Ernst Hanfstaengl.[1]

The massive agitation of the time immediately preceding the coup attempt in November of 1923—the Nazi Party held forty-six rallies with Hitler as speaker that year alone—had made Hitler the "king of Munich" and had garnered the sympathies of key conservatives as well as the money of Fritz Thyssen, which allowed the party to buy the *Münchener Beobachter*, later rechristened as the *Völkische Beobachter*, the illustrated counterpart of which, the *Illustrierte Beobachter*, was (from 1928 onward) to serve as a medium for intense portrait propaganda. Hitler's trial for high treason once again gave him the opportunity to take the stage as a speaker, giving him the greatest possible rehabilitation and publicity. During the months of his incarceration he focused entirely on his book and more or less ignored the quarrels over power and policy within the nationalist movement.

If his own testimony is to be believed, it was in his Landsberg cell that he pieced together a weltanschauung for himself, reading Nietzsche, Houston Stewart Chamberlain, Ranke, Treitschke, Marx, and Bismarck, war memoirs from many statesmen and military men.[2] But above all he assembled a new self-image. Instead of being merely the "drummer" for another, as before, especially for Ludendorff, the nationally revered general, he now thought of himself as the German savior, even as a new messiah. In a book on the language of the Third Reich, Victor Klemperer has analyzed the increasingly messianic pitch, the messianic poses and gestures to which Hitler took recourse. Religious travesty became a hallmark of NS theatrics; Joachim Köhler traced this back to Hitler's obsession with Wagner (Hitler and the German people as *Parsifal*); other authors have pointed to the blasphemous reinterpretation of the Judeo-Christian salvation story.[3] The motif of "Wallenstein's Face," the strange charisma of the countenance was now anchored politically.

The first photographs by Hitler's court photographer, Heinrich Hoffmann, in 1923, which immediately proliferated as postcards as well, show Hitler as a private person in a dark suit with a steep fold above the root of the nose, or in a trench coat, his left hand on his hip, holding a hat and a walking cane. A third photograph, a half-length portrait, shows him in a pose greatly (and perhaps not accidentally) reminiscent of the former foreign secretary Count Brockdorff-Rantzau, a famous opponent of the terms of the Versailles treaty [Fig. 19]. It says a great deal about the self-confidence of the coup's authors that they had themselves photographed by Hoffmann once more in front of the courthouse; Hitler in an imperious pose next to Ludendorff. Several photos followed in Landsberg itself, which Hitler sent to his supporters with the caption "all the more!," followed later yet by pictures of Hitler's release, with Hitler standing by the car before the fortress. Konrad Heiden's remark, according to which Hitler from now on "obsessively strove for a face of normalcy," bespeaks the new strategy of a completely legal seizure of power.[4]

On the other hand Rudolf Herz has rejected the conjecture that Hitler at this point thought purely tactically, that he had calculated every aspect of his appearance and anticipated its effect. The series of sittings with Hoffmann in the beginning of 1925 had results that were not entirely accepted and were at best steps *toward* a führer image. For although physiognomic thinking dominated the period, and although Hitler bet on the effects of the mass media, he was nonetheless aware that his external appearance had to be modeled beyond all measure.[5] For the cover of the first edition of the *Völkische Beobachter*, a Hitler in a silvery windbreaker was chosen, standing before a forest of swastika flags, and Herz may well be right when he regards the jacket as an allusion to the SA uniform.[6]

Toward the end of 1926 and the beginning of 1927, long after the reformation of the NSDAP, Hoffmann tried to solidify the pictorial concept of Hitler in another sitting. He showed him in brown shirt and lederhosen, which had now become emblematic for the party, a strategy

Figure 19. This Hitler photograph probably emerged from one of Hitler's first sessions with Heinrich Hoffmann and is thus from the fall of 1923. The stylization reminiscent of the portrait of Count Brockdorff-Rantzau (below) is eye-catching. The count was at this time already the German ambassador to Moscow.

meant to make him sympathetic to the youth movement, just like the shots of Hitler in nature, leaning against trees. Not all were approved for release, but the themes set for the pictures inevitably made their appearance. Among those approved for release was the famous series of postcards with Hitler as orator, which Berthold Viertel commented upon so incomparably and which in the United States Charlie Chaplin looked at with such disgust. The series shows Hitler with highly manner-ist gestures, which he in truth never used before audiences.[7] A picture from the first half of 1927 became the template for an eye-catching poster from 1932. It was the first truly massively stylized poster portrait of Hitler: his brightly lit face fully "without chest," like a close-up from a silent movie, before a pitch-black background, captioned simply with the name "Hitler" [Fig. 20].

Allegedly, Hoffmann had inspirations for this photograph: for exam-ple, a picture of Mussolini by the photographer Caminad from 1921[8] or also the posters from the First World War calling for the purchase of war bonds with the disembodied face of Hindenburg. Both in terms of space and time, however, there is a much closer template. One year before, a volume of death masks had appeared, having been catalogued and com-mented upon by the art historian Ernst Benkard. The collection *Das Ewige Antlitz* [The eternal face] had gone through nineteen printings by 1935. It was regarded not only as one of the most impressive studies on the topic, but also as the first serious art-historical investigation by a spe-cialist. A number of sequel volumes appeared: for example in 1927, a large-format edition of the masks of the Richard Langer collection from Düsseldorf, with a preface by the psychiatrist Hans Gruhle;[9] two years later a popular edition with a preface by Egon Friedell; and several varia-tions after World War II.[10] The characteristic mode of presenting the faces common to all these volumes—only the white *en face* before a dark background—was meant to memorialize famous Europeans, among them Germans as well. It was a new version of the project of a "national portrait gallery," with the emphasis shifted from the national to the his-torical and to the task Ludwig Justi had set for it in 1913: to present an ancestor gallery between familial (aristocratic) pride and individual merit in pictures.[11] The dead in these volumes were, at least by Benkard, provided with names; they included the faces of kings and commoners, of Germans, Englishmen, Americans, Frenchmen, Italians, Russians, of musicians, politicians, revolutionaries, actors, visual artists, and even of saints. And as if wanting to follow Justi's proposal even in this detail, there were almost no women, except of course the often recurring Queen Luise and the famous Inconnue de la Seine.[12]

In terms of content Benkard's book constituted a brilliant compro-mise between the "picture series of meritorious men," presented for

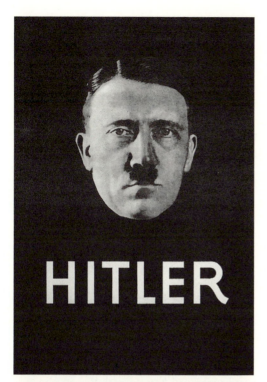

Figure 20. This poster was created for the electoral campaign of 1932 and is based on one of Heinrich Hoffmann's photographs from 1926/27. Below is the death mask of Richard Wagner, reproduced in 1926 along with more than a hundred photographs of white death masks on black backgrounds under the title *Das Ewige Antlitz* [The Eternal Face].

example at the Valhalla in Regensburg on the one hand, and the more photographically oriented bourgeoisie on the other. Just like the heads in the Valhalla, the death masks were three-dimensional objects, even if they were closer to the relief than to the bust. At the same time, one was looking at an image, a photograph of a death mask rather than at the masks themselves. In their at times dramatic lighting, they appeared like powdered faces sprung from a silent movie—but this appearance was countered in turn by the format of the collections. After all, one held in hand a large octavo format, an art volume if not a family album.

Be that as it may, with its romantically lit lily-white faces, *Das Ewige Antlitz* clearly bridged the gap to the visualizations of the "German face" demanded by the "Rembrandt German" Langbehn and provided for some time already by Benkard's colleagues in art history. Richard Hamann, for example, presented the collection *Deutsche Köpfe des Mittel-alters* [German Heads of the Middle Ages] in his institute in Marbach in 1922, and Hubert Wilm presented his *Gothische Charakterköpfe* [Striking Heads from the Gothic] in 1925.[13] Here too, and even more intensely, the photographers treated their petrified models as though they were the stars of silent movies: they doused them in dramatic lighting, they severed face from body, and shot them in close-ups. The immediacy of their facial features, familiar and highly artistic at once, began inspiring the photo volumes on living individuals at the beginning of the 1930s, in particular the works of Helmar Lerski and Erich Retzlaff.[14] In all these cases, the viewer's gaze came neither "from above" nor "from below," but straight from the front. With the exception of a few profiles, the eye-in-eye of the *en face* dominated the genre in spite of the stony faces' uni-formly closed eyes. Practiced on the book, the gaze became even more intimate than it might have been in an exhibition and approached iconic contemplation.

Quiet contemplation and remembrance of course attached them-selves to the books of Benkard and his successors for entirely different reasons. The educated bourgeois who could afford the expensively laid out work were of course powerfully reminded by the death masks of the First World War. Probably most families had lost members; but among all the publications critical of the war in these years, these volumes stood out in their reconciliatory contemplation of the beauty of the dead face. The book thus fit the stabilized phase of the Weimar Republic, in which Stresemann had mastered the crisis of 1923. At the same time, it acted somewhat as an aesthetic buffer against the passionate indictment of the war and its cost from communists, artists, and other pacifists and per-haps could effect a certain reconciliation with death.

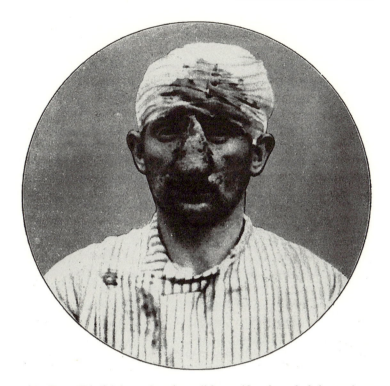

Figure 21. Ernst Friedrich, an inexhaustible pacifist, founded the antiwar museum in Berlin in 1923. Among the exhibits were unsettling photographs of soldiers whose faces had been injured in combat. The quadrilingual volume *Wage War on War!* made them accessible to a broader audience in 1924.

In particular Ernst Friedrich had, in both his antiwar museum of 1923 and his picture pamphlet "Krieg dem Kriege!" [Wage War on War!] of 1924, circulated gruesome photographs of the disfigured, blown-apart faces of war victims [Fig. 21]. This constituted a real sacrilege, particularly if we take into account that there were separate field hospitals for soldiers with facial wounds in order to spare their comrades the sight and if one considers that even in World War II officers formulaically had to inform families that their sons had fallen "face intact."[16] This different kind of "national portrait gallery," a cautionary display and obstreperously antiheroic, doubtlessly became a model for Otto Dix, George Grosz, and Max Beckmann, only that these three of course weren't exactly the darlings of those who bought the books of Benkard and Langer.

The "Holy Dogface": Hitler, Sacralized

In 1928–29, at a time when the NSDAP was already becoming a mass movement all throughout Germany, Heinrich Hoffman once again went through a series of sessions with Hitler. It was during these that the famous pictures of Hitler in the brown shirt, with the swastika armband and the Iron Cross First Class, his hands on his knee, were taken. Much like in the art-historical photo volumes of the "German face," the perspective was neither from above nor below, but rather a close-up, face-to-face. Unlike the stony monuments, however, Hitler's face in these photographs appeared gentle, even youthful, and, thanks to a slight retouching of the eyes, intense. According to Herz, this photo became a runaway success and was published several times by the NS press; Hanfstaengl's company touted it in 1933 as "long recognized as the best and most widespread image of the *Führer*" [Fig. 22].[17] The picture appeared as the frontispiece to the English translation of *Mein Kampf* and drew a memorable commentary by none other than George Orwell, an anti-communist but also an irreproachable social-democrat who was a sharp critic of totalitarianism. In his review of the book in March of 1940, four months before Hitler's attack on Britain, he writes:

I should like to put it on record that I have never been able to dislike Hitler. Ever since he came to power—till then, like everyone, I had been deceived into thinking that he did not matter—I have reflected that I would certainly kill him if I could get within reach of him, but that I could feel no personal animosity. The fact is that there is something deeply appealing about him. One feels it again when one sees his photographs—and I recommend especially the photography at the beginning of Hurst and Blackett's edition, which shows Hitler in his early Brownshirt days. It is a pathetic dog-like face, the face of a man suffering under intolerable wrongs. In a rather more manly way it reproduces the expression of innumerable pictures of Christ crucified, and there is little doubt that is how Hitler sees himself.[18]

The reaction may be utterly incomprehensible to us today, but, exaggerated by a detractor, it may give us an idea of the effect the picture had on Hitler's supporters. Upon seeing the man "eye to eye," in particular with the shiny, retouched gaze, they must have viewed him as one of them and at the same time as the savior himself. "Wallenstein's face," in the face of the "little man," was a motif of language rather than of photographic history. There was not simply that brother effect, which Thomas Mann highlighted, some doubt notwithstanding, in 1939, but moreover the pose, part demonic, part messianic, which Hitler worshippers venerated in countless embarrassing "Führer hymnals": "What does he look like?—Like one of us. / Whether big or tall I do not know. / His hands seemed finer to me / than his chin or forehead, when he speaks."[19]

Figure 22. Among all the pictures of Hitler that Heinrich Hoffmann produced, this one from 1928–29 was the most reproduced. The entrancing gaze of proximity and the glowing eyes were abandoned by Hoffmann after 1933 to depict Hitler in a statesman's poses instead.

In spite of the plethora of visual cues spread via propaganda and, thanks to Hitler's personal obtrusiveness, by the living object itself, this venerating poetry, according to Scholdt, noticeably avoided the concrete details of his external features. "Sporadically we will be told the eye color, and often even here the describer flees right away into the realm of the sacral."[20] Perhaps the image is simply more easily described than a living person; perhaps the describers' intellect, perhaps even quasi-religious emotion, was in the way of precise sensual appreciation. Most probably, however, this fetishistic reduction was possible because the veneration took place in a context of a national face cult, which had started at least after the outbreak of the First World War and even at that time had not been restricted to pictures alone. It was literally an attempt at developing a national profile, similarly pursued by a short-lived periodical named *Das Deutsche Gesicht* already in 1914, and by a book of brief biographical essays entitled *Das Deutsche Angesicht* [The German Face], which was meant to be taken along to the front by the soldiers.[21] Books with images and texts such as *Deutsches Antlitz: Gedichte zu Bildnissen Albrecht Dürers* [German Face: Poems to the Pictures of Albrecht Dürer] by Axel Lübbe, which appeared first in 1917 and again in 1921, reached deep into the sphere of German national devotion and conformed fully to Lavater's model. It was facial contemplation in Rilke manqué. The poem to the image of Dürer's mother begins: "Oh: Like the folds of her cloth / her face collapsed in the long duration"; and the portrait of Hieronymus Holzschuher seems already to describe Hitler: "See: Our right to our land / has found a face!"[22]

Hitler's face of course didn't conform either to the portraits or to these ecstatic encomia. Court photographer Hoffmann's careful mise-en-scène couldn't keep the face from seeming somewhat ordinary to today's observer, all the more ordinary for the fact that the more images one sees of him, the more obvious the mise-en-scène itself becomes. Of course, the impression would be quite different when one thought, like Hoffmann, in terms of the mass-media law of greatest effect through the greatest distribution and in terms of strategic image building. It would be different yet when one compared it to the photographic career of the Kaiser. It is in fact questionable whether Hoffmann really managed to stylize his Führer into a trademark, or whether he didn't simply help create, in league with the rituals of the Hitler cult, a "second body of the king" (Ernst Kantorowicz), mediated by the Wallenstein motif in the spirit of Walter Flex. After all, Hitler had already won overwhelming fame as an orator when, in September of 1923, Hoffmann began his portrait sessions with him. That soon a full-fledged physical and image cult developed around his person had of course less to do with his actual appearance and much more with his promise to return to the German people the lost territory and thereby the lost face; his slogan could have been: "Our right to our land has found a face."

Here of course the intimate close-up played a role altogether incomparable to the emperor's: it seduced into identification, into proximity to power, and with hitherto unknown intensity it created and reinforced the viewer's grandiose self. How long in coming this physiognomic politicization had been becomes evident in the writings of the physiognomist Kassner. In 1910, disturbed by the scandal surrounding Prince Eulenburg, in which the Kaiser found himself entangled, Kassner recognized that imperial greatness was no longer capable of existing: "An emperor is great as emperor, his imperial actions count, not those of his private life, that is speaking historically and politically." Kassner distinguishes this type of emperor from a different type—the "secret emperor"—culled from Julius Langbehn, the so-called Rembrandt German. Of this latter type he remarks sibyllically: "in these secret emperors, everything that was mere public representation among the Great Emperors has become vision instead."[23]

Langbehn's argumentation had run differently: the "secret emperor" of his famous book *Der Rembrandtdeutsche* [The Rembrandt German] of 1890 was to come in real historical terms. But Kassner anticipated the decisive point in Hitler's rhetorical attractiveness years before the man himself appeared on the stage; he did so very much in the spirit of vision-plagued expressionism: "there is for the secret, eternally present man no greatness other than a vision. It thrusts open the source of his being and only so the vision can be valid, and such a man is then holy in the sense of antiquity, in the sense of eternity, like the children or the animals. He is, one would have to say, protected and impenetrable due to his vision."[24] Thus Hitler presented himself as a "secret emperor" qua visionary—in the excellent company of authors such as Kassner, himself no friend of the regime, but also Oswald Spengler and Ernst Jünger: first as the "drummer" of a coming *Führer*, who in the end he himself turned out to be, then later increasingly in conditioning his surroundings into a horde of "apprentices" to this vision. Whoever looked at his representations, face to face, and who searched in himself for the echoes of his speeches perhaps had a "second face," a vision, rather than simply partaking in power, for at the time Hitler had none.

One of the prime testaments to the strategy of staging the Führer not as a possessor of power, but of a vision, is a late photograph from 1932: a close-up from slightly above, with shiny eyes casting a deep, partly worrying, partly threatening glance into the eye of the beholder [Fig. 23]. It appeared first on the cover page of the *Illustrierte Beobachter* on the occasion of the presidential election of March 13, then as a dust jacket cover of *Mein Kampf,* and eventually found itself in a photomontage

Figure 23. The photograph for the title page of the *Illustrierter Beobachter* dates from 1932 and comes out of Hoffmann's studio.

almost cheek by cheek with Hindenburg on a poster for the election for imperial chancellor.

The sacral component begins accompanying Hitler at the latest with the benediction of hoary Chamberlain. The concrete physiognomy of the venerated may have provided little reason for it, but the diffuse religiosity that tinted the zeitgeist between 1918 and 1945 and that generally sought its home in the countenance provided a support for it and at times may have inadvertently inspired it. In 1929, for example, the year of the world economic crisis, one of the most widely read books on the topic appeared, *Das Menschengesicht* [The Human Face] by Max Picard. Picard, offspring of a converted Catholic family, art historian and psychologist, develops in this highly complex book the idea of man as God's image and calls to account just that process of naturalization that had reduced the face to a landscape or to cosmological readability:

This is what distinguishes the human face before Christ's appearance from a later one: the human face before Christ looks as though everything that appears in it may as well show itself in a landscape or in a tree or in a stone or in a celestial constellation, and it is not by accident that Greek faces look like transformed marble, and the blocks of marble like transformed people, people asleep, or people buried in a bright earth; and it is not by accident that the Greek gods transformed themselves and people into animals and trees: The human shape was something that one could exchange and replace; man was loose, not secure in his shape, he merely waited that he be called out of it. Since Christ, however, everything pertaining to people can only happen in the shape of the human being. Since Christ, the border lines of the human shape are limits [*Grenzlinien*], crossing them means crossing into nothingness.[25]

With his vision of the end of the human face, Picard hit a nerve at the time. Siegfried Kracauer and Karl Wolfskehl reacted to this cipher; long after the war, Emmanuel Levinas developed his own existential philosophy based on "the face."[26] In 1937, Picard wrote a book entitled *Die Grenzen der Physiognomik* [The Limits of Physiognomics], in 1946, a book entitled *Hitler in uns selbst* [Hitler in Ourselves], which garnered a lot of attention and included a long chapter on Hitler's face. Picard's apotheosis of 1929 tells us that in the convergence of biology and film, of pictorial photography and phrenology, the human face emerged as an "endangered species." Decrying its disappearance turns the dominant cultural pessimism into a biological one, escape from which was in turn only possible by means of religion, or at least iconic perception. In the same year as Picard, 1929, August Sander published the first excerpt from his great sociography of the German people under the title *Antlitz der Zeit* [Face of the Times] with a preface by Alfred Döblin and with a now famous reception by Walter Benjamin, who said that the photographer may become "unexpectedly timely." For "sudden shifts of power such as are now overdue in our society can make the ability to read facial types a matter of vital importance. Whether one is on the Left or the Right, one will have to get used to being looked at in terms of one's provenance. And one will have to look at others the same way. Sander's work is more than a picture book. It is a training manual."[27]

Of course there were entirely different views cast on the German face, preparing the ground for later outbursts of hatred against Hitler's appearance. Another publication of 1929 was the famous photomontage *Deutschland, Deutschland über alles!* by Kurt Tucholsky and John Heartfield, which meant to cut through and belie the saccharine kitsch in the discourse on the human face. Nonetheless, these authors too took recourse to the physiognomic article of faith, that the outer says everything there is to say about the inner. The photo volume was published by Neuer Deutscher Verlag and showed a truly disturbing "national portrait gallery" in particular satirical group photos. The montage "Animals Looking at You" [Fig. 24], for example, alluded to the contemporary best-seller *Tiere sehen dich an* [Animals Looking at You] by Paul Eipper, a harmless guide to animals for young people that translated the physiognomic gesture into a love of animals. The same title was further

Figure 24. The photo volume *Deutschland, Deutschland über alles* (1929), with texts by Kurt Tucholsky and photomontages by John Heartfield, remained a lone, but also cruelly satirical, masterstroke by the left. Below: "Animals Looking at You."

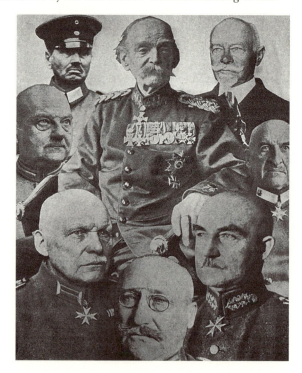

and much more disturbingly purloined years later in an anti-Semitic pamphlet by Johann von Leers as *Juden sehen dich an* (Jews looking at you). Already in their time, the authors of *Deutschland, Deutschland* saw the general mood necessary for this transformation; a photo entitled the "Leaders of the *Stahlhelm* [steel helmet] Convention" [Fig. 24] is commented on under the title "Faces":

The man on the right has possibilities.

We should look carefully at all the other faces, one by one. Especially at those that begin to be lost in the background shadows. A few stand out clearly. Let's look at this scene, and ask a few questions.

Would we want to be judged by the likes of them?

Would we want to be dependent on these men's notions of right and justice?

Can we imagined that even one of these men has ever wondered about the nature of human existence?

Can we imagine one of the faces bent—for instance—above a dead horse to ask, "What's death all about?"

Could we imagine any of these eyes ever expressing anything that we could call "human kindness"?

Could we imagine any of these men lying in a meadow and feeling in the humming of bees what nature means?

We can't.

The uniform isn't even the final external expression of their lack of soul. The uniforms are too big: even a uniform has too much room inside it. Something exists that could be called the Escape into Uniform. The uniform works like a visor: it hides fear, gives protection, provides internal support. They're deserters from civilian life.

This is the nation's flower. The fruit looks it.[28]

Joseph Roth put this even more urgently when expressing his worries about the new faces of German literature in December of 1930:

From that ghostly fog that has nonetheless enveloped millions of our fellow Germans a new literature emerges to the light of day, a literature with the names of writing ghosts, who are popular because they have "chastity" on their escutcheon and full-bearded "masculinity," and because they anticipate the future of the Third Reich. How much poison in violet-blue chalices?

From the charged countenance of the fascist dictator, so clearly Mediterranean [*welsch*] but magnanimously subsumed under the Nordic label, whose chin looks like an upside-down steel helmet, to Hitler's physiognomy, which anticipates all the faces of all his voters and in which every one of his followers can look as though into the mirror, everything is already there, already in store, [Gustav Friedrich] Dinter and [Joseph von] Lauff, the beast and the mind, the guilt-edge and the bloodstain. Table, spread yourself, bricklebrit, cudgel out of the sack! No, my dear friend! The noble portraits of long-decayed bearers of culture now disappear in the galleries before the deluge of living, contemporary faces, in which merely the lead article in a brainless provincial paper has left its traces, and over which that green hat sits, ineradicable, pert, as though the crowning achievement of a confectioned nature. Tradition is well preserved all around, and for a little money you can even see it. It was right to take her into protective custody against a present that so suspiciously insists on referring back to its lost, almost severed past.[29]

Physiognomic discourse thus oscillated between extreme suspicion, even hatred on the one hand and ecstatic contemplation and devotion on the other, and it was something that the left resorted to as well. It was a discourse that always bordered on racial platitudes and populist cliché, but which also brought into play the motifs of ancestral pride, intersubjective recognition, and of remembrance, even when (or perhaps especially when) satirically reversed as in the case of Tucholsky and Heartfield. Their motto, "When you look at the images for a few minutes, they will start to speak,"[30] was just as valid and perhaps more so for the facial devotion among conservatives. With its wide circulation and its imaginary intimacy, however, it was also an oddly contrapuntal and subversive counter to Weimar democracy. For it doggedly held on to the fiction of a society of proximity, whereas the new constitution by contrast depended on distanced sociality, on a basic objectification of the political power of judgment, and on the development of deliberative capabilities. Physiognomic interaction and the hermeneutics of character begins with the living vis-à-vis and therefore with proximity. But especially since the first electoral campaigns of the republic were fought and won with posters, newsreels, tabloids, and postcards, and thus always again with faces, the fiction of a society of proximity was kept alive. Of course no *strictu sensu* physiognomic exchange can develop without the countergaze, but everything that is read into the representation or artworks can nonetheless at least simulate proximity. The career of the close-up in film and photography bespeaks the tendency to such simulation, as do the devotional contemplations of death masks and the overflowing facial prose and poetry of the period. That such a simulation of corporeal intimacy will eventually drain its object of its significance entirely, and will even traumatize the viewer, was noticed early on—for example by Benjamin. Whether the development of interactive communication has really given rise to a more "natural" state is still in question.

A Normed Face, Arrived at Scientifically

When Hitler was allowed to leave the fortress of Landsberg at the end of 1924, he had already attained the status of beloved Führer—without the loudspeaker and as yet still without many visual aides. Georg Schott's *Volksbuch vom Hitler* from the same year portrays a genius, a religious man, an educator, a rouser, a liberator, humble, faithful, and strong-willed, a preeminent political leader. As early as 1922, Rudolf Hess in his *Preisschrift* with the title "What Must That Man Be Like Who Returns Germany to Its Old Greatness?" had minted the formulations for this fanatical devotion: "With pride we declare that one single being is beyond any criticism and that being is the Führer. This is because everybody knows and feels that he is always right and that he will be right. Our national socialism is for everybody anchored in the unconditional loyalty and devotion to the Führer, a loyalty and devotion that won't ask for the why, but rather contents itself with silently obeying orders. We are convinced that the Führer follows a higher calling, which mandates his taking Germany's fate into his hands."[31]

Hymns of praise such as those of Hess and Schott were showered on a man whom less partial contemporaries describe as downright unattractive. Take, for example, the historian Karl Alexander von Müller, who met Hitler after 1919 at the Hanfstaengels's and later testified before the courts: "His gaze bespoke even back then the consciousness of his public successes: but something awkward attached to him nonetheless, and you got the unpleasant sense that he knew it and scorned you for noticing. The face too was still thin and pale, with an almost suffering expression. Only the eminent water-blue eye at times had a relentless hardness to it, and above the *radix nasi*, between his two strong eyebrows, lay a fanatical will, almost bunching up."[32] An eyewitness such as the president of the Bavarian Academy of Science, Max von Gruber, who styled himself something of a specialist in racial hygiene, came to an even more devastating judgment in a report from the same time: "I saw Hitler for the first time from up close. Face and head bad race, mixed blood. Low, flying forehead, wide cheekbones, small eyes, dark hair. Short brush of a beard, barely as wide as the nose, gives the face a particularly challenging air. Facial expression not that of someone in full command over himself, but that of a raving lunatic."[33]

Even if a more realistic picture of Hitler probably wouldn't have been quite as scathing, Hitler was quite wise in his choice of a personal photographer and in the clever visual propaganda surrounding his person. Heinrich Hoffmann's position was precarious: Technically speaking, he was supposed to create a transmission of the speaker Hitler into the image, not simply depicting his pose—as in the postcards from 1927— but getting his figure and face to "speak." In other words, Hoffman had to translate the auditory audience at close quarters, which formed an ecstatic, increasingly tight-knit circle, into a visual audience at far greater remove, without losing the qualities of the former. The pictures were to invite *listening* rather than a visual inspection [Fig. 25]. Due to the physiognomic scripts in each realm—that of the ear and the eye—which Germans had submitted to for centuries, Hoffmann found propitious conditions so to speak. The highly official search for an embodying

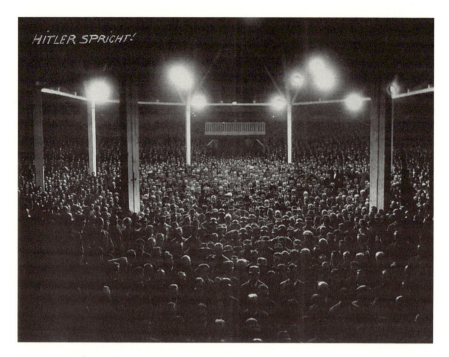

Figure 25. Posters like this one, which showed only a mass of listeners but not the speaker, created insistent advertisement for the invisible Hitler. Five thousand listeners turned up for the event in the Circus Krone. Hitler's talent in voice and rhetoric was essential for the acceptance of his not-so-Aryan face.

"German face" may have had a hand in this. The much-cited Rembrandt had helped formulate the goal via Julius Langbehn, but he had failed to deliver the object itself. In 1928, Langbehn's pupil Momme Nissen therefore abandoned Rembrandt entirely and proclaimed "Dürer as Führer."[34]

Rudolf Herz speaks of the party's strategies in collaborating with Hoffmann. Hitler wasn't supposed to remain invisible. The very first pictures taken were advertised in the *Völkischer Beobachter*: "The official portraits of Adolf Hitler will appear beginning Saturday, September 22, 1923" in three different formats appropriate for different incomes. The image cult was kicked off; the task was modeling a savior. One of the questions addressed in 1925, anticipating the publication of the first volume of *Mein Kampf*, was whether Hitler was better associated with Bismarck photographically or whether he should appear as a "youthful figure of light, as a spiritual and inspired thinker"; at that point it was decided on the latter.[35] A series of shots of Hitler in lederhosen followed in 1926–27;

however, for good reasons they never saw release to the public, except one that was dark in mood and underexposed.

Pictures like these were nonetheless flanked by an already up-and-running party propaganda machine. The year 1926 also saw the publication of a first photo pamphlet with Hoffmann's pictures of the "movement," of important events, Bavarian politicians and right-wing supporters, but of course above all of Hitler. One didn't get to imagine him invisible speaking at the Circus Krone, but one saw him alone next to Ludendorff in a full-page portrait. *Deutschlands Erwachen in Wort und Bild* [Germany's Awakening in Image and Word] invoked in its introduction already a religious mood: "A man stood up from among the people, spreading the gospel of love for the Fatherland."[36]

All four images of the years 1923–26—the inspired youth, the man in lederhosen, the man next to Ludendorff, the invisible yet all the more charismatic public speaker—represented Hitler as the epitome and the embodiment of certain close socialities or communities: the youth movement, rural Bavaria, the army, and, most intransparently, the community of his listeners, which had already become a mass. At this point, important questions were still contested and as yet undecided: whether he didn't simply suit the image, but could also function as the embodiment of this society leaning toward community, as an all-inclusive embodiment, in other words whether he could represent "the German face" in a national sense.

A photo pamphlet Hoffmann published in 1924 under the title "Whom Should I Vote for? A Guide for the Inconvincible" demonstrates how intricately linked this embodiment was with the traditional image worlds of the individual groups. Herz calls it a "special case in photographic publication," which "went well beyond the documentary claim of photography." This was due to its method of pictorial argumentation: "The predominant mode was the simple juxtaposition of two photographs, along with an ironic to sarcastic commentary meant to provide illuminating assertions about the claims and reality of the politics of the other parties."[37] This manner of making pictures speak came on the one hand from the contemporary montages by avant-garde filmmakers, but on the other hand dated back to Paul Schultze-Naumburg and the turn of the century: "I suddenly saw the basic outline of a great educatory project before me, which I would pursue for decades from then on," he recalled later, "the method of ocular impressions by means of the photographic image as a proof of good and bad."[38] Since the beginning of the century, the former painter published texts and pictures on houses and gardens, landscapes and interiors under the title "Kulturarbeiten" ["Studies on Culture"]. In his allergy against all things ugly, Schultze-Naumburg was a first-rate physiognomist. A house for him had a face—and this face could be evaluated like that of a sick person; the way to convince the audience of the validity of his appraisals was to juxtapose pictures of good and evil or bad. There was no search for a cognitive "chock" in these comparisons; one image revealed the other to be a mask. Even if the physiognomic rage among the Weimar conservatives went along with a hatred for the idea of the mask—in speaking of faces, countenance and face always meant "honest" constants. Rudolf Kassner even called the face an adnate mask—in this didactic of the visual chock, the idea of a mask is maintained, even dangerously sublated. It was no longer the idea of play, but that of deception that remained associated with it; false and hostile faces had to be disfigured into recognizability.

Even if, as Herz stresses, Hoffmann soon abandoned this form of pictorial propaganda,[39] Goebbels continued using it with great success, both in anti-Semitic propaganda beginning in 1933, and in war propaganda of the years after 1940.[40] For somewhat inexplicable reasons, the cultivated and cultivating reformer Schultze-Naumburg contributed to this propaganda in the shape of his 1928 book entitled *Kunst und Rasse* [Art and Race]. In it, he showed portraits of moronic and ill people next to portraits of modern artists in order to demonstrate the latter's degenerate psyche grossly abusing the claim to evidence and documentation, which inheres in physiognomy of any kind, and which photography universalizes beyond measure. This evidentiary status is of course of central importance to natural science—and it is from science or, more precisely, medicine that Schultze-Naumburg took the photographies for his book. In his 1920 study *Erkennung der Geistesstörungen* [Recognizing mental illness], Wilhelm Weygandt, a psychiatrist in Hamburg, provided more than one hundred photographic portraits as well as typifying charts, following the influential English anthropologist and early race "scientist" Francis Galton.[41]

Galton's importance in the history of physiognomic perception does not only rest on his status as one of the first and most insistent proponents of eugenics. His method of visual demonstration revolutionized the way people look at human faces, even if not right away. As an imaginative user of the young art of photography, he invented the so-called composite portrait: a kind of icon or *paradigmatic visualization* for a whole group of people, such as criminals, or people suffering from tuberculosis or mental illness, but also of perfectly normal families. It was a kind of paradigmatic image, but in truth an averaged face in the sense of a statistical norm. Insofar as Galton merged the features of several individuals into one photographic plate, the differences between the faces canceled each other out; what remained, what almost lit up, were the similarities, as something of the hereditary gestalt. But since this averaged face too made its appearance in the shape of a photograph, it undercut the photograph's documentary, evidentiary validity; the construct, the gestalt became personified. It is the ancestor of the famous "composite portraits" of Jewish students, which Hans F. K. Günther's 1929 book *Rassenkunde des jüdischen Volkes* [Racial Studies of the Jewish People] reproduced and on which its arguments drew. Galton's technique was basically a poetic device, namely a classic personification, but that wasn't admitted. Instead, Galton used his project for eugenics, and it has remained the methodological standard until the present day.

It only makes sense that Galton should have played a special role in the project of the national portrait gallery, that representation of "merit and ancestral pride" imitated throughout Europe since its inception in 1856. In presenting his photographic experiments, Galton suggested that his countrymen begin scientific family albums: in this way, averaged faces of fathers and mothers and children could be arrived at, eventually even faces of entire families. This would be a way of ascertaining the features most frequently passed on, of comparing these features with the relative success of the families in question, and of thus supporting Darwin's theses. A national portrait gallery of biologically selected men of merit was in the offing, of course under the condition that all pictures be taken in one and the same way, namely *en face*, in the profile, and at the same distance from the lens.[42]

Thankfully, Britons did not take up Galton's suggestion, but continued to take pictures of their lived existence from all angles and distances. The fallacy, however, that through a complicated process one could produce an average face, and that one could pass this face on as a norm by means of photography, had a career in and through the discipline of psychiatry. Wilhelm Weygandt's book on the recognition of mental illness works with photographs of individuals, but also with color plates on types. These typified pictures don't differ from the individual pictures in terms of accuracy, probably because they had been created using Galton's manner if not his method. The contrastive juxtaposition of such pictures of the norm with the individual ones thus misleads their viewer. He is supposed to see a type next to an individual, but he actually sees two individuals next to each other.[43]

Medicine and anthropology were the godfathers of the new parascience of "race studies" [*Rassenkunde*]. After all, *Rassenkunde* also had to manage somehow with the contemporary techniques for verification and demonstration, no matter its ideological precepts. When Heinrich Hoffmann first presented the "German countenance" Adolf Hitler, he thus always had a fifth column among his ranks. Hitler's reluctance to have his picture taken could be explained like this, instead of referring simply to the warrants out for his arrest in several places following the coup attempt. That racist thinking shared the claim to evidentiary status of a popular science made Hitler's physiognomy a problem. And precisely because German society from 1918 onward, independently of academic racial discourse, developed in its educated as well as its uneducated circles a real physiognomic syndrome, because it searched obsessively for "the face of the ruling class," the "face of the century," the "face of our time," the "German countenance" or "face," and so forth, the presentation of the not quite Aryan-looking face of the Führer became a problem for propaganda.

That Chamberlain helped Hitler by fetishizing his hands and eyes and being silent on the rest is hard to overestimate, but it doesn't amount to more than one important service among many other necessary ones. Under the eyes of Theodor Wolff, for example, Hitler would not have shown the excellence of an aristocratic family line; in the eyes of Robert Müller he would have had nothing of the cubist *tête carré* of the Junker caste; in the eyes of Wilhelm Bölsche nothing of that planetary brow, to say nothing of the moral law behind it. But even the simple-mindedness of the peasant's skull, tanned by work and weather, was not to be found in this face, nor anything of a particular region or landscape, token of a general kinship with a people. Hitler apparently didn't really look like anyone—and still, again and again he made the impression of the little man in whom everyone can see himself. And still he seemed to try to count, if not as the normative face, then at least as the visual embodiment of all Germans.

The scientific facial norm of racial studies is of course mutually exclusive with the living individual as the embodiment of a group. One cannot play the role of the other; for one is ahistorical and the other is nothing other than history. That the NS regime promoted both equally, although its own Führer was obviously incapable of unifying them, might at first glance be taken to be a dilemma particular to the regime. It might also, however, point to a physiognomic dramaturgy, the effect and consequent execution of which bear further investigation. That in particular the educated of the period continuously looked for such signs was nothing if not an index of the physiognomic obsession of the period, an obsession that increased with Hitler's rise. This obsession was at first linguistic rather than visual, one trying to hold to the central qualities of the society of proximity, in contradistinction to the racist phantoms of anthropology; among them, the idiomatic structuring of the physiognomic field according to categories such as candor ("looking a thing or a person in the eye"), immediacy ("standing or speaking face to face"), impertinence ("lying to someone's face, jumping or laughing in someone's face"), shame ("losing face"), and distance ("saving face"), the last two having been retained from the vocabulary of honor common before the First World War.

Excursus on Abstraction and Empathy

The sense for the normative face and the individual countenance are of course perfectly reconcilable on the aesthetic level. Someone who enjoys the abstract faces of saints by the painter Jawlensky will not necessarily dislike Max Beckmann's excessive self-portraits. As a matter of fact, ever since the art historian Wilhelm Worringer published his influential study *Abstraktion und Einfühlung* [Abstraction and Empathy] as a "contribution to the psychology of style" in 1908, the sense for types and the sense for exemplars were thought of as the two basic poles of human receptivity to art. Worringer wanted to apply each of the two poles to such binaries as weltanschauung-religion, or pantheism-monotheism. The book clearly struck a nerve at the time: in 1919, it was already in its ninth edition; more editions followed from 1948 to 1999. Even though the theory was that of an art historian, it wasn't in the least two-dimensional visually. Rather, Worringer marked the introduction of a spatial dialectic of proximity and distance, which appeared to be modeled on the opponents of sociologist Ferdinand Tönnies's famous distinction, which he described in 1887 in his *Gemeinschaft und Gesellschaft* [Community and (Civil) Society]. Empathy seeks proximity, even "objectified enjoyment of self", abstraction in contrast seeks distance, if not distancing. Empathy applies to space as an organic "world around" [*Um-welt*], while abstraction worships geometry. The "absolute artistic volition" [*Kunstwollen*], Worringer claims, is nothing but "one great mental aversion to space."[44] Akin to the religious sensitivity to transcendence, it tries to flee space altogether as a confusing, complex, trap-like dimension. This abstracting absolute artistic volition corresponds to configurations such as pyramids, mosaics, and ornaments, which are removed from if not hostile to life and are in any case denatured objectivities. The observation that this denaturing artificiality historically predates the "drive to empathy," which itself may go astray in the naturalism inherent in art, has remained unrefuted. Ernst Gombrich, in his great study on ornaments, still describes this element as a downright anthropological dimension of orientation, contrary to Adolf Loos, who had coined the formula (also a medical physiognomy of sorts) of the "ornament as crime" just a few years after Worringer. It is this developmental history of the "willing of art" from the ornament to the soul that so clearly sets apart Worringer's binaries from those of Tönnies. For Tönnies's community is older than society, the latter arising only within urbanity, where the individuals recede into the neutral status of *flânerie* or anomie, in any case that of an unknown third party.

In no case does this pendulum motion between "abstraction and empathy" assume more unfathomable or more interesting guises than

in that of the face. Even Galton's norm face, abstracted from a certain
set, may be enjoyed aesthetically; and it is certainly true that facial figu-
rations dominated cultural prehistory in the form of masks, which were
discarded with civilization. According to his own testimony, Worringer
found inspiration for his theory in none other than Georg Simmel,[45]
perhaps (even though Worringer never specified) by Simmel's early
study, "The Aesthetic Meaning of the Face." In the study, abstraction
and empathy are distinguished but conceived of as inextricably linked.
The "geometric locus of the inner person, insofar as it can become visible," the *abstractum* of the face, appears as the complement to the mimic
excitations—the occasions for empathy.[46] Over and over, the gaze is
drawn into a mimic scene and can then rest on the scene's bony set. As
though Simmel wanted to impute an abstracting drive to the face itself,
he shares an odd economic observation: human features express themselves according to the law of least resistance. The smallest change may
mean a new action, perhaps even an entirely new play on this stage. How
to unify the geometric and the mimic perspective, and whether they are
separable at all, is not discussed in this concept. It is thus left to Worringer to distinguish the two, to declare them two entirely contradictory
ambitions—a view he bequeaths to gestalt psychology.

Simmel's account, however, manages to harness something else theo-
retically. At base he is still dealing with the old class/estate principles of
the view from the top down and the other way around: mimic perception as the slave's empathy for the master or mistress and physiognomic
perception as the abstracting view of the master over the servants (in
particular the female ones). For the bourgeois middle classes these turn
into *abstracta* of (social) proximity and distance, individuality and—
perhaps measurable—geometry. The old art historic tradition of the aesthetically measured man begins to announce itself once more. But is there
a space in between? Between pure numbers and the affective content,
between abstraction and empathy, the notion of the "face as landscape"
must have functioned as a sort of compromise, at least in the popular
literature of the period. Perhaps it was an attempt to overcome the
estates-like division of labor between the fearful study of expression and
arrogant "body criticism," as Barbara Stafford has called it. When Bölsche latches on to Haeckel's cosmic brow, when Walter Flex turns Wallenstein's face into an open field, when Stefan Zweig molds the earth of
Dostoevsky's face,[47] or Rudolf Kassner the rocks in Nietzsche's,[48] and so
on, they create neither a purely aesthetic-geometric abstraction, nor do
they arrive at an individual affective profile. Instead, the face becomes
transparent. It opens the view to the outside; it shirks the dialogue face
to face and seeks instead a field of honor or religion; it disappears like
water in the ground. And what can count as the true "image giver"

here—the landscape or the appropriate symbolic field—remains a mystery. Perhaps the face in the picture—the face without a voice, that is—turns out to be just that kind of reversible figure that plays abstraction and empathy against each other and nonetheless yokes them inextricably to one another.

Hitler's face of course has never been analyzed using Worringer's method. The aesthetes of the time thought him abhorrent; the believers, however, sang his praises, but less in order to portray him than to adulate him. Günther Scholdt speaks of the legions who devoted themselves to "Führer hymnals," the effects of which "were probably devastating."[49] The cruder the exaltation, the greater the landscape or the cosmic space into which the visage seemed to open: as the vision of a coming field of honor. "And where the cosmos storms around its axes, / one came down to us his face alight."[50]

The Face of Dignity: Helmuth Plessner

The notion that "honor" and dignity can be expressed spatially is of course not new. Distance to people of esteem and to dignitaries is not the exception but the rule. But under the conditions of the interwar period, there emerged charismatic leaders such as Hitler who did not solicit esteem but adulation, who exuded enthusiasm rather than dignity, and who bound large, and in particular young, groups of people to themselves. It is this scene that one of the oddest physiognomic projects of the time, the book *Grenzen der Gemeinschaft: Eine Kritik des sozialen Radikalismus* [Limits of Community: A Critique of Social Radicalism] by the anthropologist and sociologist Helmuth Plessner from 1924, takes as its point of departure, without making explicit reference to Hitler. Explicitly conceived as an answer to Ferdinand Tönnies, the study criticizes "those active consequences" that the contemporary youth movement, as a sociality of idealized closeness, seems to draw from the political realities of the day.[51] These radical utopian hopes for an honest and confraternal society become the target of Plessner's Kant-inspired critique. In keeping with the motto that "if there are dialectics of the heart, they are certainly more dangerous than the dialectics of reason," Plessner addresses the inheritance of Nietzsche in German discourse. "The mistake lies in a one-sided biological direction of view. One does not escape the fate of Nietzsche's teaching so long as one recognizes strength only as strength and weakness only as weakness. For the vital differences of degree and type require a specific form of abstraction to count as valid moves in the game of humans."[52]

This sublimation Plessner goes on to depict as a subtle physiognomy. "Strong is whoever affirms the entire essential complex of society [*Gesell-*

schaft] for the sake of the dignity of the individual and the social whole; weak is whoever sacrifices dignity for brotherhood in the community."[53] At the time, Plessner meant by the affirmation of society something quite contrary to Spengler and many others: the affirmation of civilization and of technology as the emerging or already dominant modes of social cooperation. That they at the same time require "alienation" and distance runs counter to the eudaemonism of the proponents of "community," but it conforms to the commandments of ethics. The idea of the game and the rules of the game replace existential seriousness, asking the youth movement to become serious about the idea of the game as well. It is not by accident that Plessner applauds the "ethos of grace and ease."[54] And in contrast to the false immediacy of the reigning facial contemplation, he pleads the case of the mask: "Belonging to the basic character of the societal ethos is a longing for the mask behind which all immediacy disappears."[55] Of course, Nietzsche too could have been adduced for this thought, but Nietzsche is for Plessner (at least in this book) too biologistic, too close to an inadequate thinking "along the guideline of the body." Under the title "The Fight for a Genuine Face: The Risk of Ridicule," chapter 4 of Plessner's book sketches a life-worldly situation of the kind that first became imaginable only in the Weimar Republic: At this time, it claims, the psychological body-subject wants both to appear and to hide. Why hide? Following Georg Simmel ("Among the characteristics of the present moment, one is unmistakable: that, in an ever increasing number of values, we turn to excitation and insinuation instead of manifest fulfillment, which wouldn't allow our imagination to fill in any blanks"[56]), Plessner sees the human soul as ambiguous, polyvalent, inexhaustible, full of potentialities: "Looked at from the outside with regard to its becoming seen, the soul is the greatest riddle, eternally polysemous; it slips away from us barely comprehended."[57]

Naturally, such a soul doesn't want to be nailed down on any one form of appearance. But it must appear—birth itself forces it to. But what does this form of appearance say about the elusive many-shaped interior? Even our innate physiognomic sense sins against our soul:

What we do not want to remember nor want others to remember is engraved on our faces with the chisel of nature. What should become visible according to our intention must, however, struggle with great effort into the light and withstand the danger of exposure to others. To the extent that the soul strives to achieve its own formation and development, the organic body is a poor and inadequate symbol for the personality. Where it symbolizes it says too much; where it should symbolize it is silent. It interposes itself as a supporting objectual body between the spirit/soul subjects.[58]

This axiom of bourgeois interiority finds its inspiration not in Simmel's psychology alone. Simmel's phenomenology of the gaze, of gazing upon, of avoiding the gaze, or averting it to the ground, is extended by Plessner and pushed to a baffling conclusion. Taking his departure from the psychology of shame, to which all physiognomics ultimately leads because it wants to turn the inside out, Plessner concludes that there is only one situation, a social one, that could reconcile soul and body in unity: "*Only because there is human dignity*, [that is] the idea of a harmony within the soul and between soul and expression, soul and objectual body, [. . .] do we experience so much in ourselves and others as something insufficient[. . .]. Dignity concerns at all times the person taken in his entirety—the unity of what lies inside and outside—and describes the ideal constitution to which one strives [. . .]."[59] It is this dignity that is threatened, by the comical, but also by the caricature, which often enough one's own insufficient body gives rise to. It seems that Helmuth Plessner was the first one to speak of the inviolability of this dignity:* "Maybe—we venture only to suggest—the dialectical dynamic of psychological life, with regard to its practical determination and knowledge, is rooted (comprehended most purely) in an aesthetic inviolability that seduces one to violate it."[60] The book goes on to develop very stringently the idea of dignity as a "saved face" and the social rules as methods of saving face. But still, Plessner is not concerned with a determination of the *culture* of shame, in which the notion of the face figured as a mere metaphor. Plessner's line of argumentation remains physiognomical, after all he was originally an anthropologist and, during this very period, he was at work on a theory of the "mimic perception of a foreign I" and thus understood the human subject always also as a body–not as a body of blood and race, but nonetheless one that appears and wants to appear, with its "inviolability that tempts violation." Nietzsche's "guideline of the body" is thus transformed into a guideline of corporeal dignity, a liminal sociological term somewhere between "community" and "(civil) society," proximity and distance. After all, that which tempts violation has to come close enough, and the notion of inhibition presupposes a psychic apparatus that literally wants to com-prehend.

Plessner thus gives us—following Thorstein Veblen—perhaps the first theory of "visual publicity" in the sense of an expanded "civil public sphere" in which everybody wants to count as an appearance before everybody else, wants to present himself as such. But since there is also always closeness, the weaker spirit needs an "armor" or a "mask" so as

---

*The first article of the German Grundgesetz [Basic Law] states that "Human dignity is inviolable. To respect and protect it is the duty of all state authority" [translation Axel Tschentscher, Jurisprudentia Verlag Würzburg]. The author is here alluding to that formula. Trans.

not to be hurt. The stronger one creates a "genuine face" in his own works, and the strongest finally "unintentionally will imbue the infinite with his own characteristics and awaken on his face the memory of a divine visage."[61]

The pathos of facialization apparent in these formulas bespeaks how closely fenced in the field of honor was with physiognomic vocabulary, if it wasn't thought as second-degree physiognomy *tout court.* Granted, this social order of recognition and prestige is in Plessner's vision ruled by somewhat antiquated strategies such as tact, diplomacy, ceremony, and politeness, strategies from the centuries that could still make reference to "a struggle" that "should not be fought for the sake of existence [*Dasein*], but for the sake of essence [*Sosein*]."[62]

Plessner's recourse to tact and politeness of course covers up the fact that in 1924 the "visual publicity" that had gone along with the Weimar Republic could not make appeal to knighthood in shining armor, but rather called for an entirely different type: a person who could sculpt or conceal his or her appearance through habitus. What was required was thus in actuality the actor—a topic of Plessner's later sociology. It is not by accident that, at the time, the most exhaustive description of a face bearing as an imprint all the features of the inexhaustible individuality that Plessner and Simmel celebrated was the death mask of an actor. In his 1929 introduction to one of those small portrait galleries in book form that followed Benkard, Egon Friedell describes Josef Kainz, who had recently died an early death:

In my study hangs the death mask of Josef Kainz, taken by his colleague Otto Tressler. It is so positioned that whenever I raise my eyes they must hit upon it, and I thus end up looking at it probably more than a hundred times a day! But every time the mask is different. Just as the sea takes on ever variable colors under the keel of a ship, at times orange or fleshy pink, then crimson red or glass blue, then again milky white, vivid green, sulfurous yellow, or varnished black: this is how the countenance changes its expression continuously and in the most surprising fashion. At times it looks like the portrait bust of a Roman emperor: cunning, dissolute, and degenerate; one moment later like the image of an ecstatic saint, before whose distant eyes the pearly gates jump open; one time it may show the dulled features of an age-old woman, another the ferocious grimace of a cynical comedian; and in between it is a poet in reverie, a philosopher lost in thought, an ascetic with a pained smile, a boy with a guileless laugh, a quietly contemplative madman, a lewdly grinning faun. Every now and then it is all these together, mixed perversely and strangely iridescent. At yet other moments it is nothing at all, nothing but an empty plaster cast. And indeed one may look at this strangely multifarious impression that dead Kainz's image leaves with us, as a symbol of the effect Kainz elicited while still alive. For he too was insuperable in the art of showing a different skin in each different role, yes even in each different scene, to dazzle the eye with the incessant change of color and lights. And yet it has often been claimed of him that he was in all his roles the

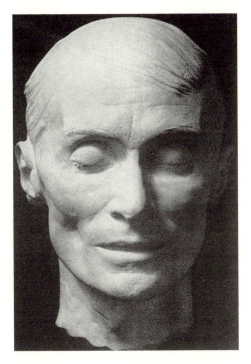

Figure 26. One of the most beautiful death masks of the era showed Josef Kainz, one of the most revered actors at the Burgtheater before the First World War. With its multifarious mimic qualities becoming evident under changing lighting, it created a link to the portrait of the silent movies, extensively discussed by Béla Balász, the Hungarian critic and director.

same Josef Kainz. Indeed he merely restlessly changed the outward expression of his essence, merely put on a new enchanting mask each day, behind whose splendor hid always the same man in the dark[63] [Fig. 26].

In 1924, Plessner could not have guessed that of all things it would be an unmistakable *death* mask that would function as the visual embodiment of the ambiguous *theatrical* mask. What is turned inside-out here he still conceives of as "entirely inner" and highly vulnerable. But it is hard to argue with the suspicion that Plessner too construes the "rich" inner life of the individual according to the philosophy of culture of the *fin de siecle*, and that he puts inside what was at that time already outside. Not just Rodin, but also Rilke asks shortly after 1900: "For who knows *what a face is*, and is our notion thereof not mere prejudice, a limitation of the staggering number of forms that could constitute a face in their inexhaustible combinations?"[64] It is an argument he mutes a bit in the novel *Malte Laurids Brigge* (1910), but applies to the modern metropolis: "Have I already mentioned it? I am learning to see. Yes, I am starting. It's not quite there yet. But I will make use of my time. That, for example, it never came to my mind how many faces there are. There are huge numbers of people, but even more faces, for each has several."[65]

On first glance, this kind of facial prose may have little bearing on a culture of shame, and even less on a culture of guilt, because there is no mention of either conscience or misdeed. Much rather it seems to reflect the emergence of an "externally directed society," as Rilke's friend Rudolf Kassner, himself a passionate physiognomist, diagnosed it: "Apart from the thespian and the movie actor, who still has a face today?" In his speech on the foundations of physiognomy of 1922, he sketched the beloathed actor's rise to the top of the social pyramid, using unusually modern vocabulary: "I want to say, the secret, most tacit [*nie ausgesprochene*] purpose of all institutions was directed against the actor and was hostile toward him. The actor alone gained from the decadence and decline of most institutions and could thrive. Among the types, he is the one quickest and easiest to develop. He makes his appearance almost automatically, once all the other types are missing or lacking (physiognomically speaking). Only one type rivals him in the speed of his development: the athlete. The types are, as it were, the interior and the exterior of the face of our time."[66]

Kassner has offered a description and diagnosis—if not an outright explanation for the facial discourse's extraordinary career in the Weimar Republic—that have lost none of their relevance today. The countless treatises not only about the recognizability but especially about the fungibility of face and character are here at last given a sociopsychological explanation. What this explanation accounts for is why the different iconizations of the epoch (the racial norm of the face, the face of the saint, and lastly the face of dignity) found such passionate reception, even if at the same time ideal hopes attached to the face of the "great individuals." One spoke of faces and meant stable referents; one spoke of instances and meant secure institutions: science, religion, a sociality of recognition, to say nothing of the referent and institution called "Germany," with its "eternal countenance." Of course Hitler could not provide any of these visual embodiments, but the discourses about them all lead eventually to him. Even at a very cursory glance, he didn't conform to the Aryan racial image, and yet he made it the norm for others; only his most fanatical devotees thought him holy, and yet he staged himself as the German messiah; the idea of human "inviolability" [*Unantastbarkeit*] ran counter to everything he said and did, and yet he took conservative voters by storm through an angry restoration of inviolable, German national self-certainty.

Sebastian Haffner has pointed out that Hitler completely lacked a sense for institutions, that he had a gambler's disposition toward the future. No contingency plans were made in the case of his death; his political projects weren't conceived beyond his death. There was no attempt to provide for coming generations; little attempt was made to secure social structures beyond theatrical rituals because "the Führer" had declared himself the incarnation of these structures.[67]

Of course, all this emerged only later. When Rudolf Kassner wrote his comments in 1922, he wanted to, by a macabre turn, point to the two enemy figures of his time: the Jews and the Americans, the actors and the athletes. But the main profiteer from the tearing down, the replacement, and the creation of the social framework at the time, and the person who was to accelerate the pace of these developments, was none other than Hitler himself. Nonetheless, with the portrait sessions with Heinrich Hoffmann in 1928–29, Hitler no longer presented himself as an angry orator or as the determined drummer, but rather as a "national comrade" in the brown shirt with shoulder strap, the Iron Cross First Class, and the German equivalent of the Purple Heart: and Orwell took the occasion of these pictures to impute to Hitler a Jesus thematic. Today, Rudolf Herz believes the series to be "perhaps the most convincing contribution to the photographic definition of the Hitler mythos at the end of the 1920s"; according to him this series "humanized the tough fighter type and [managed to] stylize Hitler's physiognomy into a trademark."[68] Humanization and trademark— whether these two go together at all is of course another question. According to Herz, Hitler furthermore underwent a sort of "learning process in self-presentation" in the course of these sessions, looking to solicit sympathy and—in slight association with the American type—to present himself as a self-made man, even as a civilized "superior statesman." The dramatis personae were now almost complete—now all that was missing were the Führer's costume and masks.

Chapter 4
Self-Images 1929–1939

The Führer's Countenance

The years between 1929 and 1939 witnessed the unprecedented spectacle of Germany's complete social, economic, and parliamentary collapse—and a panicky coping mechanism that took the shape of the meteoric rise of the NSDAP with Hitler as its Führer and from 1933 onward as German chancellor. The trench warfare of economics and power politics notwithstanding, Hitler—at least in the eyes of the outside world—held fast to his mission: the displacement of the Jews and the revision of the Versailles treaty. As early as *Mein Kampf* he had declared revenge for Versailles the precondition for the success of his movement and thus made a motivation shared by the entire political spectrum of the Weimar Republic his own political territory. The party's fourth annual convention in 1929 in Nuremberg was scheduled to coincide with the ten-year anniversary of the humiliation. These revanchist demands went along with the *Lebensraum* [life space] fantasies of his book: the colonization of the East concomitant with the merciless expulsion and expurgation of Bolshevism and of course, again and again, of the Jews were the mainstays in Hitler's speeches once he was allowed to give them again. The 1929 rally was a demonstration of strength, the party having by now reached 130,000 members, some 30,000 or 40,000 thousand of which came out to Nuremberg at the beginning of August. During the same summer, a campaign began under Goebbels's aegis for a referendum against the Young plan, which provided for a reassessment of German payments of reparations; the campaign was meant to open old wounds, heating up memories of the Versailles treaty, and it succeeded in doing so.

Hitler recounted the stations in Germany's "re-erection" ten years later in a speech before troop commanders: leaving the League of Nations, rearmament, proclamation of the freedom to militarize before other countries, remilitarization and reoccupation of the Rhineland, and solution of the "Austrian and also the Czechoslovak problem," meaning the occupation of eastern territories. According to his speech, he had decided on these steps years earlier, had hesitated at times and moved faster at others, but in any case, he claimed, they were "long-laid plans."[1]

The remilitarization went along with a neutralization of civil society: the burning of the Reichstag took care of the Communists, the Enabling Act dispensed with the Constitution, the self-dissolution of the parties dismantled the political organization, the law on the "reconstruction of the Reich" reorganized the federal system of state government. Paramilitary groupings and closely surveyed societies of proximity replaced its free social structure: SS and SA, Gestapo, SD, Hitler Youth, Führer schools, BDM [Bund Deutscher Mädel, or German Girls' League], and so on. The brutality of state power emerged clearly in the 1934 "Night of the Long Knives" and in the pogroms of November 9, 1938; systematically murderous anti-Semitism had been taking shape less and less covertly since 1933.

Beginning in March of that year there were open acts of violence against individual Jews and Jewish stores; in the same month, the first regular concentration camps in Dachau and Oranienburg were created and the ministry of the interior installed a department of "racial hygiene." In April, there was a countrywide boycott of Jewish businesses; at the same time the "law for the restoration of professional civil service" was passed, a law aimed in particular at Jewish public servants. At schools and universities, the proportion of Jews was reduced to 1.5 percent. Further, that same year brought a law of derecognition, expatriating many Jews from the East and the West. The regime's opponents and victims began fleeing Germany en masse.

In 1934, President Hindenburg died. Hitler unified the offices of chancellor and president in his own person and had a referendum in order to confirm the measure: 89.9 percent of Germans voted for it, with some 95.7 percent of Germans turning out at the polls.

From January of 1935 on, there were special guidelines for race-political education in the schools; in June, a general compulsory military service was introduced, nullifying the stipulation of the Versailles treaty unilaterally. In May, Jews were excluded from the Wehrmacht; in the summer, the boycott against Jewish stores was intensified; in September, the Nuremberg Laws deprived Jews of all their civil rights. In the years that followed, the freedom, property, and options a Jewish citizen might have had were systematically curtailed and penalized. The so-called race laws found their culmination in 1935–36 in the "law for the protection of the hereditary health of the German people," prohibiting marriage between the handicapped and the healthy, the SS program Lebensborn for the promotion of Aryan procreation, and the *Blutschutzgesetze* [blood protection laws] against Sinti, Roma, and people of color.

The pogroms of the so-called Kristallnacht in November of 1938 led to the murder and deportation of tens of thousands of Jews into the concentration camps, to the destruction of almost all synagogues and of more than seven thousand businesses. The entire Jewish press was outlawed and Jews were forced to pay "compensation," meaning the confiscation of Jewish fortunes and the "Aryanization" of businesses. With these abhorrent accomplishments behind him, Hitler gave a secret speech before the high command of the Wehrmacht that very month, in which, in order to prepare for the coming war, he developed his plans for expansion in the east quite succinctly.

*   *   *

His devoted audience of course saw an entirely different side of these years: disappearance of unemployment, the creation of the autobahn, the grand displays of athletic and aesthetic prowess in the Olympic Games, and so on. In of September of 1936, the Nuremberg Reichsparteitag der Ehre [Convention of Honor] took place; it was followed the next year by the rescission of the German signature under the declaration of guilt of Versailles. It had thus taken Hitler four years to give Germans back the "face" that they had lost, according to a large majority, in the First World War. That this metaphor was taken at face value had to do with that obsessive literal-mindedness that Hitler displayed again, in June of 1940, after the defeat of France. As soon as victory was complete, he charged General Keitel with drawing up an armistice that would mirror that of 1918. Even the ceremony was *literally* to practice revanche. The treaties were signed in the same old salon car that Marshall Foch had used in 1918, at the same place, a clearing in Rethondes near Compiègne. Keitel's first words recalled "the deepest ignominy ever suffered," which would now be expunged.

The first report of this scene came from William Shirer, then a European correspondent for CBS. He gave a by-the-minute account of the event, and as always when Hitler impressed him, he described him physiognomically:

[. . .] I am but fifty yards away from him and see him through my glasses as though he were directly in front of me. I have seen that face many times at the great moments of his life. But today! It is afire with scorn, anger, hate, revenge, triumph. [. . .] Suddenly, as though his face were not giving quite complete expression to his feelings, he throws his whole body into harmony with his mood. He swiftly snaps his hands on his hips, arches his shoulders, plants his feet wide apart. It is a magnificent gesture of defiance, of burning contempt for this place now and all that it has stood for in the twenty-two years since it witnessed the humbling of the German Empire.[2]

This highly significant, almost salvific mise-en-scène could not but hit its mark with the public. It was a typological gesture straight out of biblical hermeneutics, which reads the prophecies of the Old Covenant as fulfilled or revaluated under the new one. In conscious, even competing reference to Judeo-Christian thought, Hitler undertook leadership in his own perverse salvation story. With this kind of "leadership" he at once neutralized that social area, which solicits literal attention as such: the area of right, of faithfulness to the letter of the law.[3] None other than Carl Schmitt, the crown jurist of the Nazi years, described this disempowerment of civil society in 1933 and gave reasons for it:

This concept of leadership [*Führung*] comes out of the concrete substantial thinking of the National Socialist movement. It is characteristic that any representation fails and that every accurate representation at once exceeds representationality and instead corresponds to a leadership in the thing itself. Our concept neither *needs* nor is *capable* of mediating image and representational comparisons. It neither stems from baroque allegories and representations nor from a Cartesian *idée générale*. It is a concept of immediate present and real presence.[4]

How present this bankruptcy of metaphorical thinking was throughout the NS movement, becomes clear through a travestying detail from the same year, 1933. Ernst Hanfstaengl, Hitler's friend from his early Munich days and now *Auslandspressechef* [foreign press chief], published a coltish collection right after Hitler's seizure of power. *Tat gegen Tinte: Hitler in der Karikatur der Welt* [Deed Against Ink: Hitler in the Caricatures of the World] attempted to "refute" each caricature with irrefutable arguments, in the style of the visual propaganda of Schultze-Naumburg. One of the first of these caricatures was not from abroad at all, but rather from *Simplicissimus*, which had commented on Hitler's rise to power since 1923 and had been much quoted abroad. The title page of April 1, 1924 showed Hitler on horseback, waving a flag and parading through the Brandenburg Gate: a black knight is next to him; Friedrich Ebert, then president of the Reich, is in chains below him; and up front on the left a warrior is brandishing a saber and standing over a man on the ground, apparently a Jew [Fig. 27].[5] The drawing's title was "Hitler's Entrance into Berlin," intended as a parody of the failed coup attempt of November of 1923. At the same time, the image was a travesty of the giant canvas entitled *Kaiser Wilhelm Victorious*, painted by Ferdinand Keller in 1888 (the so-called Year of the Three Emperors, in which both Wilhelm I and his son, the emperor Friedrich Wilhelm, died and in which Wilhelm II ascended to the throne[6]). According to the physiognomist Müller, this painting with its shining white steeds, inspired Walther Rathenau to remark at the start of World War I that if the emperor—

Figure 27. An exceedingly eloquent example of the densely structured allusive technique of *Simplicissimus*, this Hitler caricature of April 1, 1924 refers to a painting by Ferdinand Keller from 1888 entitled *Kaiser Wilhelm Victorious* and comments—somewhere between derision and admiration—on Hitler's coup attempt of November of 1923.

Wilhelm II—were to ride triumphantly through the Brandenburg Gate
with his paladins, world history would have lost all meaning.[7]

According to Hanffstaengl's 1933 book, it was this multivalent, overly
allusive caricature from the *Simplicissimus* of April 1, 1924 that he
brought to Hitler in Landsberg Prison: "Beyond the political ignorance
apparent in the image, there was something else in it that preoccupied
me, namely the thought that this may perhaps be an involuntarily visionary perception of future events. When in this context I uttered the words
'yes, that's what it'll be like one day,' it was this caricature that became
for all of us the secret motor that drove us to make happen that which
seemed back then, in April of 1924, impossible."[8]

Not picture thinking, but the direct translation of images and visions
into action, with "hair-raisingly literal-minded consistency,"[9] numbers
among the most central gestures of the NS movement, suturing the ele-

ments of its political religion. The revision of the Versailles treaty, the reconquest of the territories lost in it, and the conquest of open spaces in the East had comprised Hitler's unshakable visions since 1918. How closely his thinking bordered on Jewish messianism, even to the point of blasphemous quotation, was apparent even before Adolf Eichmann's Jerusalem trial between 1960 and 1962. In her study, Hannah Arendt described Eichmann's revolting "Zionist phase," in which he adduced his reading of Theodor Herzl's 1896 magnum opus *Der Judenstaat* [The Jewish State] to claim that Hitler had in no way meant to exterminate the Jews, but rather aimed to drive them into their own region, to give them "a place of their own, soil of their own" in conformity with the precepts of Zionism.[10] There were no moral concepts attached to this, no utopia of human dignity or salvation; much to the contrary. The human being and the soil it dwelt on had become almost synonymous.

The physiognomic literature of the years between 1930 and 1939 makes that clear, as well as how intensely this literal transposition of visions led to its own physiognomic rituals. All of them display the emerging, the just regained German face in a purely physical sense, showing the German self-image flaunting itself not "from above" and not "from below," but in general "from up front"—as though the *en face* pose was meant temporally, as though the years since 1918 had been nothing but one long warm-up for the leap into identity.

At the same time, the suspicion that the face of the Nazi leadership perhaps did not embody that identity or its Aryan self-image at all snuck even into the very first review of the first exhibition of "Führer heads" in 1933. The Berlin *Lokal-Anzeiger* of October 21 commented, without mentioning the Aryan type in one word:

In the palace, the Reichskartell der Bildenden Kuenste [Department of Fine Art] opened an exhibit that unites numerous pictures and depicture of great leaders of the National Socialist movement. It gives interesting insights into *how our artists physiognomically come to terms with the problem how to make the heads of the leaders of the new Reich palpable* [anschaulich] *in their individual temperament and personal essence.*

Of the Reich's president Hindenburg, we find one painting by Hugo Vogel, a chalk drawing depicting the then field Marshal at his headquarters in 1916, and a new coal drawing by Bruno Breil. The portraits of the Führer are quite numerous. Walter Miehe depicts him in a coat standing up, Holleck-Weithmann emphasizes the linearity of his decisive head, Karl Bauer gives a characteristic etching of his profile. Carl Hachez, Erich Kux, Willy Meyer, and Otto Priebe depict him in various graphic techniques. Besides the famous busts of the chancellor by Pagels and Stark, the most impressive head [on display] is a bronze by Ernst Seger, though Walter Wolff too has created a bronze bust. Hermann Göring is rendered by Holleck-Weithmann and Renfordt; his willful head can be seen in one of Pagels's bronzes. Very lifelike is R. Sagekrow's watercolor of Dr. Goebbels's countenance; Ludwig Manzel created an exceptional bronze medallion. The bronze bust by Hanna Cauer shows Dr. Frick in an antique toga, Walther Darré was drawn by Franz Triebsch, Paul Gruson did a sculpture of Dr. Lippert, Alfred Rosenberg appears standing up, painted by Luitpold Adam.[11]

Hardly any of these painters has left any other traces; whether the works here catalogued still exist in some museum storerooms is doubtful.

The objective emerged more clearly six years later, when Hitler's fiftieth birthday gave the occasion not only for a full exhibition of Hitler portraits in Frankfurt but moreover for a photo volume by Heinrich Hoffmann.[12] *Das Antlitz des Führers* [The Führer's Countenance] of 1939 comprises sixteen portraits beginning in 1919, with captions detailing the stages of Hitler's rise to power and success: 1919, 1923, 1926, 1928, 1929 ("the Führer storms without surcease from rally to rally"), 1933 ("At the turning of the tides: one hour after his appointment as chancellor . . ."), 1934, 1935, 1936, 1937 ("We are one people, let us now be one empire"), 1938, 1939. The first picture in this series is already slightly misleading, for it shows a natty young Hitler [Fig. 28], photographed in his first session with Hoffmann in 1923,[13] while the caption claims: "In the year of Germany's deepest humiliation, in the year of civil war and the Weimar national convention, Germany loses through the imperious dictations of Versailles both freedom and honor. In this year of desperation, one unknown soldier of the gray front decides to turn Germany's fortunes all by himself. One man rises against the world. . . ." None of this can be gleaned from the photograph; it is meant to appeal to entirely different circles than the text. Nonetheless, the choice of photograph is canny. Hitler appears in the book—almost like Wilhelm II—in a continuously changing wardrobe. In dark suits, in a long coat, in the brown shirt, in a suit with party insignia, in a leather get-up, in a trench coat with a dog whip, in uniform. The last photo, taken during the 1933–34 sessions, has the caption: "Our world power: Adolf Hitler!" It has Hitler looking very seriously, almost like a visionary, toward the text [see Fig. 28].

The photo volume had a first printing of two hundred thousand copies. Reichsjugendführer [Youth Leader] Baldur von Schirach wrote in the preface:

What German could look upon these images with anything but deep emotion! For doesn't his countenance mirror to all of us our own life as it rose from the depth of the German collapse through distress, battle, and labor to its present heights. . . .

When we read in these dear features, we learn of our cares and our determination regarding our existence; and moved and shamed we recognize the face of a man who never wanted to think of himself.

It is this selfless, exclusive thought devoted only to Germany, which here impressed itself onto *the* German face par excellence, so that in the future no

Figure 28. The date of the first photograph, taken by Heinrich Hoffmann, remains unclear. According to a picture volume of 1939, it was taken in 1919, but this is highly unlikely because at the time Hitler was still a soldier rather than the dapper fellow of this picture. The *Illustrierte Beobachter* of 1936 dates the picture to 1921, but if this is true, Hoffmann could not possibly be the photographer. He himself claims in his memoirs that he took the picture in 1922, even though he managed to convince Hitler to sit for him only in 1923. The second photo, which was the last image from *Das Antlitz des Führers* [The Führer's Countenance], came out of the sessions of 1933–34. It became the template for a poster bearing the tag line "One *Volk*, one Reich, one Führer."

German will be able to recall his homeland without seeing the Führer's face before him. We don't want to waste words here on what can only be experienced by the heart! He who leafs through the pages of this volume will perceive the stylus of God, as it turned, with a few mysterious strokes, a single human countenance into the sublime symbol of an entire people—from the picture of the soldier returning from the world war to the portrait of the creator of the Reich who fulfilled, yes exceeded, the hopes and dreams of a millennium. He will then, through his own fidelity, dutifulness, and obedience, try to be worthy of this Führer.[14]

Heinrich Hoffmann's volume, *The Führer's Countenance*, appeared at the conclusion of a decade that had seen the physiognomic tendencies of the 1920s solidify along racist lines and divergent tendencies silenced. The project of a "national portrait gallery" had been transformed into a biological version in the shape of "ancestral research," charged with the doctrines of descent and relation, and with the selection of the SS whose members had to document a spotless family tree going back to the year 1800. A futuristic version of this biological family tree was created by Heinrich Himmler in the shape of the Lebensborn, with the aim of promoting the procreation of the elite. The Stiftung Ahnenerbe was similarly biologized and medicalized. Founded by Heinrich Himmler and Walther Darré, it was repurposed from 1939 onward for so-called war-connected ends, later for human testing as well.

Also beginning in 1937, schools were given new guidelines. In accordance with the ideas developed in *Mein Kampf,* racial studies became central, including weekly training in recognizing and distinguishing "Aryans" and "non-Aryans." This physiognomy was applied to the extent that, according to Hans Blumenberg, so-called physiognomists were dispatched during the war; they traveled to France in order to track down Jews.[15] The clearest physical stigmatization, the yellow star, was forced upon Jews in Germany beginning in 1941. It appears that they were not as easily identifiable as physiognomics and racial doctrines would have it, while at the same time it was difficult to make out the "Aryan" in Hitler, Goebbels, and others. In 1963, Joachim Fest opined that it remained doubtful to what extent their appearance was reconcilable with the pure theory, and that "this must not be seen as too binding. . . ."[16]

In any case, the commemorative stamp for Hitler's fiftieth birthday showed Hitler with his military hat. Baldur von Schirach's canny formulation that it had been "thinking of Germany" that had given the Führer "the German face par excellence" thus was not the whole answer.

Seeing in Figures [*Gestalten*]: Ernst Jünger and the Future

From a physiognomic perspective, three central projects of the Weimar years imploded in Hoffmann's sixteen-picture Hitler hagiography: The project of a national portrait gallery terminated in its absolute reduction, taking the portrait of the "creator of the Reich" as the visual embodiment of an entire people. The same went for the project of physiognomic regional studies: "the Führer's countenance" as home(land) and mental ground/soil on which one could look without shame but rather with pride. The third was the project of the "New Man," seen by the visionary's "second face [*zweites Gesicht*]" in "thinking about Germany." This second face's physiognomic prophet since the beginning of the 1930s was no photographer or painter, but none other than the author Ernst Jünger. Unerringly he had in a sense set the tone for the 1930s with his book *Das Antlitz des Weltkrieges* [The Countenance of the First World War]: a collection of two hundred photos, plus maps and chronology, as though to recapitulate one last time the calamitous point of departure for the politics of revanche. Hitler reportedly thanked Jünger upon receiving the book and allegedly read and praised it as well.[17]

No greater contrast is imaginable than between this volume and the images of World War I that Grosz and Dix and many other eyewitnesses returned with in 1918. For Jünger, highly decorated, the First World War had become natural history. A new aesthetic enters the stage when he writes in his introductory essay on "War and Photograph": "One must not expect more from photography than it can deliver. A fine imprint of external events, it resembles the imprints the erstwhile existence of strange animals has left in the rocks. Those may well provide material for contemplation—but what the life of the great animal and what its secret movements were like: this only the imagination can tell us. . . ."[18] Not, in other words, historical knowledge. What is meant here is rather already the imagination of the physiognomic visionary and reader of figures, as Jünger was to present himself in his 1932 book, *Der Arbeiter: Herrschaft und Gestalt* [The Worker: Dominance and Figure]. It was a brilliant essay on a "type" to come, a type that had less to do with any actual laborer than with the hybrid inheritance of the New Objectivity, the highly equipped man in uniform and workman's suit. With the Janus face of the sentimentalist who is really a futurist, Jünger paints a rather accurate picture of physiognomy since the eighteenth century: originally geared toward the individual and toward empathy, it subsequently lost its unity and eventually reached its clinical end point in the modernist portrait. It was a premonition of the concept of "degenerate art," if only touched on briefly by the author. As though to dispel Rudolf Kassner's worry that a face may only exist within the institutions, while outside of them accident and acting rule, Jünger evokes the new situation of society at work, in which the institutions of the life world emphatically mask the face rather than liberating it. The mask, Jünger writes, "makes its appearance in manifold ways, in situations in which the specific character of work asserts itself—be this in the shape of the gas mask with which entire populations are being outfitted, be it in the shape of the facial mask for sport and high velocity, something owned by every motorist, or be it in the shape of the protective mask at a workplace made dangerous by radiation, explosions, or narcotic substances."[19] The masking of the person of action, Jünger asserts, reaches into everyday life and even into recreation time and takes on a "metallic" quality in the case of the man and a "cosmetic" one in the case of the woman. In either case the mask has anti-individualistic tendencies, expunging even sex characteristics; it is the unmoved expression of the "type."

What is more ominous than this type is the vision Jünger has of its discoverer. Worringer's schema of "abstraction and empathy" is destroyed here: on this reading empathy, the careful glance "from below," disappears from the repertoire of visual activity. The perception of types as the epitome of "figure" [gestalt] puts the "seer" into a bird's-eye view beyond good and evil: "Seeing in figures is a revolutionary act, insofar as it recognizes a being in the full and unified plenitude of its life. It is the great advantage of this process that it takes place beyond either moral and aesthetic or scientific values. In this space it is not of primary importance whether something is good or evil, beautiful or ugly, false or true, but rather what figure it belongs to."[20] Apparently Jünger—who ten years later agreed with Carlo Schmid that Germans had "no physiognomic instinct"[21] because they had elected Hitler—at this time still thought Hitler had the power of this seer to recognize the new type and to detach it, perhaps even tear it, from its old entanglements. Or was this a self-portrait?

In any case, the magic word "gestalt" [figure] dominated biopsychological discourses, in particular in the sciences. According to one reading, the concept originated in the work of Christian von Ehrenfels (1859–1932), who applied it to the musical scale model, which could take its departure from any one note and which would nonetheless repeat the same recognizable unity. The figure as a perceptual concept, as perception's typological faculty, was contrasted with the fluctuation and instabilities of physiognomic perception. Names like Wilhelm Dilthey, Max Wertheimer, Wolfgang Köhler, and many others are associated with this line of inquiry; among them a long row of emigrants, not all of them Jewish. NS science by contrast favored the concept of "wholeness" [Ganzheit], which allowed the racial integration of the individual into the "body of the people." Praise for figures shifted from the individual to the group, be it "Aryan" or "Jewish." Zionists too spoke of the "figure of the Jewish people," which could show clear contours only with its own country beneath its feet. The seeing in figures in NS ideology segued into other activities. Instead of "gestalt," scientists spoke of "psychic selection"[22] and meant by this nothing other than biological selection in the context of a psychology of perception, with the same brutality proclaimed by Jünger.

The phantasm of clear and clean boundaries proved multipurposed. In racist argumentation it went so far as to suggest hygiene, which in turn suggested the image of unclean and murderous bacteria of which one had to rid oneself. At the same time, "gestalt" with its linear demarcations morphologically suggested nothing short of the lines in a map, lines in turn suggesting borders and claims to property [Fig. 29]. For all this, it was the art historical past of the term "gestalt" rather than, say, the idea of a musical scale that became important, namely its deduction from the silhouette. Since the end of the nineteenth century, "gestalt" inherited the concept of the "profile" from eighteenth-century anthropology—the comparative study of profiles, meant to help set apart ape and man, black and white, man and woman. It was a special kind of "ancestral line," which had as its subject not a succession or family line, but rather a line of species, which long before Darwin became engrained as *the* evolutionary schema in public consciousness. For Dürer it was already its own genre of caricature and Grandville perfected it in the middle of the nineteenth century [Fig. 30]. In Lavater's physiognomy too there was a specific art form for this: the silhouette. Not by accident did the pastor Lavater look to the silhouette as a religious, downright anagogical figure: for the outline shows, he thought, the potentialities, not however the "actuality" [*Würcklichkeit*] of an *en face* portrait. And the same rhythm of premonition and actualization animates the salvation story with its thinking in terms of *typos* (rather than *typus*). In our salvation story of sorts we have not yet seen the face of God *en face*.[23]

In this spirit, and on its own blasphemous path to a "national portrait gallery," a photo volume entitled *Menschen der Zeit: Hundert und ein Lichtbildnis wesentlicher Männer und Frauen aus deutscher Gegenwart und jüngster Vergangenheit* [People of the Times: One Hundred and One Photographs of Essential Men and Women from Present-Day Germany and the Most Recent Past] appeared in 1930, a piece of National Socialist propaganda. The selection begins in 1919 and wants to show people who have had "real significance" in post-war Germany, but it excludes the living ones who are close to the publishing house, as well as those "on which great hopes may be staked, but whose real accomplishments will lie in the future."[24] Meaning: Hitler, who is alluded to by the cover photograph of Count Brockdorff-Rantzau that strikingly resembles a Hitler photograph of 1923 [see Fig. 19] and that, as a parody, adorned the dust jacket of Grosz's 1921 *Das Gesicht der Herrschenden Klasse* [The Face of the

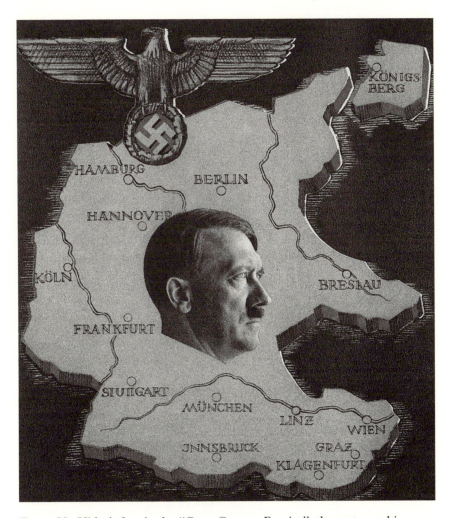

Figure 29. Hitler's face in the "Great German Empire"; the cartographic outlines of this postcard of 1938 could be read like a picture puzzle as the profile of a dog with a wide-open muzzle. The territorial metaphor of the face as landscape belongs to the very center of National Socialist ideology. It meant in the end, as Max Picard later reflected, the end of the—Christian—human face.

Ruling Class] [see Fig. 15]. The hopes the photo volume projected into the future were apparently shared by Rudolf Borchardt, when in his 1931 speech on "leadership" he imputed to the dictator the power "to reshape the entire face of the nation and to write into this face a new outline by the sword. . . ."[25]

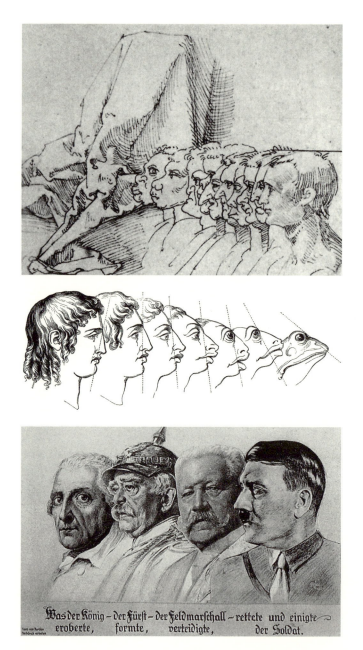

Figure 30. Lining up profiles has occupied painters since there were light and shadow. The arrangements by Dürer (profile studies around 1513), Grandville (Apollo descends into a frog, 1844) and Hans von Norden's postcard show tree-of-descent thinking graphically.

This was a skewed image of the tyrant, but nonetheless an accurate one, since after all Germany was at this point seeking to raise its profile no longer in the psychological sense, but by military means. In 1936, Jünger finally switched sides in an exchange of letters with the painter Rudolf Schlichter. At least now he hoped for an art that "would paint and draw in such a fashion" that "the slaying of the tyrant could not be far behind."[26]

Physiognomic conditioning in the sense of pattern recognition signified the decisive transition from that society of proximity associated with the *semantic field* of the face to a society of distance. In the concept of the shape/gestalt, taken in its German-nationalist usage, the "saved face" of the Chinese (to whom the German press owed the expression) makes its reappearance. Speaking along the same lines as Worringer, we are dealing with a primitivization here: away from the developed society of proximity that communicates with the existential space and its objects mimically and dialogically, back to the archaic, "anti-spatial," life-fearing realm of abstraction that buffers against confusing impressions. In terms of psychological analysis, it speaks volumes that the NS politics of *Lebensraum* operated with a signifying system marked by "anti-spatiality." That even a writer would promote the transition makes it all the more noteworthy. Profiles are best seen from the side, figures from a distance, both most clearly by a "seer." In 1937, an art historian stated explicitly: "After all, the word face has a double signification in German. It can mean the countenance, but also the 'second face,' the vision. Only a countenance that is capable of face-ing [*gesichtig*], that to some degree has the power of seeing [*Gesicht*], is truly facial. The power of seeing however is not unique to the visionary. Everything that is in the world must be seen with this power, if it is to be really seen."[27]

Just like this, as a "second face," the Führer, the primitive and life-fearing portraitist of his people, purportedly sees a German face from afar as a type (in the sense of *typos*) and works toward its realization in the sense of a salvation narrative. That in fact he saw nothing other than the "first face," a biological given connected to a geological given, namely the *Lebensraum*, was clearly apparent to everyone involved by now. The facial prose of art historians with NS leanings or merely German nationalist sympathies simply marks the successive distance between the standards of art and those of so-called life, not in the sense of empathy as in Worringer, but in the very explicit sense of scientific abstraction and of its biological counterpart: the racial profile.

The physiognomic about-turn from the *en face* to the profile meant the disappearance of just that language of empathy that, according to Worringer, was to go along with higher degrees of socialization: facial expression.[28] Someone who looks at and for human "figure" or "gestalt" for scientific or visionary reasons doesn't pay much attention to a furrowed brow, a smile or blush, or perhaps the transmission of suffering so basic to the devotion to Christian icons and to the real presence of political terror. The steely, warlike type of the future with a metallic mask under his steel helmet creates social distance and saves face only as a shape.[29] It was only logically consistent for psychiatrists of the period to conceive of facial expression as a form of articulation reserved for children and the mentally ill.[30] Experimental psychology, in contrast, had studied facial expressions since the beginning of the 1930s predominantly in the medium of film and after 1933 did so mostly in the employ of the military, structuring selection processes of officers on a scientific basis.[31] It is among the more comical lacunae of their scientific superstructure that even convinced NS scientists had to declare all-important qualities such as courage and willpower immeasurable, in spite of everything the data of facial expression, gestures, and build were adduced to show.[32] The most dedicated party-liners among them equated rather limply the play of expression and of muscle: "My intention in writing this book was limited to drawing the expression of the German face as it is founded on the labor of the muscles."[33]

Muscle labor instead of facial expression—this became one of the dominant life worldly attitudes of the time. After all, the NS state had developed under the banner of movement and expressedly *as* a movement. That Leni Riefenstahl's most important innovation in film technology was the *moving* camera, which accompanied its object on tracks or elevators, is not an accident. That it is a movement entranced by the fight, that the movement is disposed toward war, does not remain hidden. A photo volume from 1935 entitled *Das Deutsche Führergesicht* [The German Führers' Face] comprises "two hundred images of German fighters and pathfinders from two millennia," as though there had been such a thing as "Germans" since the birth of Christ. The author concludes his gallery with a photograph of Ferdinand Liebermann's bust of Hitler and comments on the sight of the Führer in a biblical tone: "An unknown soldier climbed from the trenches of Flanders, and when he went among he people he brought with him deeper than others the experience of a space, in which there was only the distinct alternative of life and death[. . .]."[34]

Similarly, *Das heilige deutsche Antlitz* [The Holy German Countenance] of 1934 thinks of the enemy automatically along with the Führer: "An Asiatic countenance HIDES the soul—German countenance IS soul. The holy countenance created by Germans thus reveals all the victories and defeats of the spirit. German spirit is motion—and so must [be] the countenance."[35] This is obviously hard to demonstrate: the volume contains pictures showing mostly biblical faces in stone and wood in photographic reproduction; if at all, mimic movement is created through lighting technique. The book is an appropriation of high art through the technology "from below" called photography.

Other picture volumes of the time show faces if not as landscapes then at least as elements of a social environment. Their make is clearly already in line with the new state. Between 1930 and 1933, volumes appear with titles such as *Frauengesicht der Gegenwart* [Women's Faces of the Present Moment],[36] *Das Antlitz des Alters* [The Countenance of Old Age],[37] *Köpfe des Alltags* [Everyday Heads],[38] *Die von der Scholle: Deutsche Menschen I* [Those from the Native Soil. German People I],[39] as well as *Das deutsche Volksgesicht* [The Face of the German People].[40] Not all of them are as possessed by the face as Lendvai-Dircksen or Erich Retzlaff, who both work on peasants in particular regions. Hans Retzlaff (no relation to Erich), who also published more than a dozen photo volumes in this genre, is more interested in traditional attire and spaces.[41] The photo volume on the women's faces, in contrast, unites once more all the prevailing tendencies: individual portrait, type portrait, and race portrait. Famous women are mentioned by name, less famous and beautiful ones are typified à la Sanders via a professional moniker (secretary, doctor, philologist)—as though labeling by type might help otherwise less attractive women. Entirely unknown but "naturally beautiful" portraits are titled simply "head of a young girl." Even Helmar Lerski, who worked in the United States before 1915 and returned to Germany only to emigrate to Palestine in 1932, switches between national poses, New Objectivity, and Hollywood shots. But national-racial themes were clearly on the rise. At least six more volumes of Erna Lendvai-Dircksen's comprehensive physiognomic regional studies appeared until 1943[42]: Schleswig-Holstein (1939), Mecklenburg and Pommerania (1940), Tyrolia and Vorarlberg (1941), Lower Saxony (1942), the Electorate of Hesse (1943). All of these pictures—incidentally downright contemplative and soulful—place regional specificity in imprint and poise above mimic expression and thus figure/gestalt over scene. They also place the group above the individual. For in spite of the intimacy of the close-ups, the volumes suggest fixed groupings rather than an open row of pictures in a gallery whose exhibits may change. August Sander's "Stamm-Mappe" [Family portfolio] evolved from a family portrait, and in the grand project of his German sociography group portraits predominate.

Photo volumes of this kind realized the project of a "national portrait gallery from below" in an odd mixture of scientific registration and sentimental family album, while the real existing portrait gallery in the Berlin Kronprinzenpalais came ever closer to dissolution. Its last grand exhibition, with 460 portraits, painted by famous painters as a national portrait gallery "from above," of course already excluding Jewish people "of merit," happened in the context of an entirely different social event, namely the Olympic Games, and thus in the context of the athlete-body and its attendant selection mechanisms.

Along the intellectual path to Olympia, in 1933, the renowned politician, physiognomist, psychiatrist, and art connoisseur Willy Hellpach published an essay in *Medizinische Welt* magazine entitled "The Racial [*völkische*] Constitution of the Countenance." He took the photographer's approach literally and delved into regional differences between Frankish and Swabian faces of the present day. But the careful tabulation segued abruptly into the vision of a type to come: "man's strongest and finest organ of expression, his face, is also a mirror, which allows us to discern good or bad breeding, well-formation or malformation of the human soul. To a staggering degree a face can reveal to the knowledgeable that its bearer is neither *eugenos* nor *euplastos*! Only generative well-breeding (eugenics) and directive well-formation (euplastics) give us THAT control over nature, which will become even more important than the objective technical one of the machine: control over our human nature!"[43]

The specter of eugenics raises its head quite clearly here. It goes well beyond the retrospective search for ancestry in art and religion as well as in physiognomic regional studies. While those extol what is out there, permitting the viewer to find herself in them and "be part of the picture," eugenics deals with the redemption of concepts, with the literal humanization of the well-formation [*Wohl-gestalt*]. Releasing metaphorical thinking from the biopolitical semantic field entrusts the human shape to technology, with lasting effects. Even if Hellpach couldn't yet imagine an "anthropotechnology," and wanted to understand the "generative well-breeding" in terms of bodily discipline, perhaps as a kind of sport, the phantasm of "control over our human nature" inscribed itself into the minds of the scientific intelligentsia from the war onward, despite the very human catastrophes of the Third Reich. In 1985, Peter Weingart, historian at Bielefeld University, reminded us of Julian Huxley's prognosis from 1965, according to which in the future "eugenics—that is the genetic amelioration of human beings—will without fail become one of the main goals of an evolving humanity."[44]

In 1932, Ernst Jünger sketched one of the decisive stations along the way. "One of the means for the preparation of a new, more audacious kind of life," he commented on his vision of the "worker," "is the destruction of the valuations of the detached, vainglorious intellect, the destruction of the education that the bourgeois age has performed on the human being."[45]

Countenance and Commerce: Hoffmann, Hitler, Riefenstahl

The more slavishly the national leadership was devoted to this program, the more beautiful and the more valuable the German countenance became, in particular its incarnation, the Führer's face. Rudolf Herz counts fifteen photo shoots with Heinrich Hoffmann in which the photographs taken were later proliferated to publishers, political propagandists, and also to painters—or were given as personal gifts in silver frames with or without a personal dedication from the Führer. Hoffmann became a wealthy entrepreneur: between 1933 and 1939 his revenue rose from 700,000 reichsmark to 4.5 million, by 1943 to 15.4 million.[46]

An almost ingenious money-making scheme was the idea of marketing Hitler's face on stamps: first on a special stamp for his birthday in April of 1937, with the text "he who wants to save a people must think heroically," then later with other special stamps following on a regular basis.[47] For ideological reasons Hitler did not want to see his face on bills or coins. Since 1941, Hitler's profile was on every standard stamp. "The philatelists of the world—and Hitler, himself a sometime philatelist, listened to them—demanded German stamps with his head on them. He thought it might be good propaganda," Picker reports in his reproduction of conversations by table at the Führerhauptquartier, Hitler's headquarters.[48] Albert Speer relates an idea by Martin Bormann: that Hitler had copyright claims to every postage stamp bearing his face; the money thus raised financed, among other things, the expansion of the Obersalzberg complex.[49]

Among the numerous photo volumes by Heinrich Hoffmann that Herz has found and described, the most successful in terms of sales (over two million copies) was a Hitler volume entitled *Bilder aus dem Leben des Führers* [Pictures from the Life of the Führer] from 1936. Like many of these volumes, this one was published by the Cigarette Picture Service in Altona, which was owned by the Reemtsma tobacco company. Going down the best-seller list, the book is followed by the brochure "Deutschland erwacht: Werden, Sieg und Kampf der NSDAP" [Germany awakes: Genesis, Victory, and Struggle of the NSDAP] of 1933 (over one million in sales); then *Der Kampf ums Dritte Reich: Eine Historische Bilderfolge* [The Fight for the Third Reich: An Historical Series of Pictures] of 1933 (eight hundred thousand); then, just in time for the victory over France, *Mit Hitler im Westen* [With Hitler to the West], with prefatory remarks by General Field Marshal Keitel from 1940 (six hundred thousand). Only then do we get to the vastly popular *Hitler wie ihn keiner kennt* [Hitler Like No One Knows Him] from 1932, which Albert Speer still thought to be the best-selling Hitler volume.

The largest income was nonetheless generated by individual photographs, with which since 1933 a "complete saturation of the political public with Hitler's portrait" was attempted and accomplished.[50] The market for journals and newspapers in Germany and abroad, as well as the growing movement toward private devotion to Hitler's face, increased the demand for Hoffmann's photographs. Veritable family altars were created voluntarily or upon suggestion by the party and Hitler's portrait was advertised as the perfect Christmas gift. Beginning in 1934, at the behest of secretary of the interior, Frick, public funds paid for the decoration of representative official spaces with appropriate photographic portraits—usually those from Hoffmann's 1937 Hitler shoot on the balcony at Obersalzberg, but also from Knirr's version or Willy Exner's painting of Hitler with the turned-up collar. There is a photo of that painting, taken by an American army photographer, showing two French people "executing" the Führer's image[51] [Fig. 31]. These kinds of assassinations or desecrations in effigy were not uncommon during the NS years; Herz points to the court records of the Munich Special Court charged with prosecuting these crimes.[52]

After Goebbel's installation as propaganda minister, film was added to this repertoire. The filmic image had since 1927 accompanied party conventions, but at least during the final years of the Weimar Republic film simply wasn't as efficient politically as speeches.[53] The *Wochenschau* [weekly newsreel] changed all that. It had established itself as a "living newspaper" and a place in public consciousness, in particular in connection with the kaiser. After him, Hindenburg became the medium's next "star"; Hitler was at first deemed relatively uninteresting, if not unwanted, since the production companies rejected him politically. This changed with the propaganda minister, Goebbels, for as early as May of 1933 Goebbels discussed the plan for a movie devoted to Hitler with Leni Riefenstahl.

The discovery and employment of Riefenstahl pushed filmic representation of party and party leader, of movement and body, into a hitherto unknown aesthetic and atmospheric dimension. With unparalleled expenditure in material and money—170 staff members and 130,000 meters of film—she shot *Triumph of the Will*, a filmic chronicle of the 1934 party rally, after producing, according to expert opinion, a mere compilation of newsreel and studio scenes the year before in *The Victory of Faith*. "Commitment to the revision of the defeat in World War I runs through the film like a thread," Dölzel and Loiperdinger write in their analysis of *Triumph of the Will*. Together with the world-famous film about the 1936 Olympic games, Riefenstahl forced an aestheticization of the NS dictatorship, which uncannily anticipated the society of the culture industry after the war.

Figure 31. At the end of the war the Allies found Hitler portraits in households everywhere, be it in photographs or in paintings—here the popular "Kragenbild" by Willy Exner. As director of the annual Great German Art Exhibit in the Haus der Kunst since 1937, Hoffmann received, according to his own testimony, between 100 and 150 Hitler portraits annually. Usually he selected only a few of them. All pictures from the Nazi years were seized or destroyed by the Allies after 1945; the propagandistically questionable ones were brought to the United States; the others are today being administered by the German Historical Museum in Berlin.

Riefenstahl's work also affected the aesthetics of the news. In contrast to Hoffmann's photo books she showed Hitler—the great statesman and Führer, who united all power in him—naturalistically rather than theatrically, in conducting the rituals of power, and channeling power through his speech—an inestimable advantage of the filmic medium. Of course, according to more recent statistics, by the fall of 1938 a mere 7 percent of Germans (excluding Austria and the Sudetenland) had access to the current Wochenschauen newsreels. Moreover, there were relatively few copies for the entire Reich—"all four providers added up to about four hundred copies." Only from October of 1938 onward were theater owners required to show the *Wochenschauen* as a prefeature. In the summer of 1938, Hitler himself had intervened into production and had criticized "that during events the shots are usually restricted to my person," while it was much more important to dignify peasants and glorify soldiers.[54]

Photo books that showed Hitler in private or as a man of the people weren't as successful by themselves as those that showed him as army commander or paramilitary Führer. But taken together, and in particular as devotionalia, pictures of the private Hitler showed a clear preponderance. Hitler, the simple man in countless scenes and situations of everyday life, with children and adolescents, hiking or at home, with his dog or blond women—all of this had long turned into a "national portrait gallery from below" all of its own. A 1936 special issue of the *Illustrierte Beobachter* shows this one-man gallery that was later recreated as *Das Antlitz des Führers* [The Führer's Countenance] by Heinrich Hoffmannn. Both versions were clearly conceived as answers to the *Simplicissimus*'s caricature from 1923: "What does Hitler look like?" Now there were sixteen portraits distributed over two full pages of the tabloid, and they showed the Führer's face in photos from 1916 to 1936 [Fig. 32]. A "gallery" neither from above nor from below, but significantly "from the gutter to the stars," it was appropriate to the unheard-of curriculum vitae of the one-time lance corporal, who in 1936 was busy celebrating the reoccupation of the Rhineland: "We see here the Führer's face in its miraculous transformation from the beginning through the years of tremendous struggle for the victory of his idea to its present form. . . . Just like the ordinary idea of this common man . . . and his unshakable belief and personal courage gave rise to an entirely new German Reich, so too did the ordinary, almost blank face of a young man eventually become the face of the Führer of the German nation and—God willing—of the peace of the European world."[55] Given his successes, Hitler's status as a man of merit was disputed less and less between 1933 and 1938—excepting of course his enemies who had either fled, were dead, or were in concentration camps. It was only logical that he should therefore grow into the "portrait gallery from above," into Ludwig Justi's "series of pictures of ancestral pride." Impulses to this apotheosis had obviously existed long before. Hitler liked to see himself—in the evolutionary schema caricatured by Grandville—in the succession of Frederick the Great, Bismarck, and Hindenburg [see Fig. 30], and (not least through self-stylization) as a mythic reincarnation of Frederick Barbarossa. From his balcony at Obersalzberg, he could gaze onto the Untersberg, in which the legendary emperor was said to lie hidden until his time had come—a myth whose suggestiveness had haunted the thoughts of educated Germans since Julius Langbehn's dark vaticinations about the "secret emperor" to come. In 1936, however, the point had been reached where, according to Kershaw, "hubris [. . .] was inevitable. The point where nemesis takes over."[56]

"Degenerate Art"

One of the most brazen and effective of all the propaganda tools invented by the Hitler regime was mentally besieging the population with the double face of the "great little man." Its Janus-face was diagnosed early and its rise was watched with fear. The figure Hitler was the opposite of Falladas's famous "little man,"[57] who sinks ever deeper into petty bourgeoisie; rather, it seemed to represent the long hoped-for "secret emperor." Whoever could identify with the "little man" thereby shared the grandiose self of the "great." Thomas Mann expressed this peculiar face-to-face perception in "Brother Hitler," as did Charlie Chaplin with his *Great Dictator*, which grants the little Jew the same face as the murderous dictator. The face of the "great little" man corresponded spectrally to the democratic hopes of the Weimar Constitution. Just as Napoleon had once been swept to the top by the revolutionary hopes of the Third Estate, Hitler received the fealty and support of a supposedly "socialist" thought. His rise was the stuff of legend and seductive to any cult of grandiose self. That the former flophouse resident, who had spent his first thirty years doing nothing, could become a simple, even a decorated soldier was perhaps not all too surprising. But that he could develop into one of the most talented demagogues certainly was. What confounded observers was the loner's ability to subjugate ever greater and mutually hostile groups into states of almost religious veneration. What almost passed understanding was how this man now acted as chancellor, as commander of armies, as diplomat for seven years, from 1933 to September of 1939, and could count on ever greater recognition and authority—and that he did all this while preserving his image of the "little man of the people," which Hitler tirelessly reiterated in his speeches. Historians have recognized this riddle again and again and still been unable to account for it. While Joachim Fest continues to stress the evil in this figure,[58] historians such as Ian Kershaw have elaborated the idea of the population "working toward the Führer."[59] In fact many individual studies—on Heinrich Hoffmann (by Rudolf Herz), on Goebbels (by Felix Möller), on the Wehrmacht (Hannes Heer's heavily criticized study), or on police battalions (Christopher Browning), on poets and philosophers and many others—have pointed to the collaboration of large social groups and individual "talented" criminals.

Physiognomic discourses, both among the educated bourgeoisie and among professional physiognomists, similarly and centrally worked "toward" Hitler. In word and (photographic) image, they translated the

Ein Antlitz-

Es handelt sich hier nicht um eine psychologisch-geleitete oder eine phrenologische Studie. Wir sind nach 14 Jahren seines Kampfes um die Macht und 3 Jahren seines Aufbauwerkes in der Persönlichkeit des Führers so veranlasst, mit seinem Antlitz, so innerlich verbunden, auch der verabelte und härteste seiner Kämpfers, wie ein Sohn mit dem Antlitz des Vaters. Wir können das Antlitz des Führers nicht anders lesen, als wie das ganze deutsche Volk es sieht: mit dem Herzen. In unserem Herzen aber ist, wenn kein Bild vor uns auftaucht, in welcher Form und aus welcher Zeit es auch sein mag, nichts als rückhaltlose Bewunderung, bedingungslose Anerkennung seiner beispiellosen Leistung und aus ihr herzens Hingabe ohne Grenze.

Es hat nie ein Bildnis gegeben, das in Millionen und aber Millionen Herzen, in den Herzen dreier lebenden Generationen eines ganzen Volkes, vom Kinde bis zum Greise, so tief und bedeutend eingebrannt war und ist und bleiben wird, wie das des Führers. Sein Antlitz leuchtet in uns als die Erfüllung der Sehnsucht nach irdischer Vollendung. Sein Antlitz steht vor uns als das Antlitz des Schöpfers einer neuen deutschen Welt, des Erwechers des deutschen Volkes, des Erretters der göttlichen Idee und der in ihr wurzelnden Kultur vor der Zerstörung durch das entgötterte, materialistisch-jüdisch-bolschewistische Chaos.

Wir sind besessen vom Wert des Führers, von seiner alle überragenden Persönlichkeit, von seinem Genie. Wir sind besessen von seinem Antlitz. Und wir kämpfen mit ihm dafür und glauben es, weil wir es wollen nach

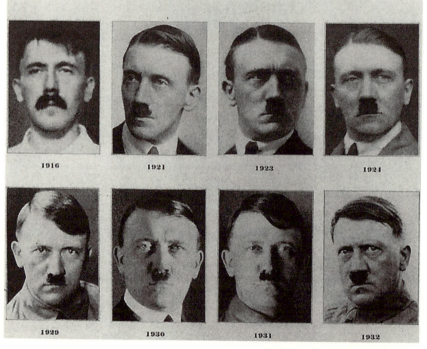

Figure 32. Hitler's favorite legend was that of the rapid rise of the simple soldier to chancellorship and to the status of the German avenger. The *Illustrierte Beobachter* wanted to illustrate this career facially (and face-to-face) in 1936 on the occasion of the remilitarization of the Rhineland. With the repetitious close-ups commented on rabidly in the accompanying text, the montage of course withheld the fact that the road to rulership tends to *distance* the ruler—a fact represented by Leni Riefenstahl in her films.

vom Kampf geformt

seinem Willen, 60 Millionen: daß auch die Welt ihn
so erkenne, daß alle Völker unserer Rasse und Kultur
seine Person, sein Ziel und seinen Kampf mit offenen
Augen und ehrlichen Herzen sehen, daß die Staats-
männer, die den Frieden und die Größe ihrer Völker,
die das Glück der Menschen erstreben, ihre Hand legen
in die Hand Adolf Hitlers, die reinste und aufrichtigste
und die berufenste, die je ein Volk gelobt.

So denken und fühlen wir, so denkt und fühlt mit
uns der deutsche Mensch angesichts dieser Bildnisse.
Sie sind unsagbar viel mehr als etwa eine interessante
Zusammenstellung. Wir schauen das Antlitz des Führers in seiner wunderbaren Wandlung vom Radegion
durch die Jahre des ungeheuren Ringens um den Sieg
seiner Idee bis zu seiner heutigen Form. Wir sehen

im Werden und Wachsen, in der Entwicklung seines
Gesichtes das Werden und Wachsen seiner Idee, das
Werden und Wachsen der Bewegung, die Entwicklung
des Kampfes, seines Wesens und Weges. So wie aus
den einfachen Grundgedanken dieses einfachen Mannes
aus dem deutschen Volke und seinem unerbittlichen
Glauben und persönlichen Mut ein ganz neues
Deutsches Reich Gestalt wurde, so ist aus dem ein-
fachen, noch fast unbeschriebenen Antlitz eines jungen
Menschen das Antlitz des Führers der deutschen Nation
und — so Gott will — des Friedens der europäischen
Welt geworden.

Seine Augen brennen in unserer Seele, in unserem
Herzen dämmert sein Wort, in unserem ganzen Leben
lebt seine Tat.

1925 1926 1927 1928

1933 1934 1935 1936

idea of the nation from a linguistic category into a facial one. For even if the idea of the "Aryan race" was not truly a national one, it was beyond all the seemingly supranational rhetoric, above all the German *nation* that was vying for dominance here. Whether this was simply a substitution of an outmoded culture of guilt by a new psychology of shame will for now go unaddressed. The facial obsession that Hitler had added fuel to since 1919 by making appeal to pan-German fantasies of *Lebensraum* in the East and simultaneously proclaiming the displacement (not yet the annihilation) of the Jews had at first a purely linguistic point of attack: It was the idea of a "lost face" as a "field of honor" that Germans had to regain. In time, and owing to the physiognomic rage among the educated classes, it became clear that Hitler, far from any metaphoric interpretation, was calling for redemption and restitution on a literal level, that he was turning the face into a territory, the territory into the desired space. He was a man of deeds and not of ink, as his friend Hanfstaengl put it—or perhaps simply an unimaginative "eideticist," as he has been described more recently.[60] For didn't the architect of this restructuring of a linguistic nationality into a facial one have to be a physiognomist himself?

In her generally unreliable recollections, Leni Riefenstahl tells of an evening with Hitler in August of 1939: they watched newsreels from Moscow, which at one point showed a full-screen profile of Stalin. According to Riefenstahl, Hitler commented: "That man has a good face—one should be able to negotiate with him." One week later the nonaggression treaty was signed between Hitler and Stalin, and Riefenstahl seemed to believe that it was Stalin's face that had convinced Hitler.[61] Here the two lines of the Führer who decides everything, on the one hand, and admirers "working toward" him, on the other, run together as though in a parody. For if anyone gave Hitler a "good face," perhaps the most efficacious face ever, it was Riefenstahl. And if anyone believed in a "good face" in the sense of a disclosure of character, it was her. There are few reports that Hitler actually said such things, even if Goebbels noted in March of 1940, very much along the same lines, that "the Führer saw Stalin on film and he thought he seemed likeable. That's really when the German-Russian coalition started."[62]

The regained, literalized "German face" was by now impossible to ignore. It was by its nature not a self-portrait, but a *grandiose self*-portrait, one getting ever larger. In 1936, for the parliamentary election in March, a slide projector projected a 50-meter-square portrait of the Führer onto the façade of the Munich town hall.[63] That same year, on the occasion of the Olympic Games, Eberhard Hanfstaengl, then director of the national galleries, held the exhibition *Great Germans in the Pictures of Their Time*. It was one last attempt to rethink the German line of descent according to the formula of "merit and ancestral pride," a project that thought of itself explicitly as the continuation of Justi's "collection of models," as Hanfstaengl remarked—expressedly without photographs. Of course, all the paintings appeared as photographs that year anyway in the exhibition's companion volume entitled *Die Großen Deutschen im Bild* [The Great Germans in Images].[64] It was followed one year later by *Das deutsche Antlitz im Spiegel die Jahrhunderte* [The German Countenance in the Mirror of the Centuries], a "grand exhibition of the city of Frankfurt, with the cooperation of the NSDAP department for race policy." From art history came a pocket-sized gallery in the shape of *Das deutsche Gesicht in Bildern aus acht Jahrhunderten deutscher Kunst* [The German Face in Pictures from Eight Centuries of German Art],[65] and Erna Lendvai-Dircksen showed *Das deutsche Gesicht des Ostens* [The German Face of the East]. In the same year, 1937, Hitler's face presided over an exhibition designed by Egon Eiermann called *Give Me Four Years' Time*. At eighteen meters in height it was the largest format ever shown. Its expression marks it as an obvious precursor to the pensive face that George Orwell turned into a main actor in his novel *1984* some ten years later [Fig. 33].

That same year, Hitler opened two further exhibitions in Munich: the famous arrangements *Degenerate Art* and the *Great German Art Exhibition* in the Haus der deutschen Kunst. The latter was a "competitive exhibition" [*Leistungsschau*] of German creativity, which was to repeat annually from now on and demanded new Hitler portraits each year. As yet there were few war pictures, and the nudes of the later years were missing as well. The exhibition comprised around 900 objects from 580 artists, but looked at by the light of day it was nothing but a monstrous staging of the Führer's face, which had at last made its way into the hallowed halls of art.[66] In Munich numerous images and busts of the Führer were on display: for example, by Hermann Barrenscheen (*The Führer*, in oil), Hermann Hahn (*The Führer's Bust*, bronze), Hermann Otto Hoyer (*In the Beginning Was the Word*, oil), Richard Klein (*Führer*, bust, bronze), Heinrich Knirr (*Three Führer Paintings*, oil), Hubert Lanzinger (*Image of the Führer as a Standard-Bearer*, oil), Ferdinand Liebermann (*Führer*, bust, bronze), Richard Lindmar (*The Day of Potsdam*, oil), Karl Rickelt (*Führer*, oil), and Hand Schwegerle (*Führer*, bust, bronze).

Except Karl Rickelt from Cologne and Richard Lindmar from Berlin, all these artists hailed from Munich or somewhere else in Bavaria. The most famous piece was the bust by Ferdinand Liebermann, already the frontispiece of the catalogue of the Olympia exhibition in 1936. Lanzinger's "Standard-bearer," which was quickly removed from the exhibition, made its reappearance in the Berlin Alte Museum in 1999 in the exhibit *German Art of the Twentieth Century*. Then there was Heinrich

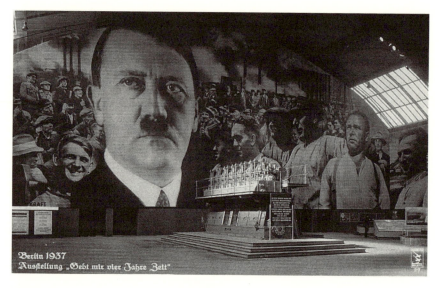

Figure 33. The worried, even unhappy expression on Hitler's face in this, its largest depiction ever (at eighteen meters in height), seems strangely at odds with the enthusiasm of the technological exhibition in the context of which it was on display. Its title, "Give Me Four Years' Time," came from a Hitler speech of 1936. After four years of triumphal "re-erection" his thought was now bent on rearmament and on coming wars. The photographer of this picture is unknown.

Knirr's painting of the Führer, allegedly the only one Hitler posed for voluntarily.

Heinrich Hoffmann, who, at Hitler's behest, had taken over steward-ship of the exhibition and overseen the selection of submissions, reported that 100 to 150 Hitler portraits were submitted annually, but that only few of these were shown. According to research by Otto Thomae, in the years between 1937 and 1944, a total of 31 paintings of Hitler were published—or perhaps more accurately: were staged photographically. Most appeared in the pompous periodical *The Art of the Third Reich*. Adding about fourteen portraits that appeared either in the journal or the *Völkische Beobachter*, and taking into account that further depictions may still emerge, we end up with about 50 published portraits of Hitler—usually modeled on Hoffmann's photographs or after the imagination. Around a third of these portraits would have been busts, among them those of Arno Breker and Fritz Hub.[67]

The great number of exhibits (two hundred in 1937 alone), of which many depicted Hitler or other party greats, recalls a particular form of the Valhalla of 1842, thus the first national "men of merit" gallery of the nineteenth century even before the empire. This template remained the driving motif not only in the following exhibitions until 1944, but also for the party's art journal. With sepulchral rage, the journal memorialized the growing loss of life; dramatically photographed sculptures dominated the scene.

Among those physiognomically "working toward" the "German face" were not only biologists, psychologists, and criminologists, but artists and art historians, photographers and filmmakers, advertising firms and propagandists. In hurrying obedience to the expurgation of Jews and "unfit life," this group worked on the attendant expurgation of the corresponding faces *from the image*. Even so cultivated an author as Rudolf Kassner did not shy from writing a popular *Physiognomy* (1932) for the educated classes, without Jewish faces but with a clear message: the interior is the exterior.

In her recollections Margret Boveri tells of the disappearance of a van Gogh from the Staedel in December of 1937.[68] Ernst Benkard, art historian and staff member for the *Frankfurter Zeitung*, disclosed that the National Socialists had removed the *Portrait Dr. Gachet* from the museum. Without making reference to the theft, his colleague Benno Reifenberg wrote a column on this *Dr. Gachet*: "All lines and color lead to the face. There, in an unfathomable transformation rust-red and bright-green colors develop into the face of a person who has not avoided the sun, but in whose features the spirit has left its shadows and stretched the skin. The eyes look straight ahead, over the painter's head and beyond him. They exert command over all the movement the picture may excite. Those two eyes are deep and at once transparent as a lake; from them emanates the calm of a noble man." At the end of his text Reifenberg quoted van Gogh's letters, in which the painter imputed to his Jewish doctor the "dolorous expression of our time." "It is just this expression that is preserved by the respect and the commanding power of the painter, and from the woes of yore descendants can find surcease for their own woes too." Reifenberg was summoned by the ministry of propaganda and later arrested. The appeal to the face in the picture, the appeal to mimic empathy and especially the allusion to the suffering of the—Jewish—descendants had had their effect. Only once Ernst Benkard confessed to his disclosure was Reifenberg freed.

That episode shows how calamitously the expulsion of the expressive face from the image damaged the notion of metaphoric competence and fed into the "hair-raising literalness" Joachim Fest has attributed to Nazi thinking. When in the same year Max Picard published his book *Die Grenzen der Physiognomik* [The Limits of Physiognomics], in order to reassert this competence from a religious viewpoint, it was already too late: the project "degenerate art" was in full swing.

Peter-Klaus Schuster has shown the genesis of this infamous campaign against 110 artists with some 600 works, a majority of which depicted the human form, alone or in groups.[69] Paul Schultze-Naumburg was not the first to apply categories of medical physiognomy to the human shape in art. The schema of "sick" and "healthy" dates back to romanticism. But what began as a discussion on art was greatly expanded by the criteria of "degeneracy" in naturalistic thought. The impression could, almost had to arise that there was perhaps no such thing as art-specific standards, an autarkic world of symbols, perhaps tied back to language. Not least photography had dulled the sense for the symbolic, while promoting the need for documentary certitude. The independent symbolism of art, its iconography, disappeared and was replaced by a hereditary iconics—the face as the bearer of biological information. The portrait of the racially pure person functioned as a passport photo and the passport as a certificate of descent. Wolfgang Willrich, painter, author, and the real initiator of the exhibition thanks to his 1937 book *Säuberung des Kunsttempels* [Cleansing of the Temple of Art], epitomizes this race art. Himmler said of his portfolio with pictures of the faces of SS men "that this Nordic blood, which formed and minted these faces, belongs to the entire German people," and that "the eternal face of Germanic blood [*deutsch-Germanischen Blutes*]," as that of the ancestors, had to be maintained and propagated.[70] In fact there is a photograph from 1933 of Hitler among young SS officers, in which he strikingly resembles them in his martial pose [Fig. 34]. Any criticism of this naturalism was forestalled by the continuous recourse, prevalent since the turn of the century, to Greek bodily beauty, to the aesthetics of nudity.[71] It was a patently Darwinist reduction of aesthetic thought, for how should an old, a sick, a marked body, or a crying, laughing, or simply smiling human being now find its place in art without objurgation?

Hitler's programmatic exclusion of art from the development of social life came back to haunt the Reich in the shape of the art promoted by it. It demonstrates on the lowest level the dominance of figure/gestalt of facial expression, the victory of distance over proximity, the triumph of—supposedly natural—shamelessness over shame. Few things testify more clearly to the "split consciousness" with which Hans Dieter Schäfer[72] has diagnosed the Third Reich than just this side-by-side comparison of the two art exhibits, of which one was turned toward life, the market, expression, play, and experimentation, while the other was calcified in the generic poses mandated from above, or boiled down to the inscrutability of the Führer's countenance.

It only makes sense to assume that one motive for the expulsion of "degenerate art" from the German life world might have been the exorcism of those social relations that still revolved around the society of

Figure 34. Hitler at a Nazi leadership school, expressedly as "primus inter pares." The famous and oft-ridiculed position of his hands is perfect for this situation: the right arm always ready for the *Heil Hitler*. That with this gesture Hitler practically saluted himself is part of the involuntary comedy of this ritual.

proximity, around facial expression, around the psychology of shame. The German people's erstwhile "lost face," now regained for all the world to see, was a play of muscles rather than of facial expression and was not intended for reciprocating glances for an other. Other than the physiognomic line of ancestors of the German people in the works of the old masters, who after all had always (and always with great sophistication) depicted mimic qualities, the German face of the present day, the subject of racism, aspired to be pure figure/gestalt, "saved face." Not by accident was the real inventor of the notion of figure/gestalt in the nineteenth century, Christian von Ehrenfels, a committed eugenicist. Empathy and abstraction fell apart into two separate operations. Only in very few cases did their conflict still become thematic, for instance in that of Ludwig Ferdinand Clauss, once a student of Husserl. As late as 1925 he had depicted Nordic man as a "man of achievement," but then, along with his Jewish assistant, he turned increasingly to "empathetic understanding," really the gestalt-vision's diametric opposite. "With the type of the man of achievement we enter the array of types [*Gestalten*], whose styles (typical features [*Gestaltgesetze*] we think of as hereditary, that is to say as blood-dependent, and thus as a racial style." Thus he wrote in his book's seventeenth edition of 1941, but at the same time he warned insistently against superstition that "man of accomplishment" or "Nordic" referred to moral concepts.[73] But the warning was for naught and the immanent contradiction unsublatable. If people in synchronic coexistence looked at each other according to hereditary "typical features," the diachronic perspective would destroy the synchronic one. Instead of relating to one another in the terms of mimic presence, one would see only the children in parents and, vice versa, in the children nothing but the parents, grandparents, or unwanted elements in the line of descent.[74] The dogmatic stipulation of "sole worth of Nordic man" with blond hair and blue eyes had its consequences among Aryans as well. There was, Clauss writes, "among honest German people who had fallen under the spell of this very article of faith, a nagging despair over their own worth, because they were unable to find the desired qualities when looking into the mirror. Some desperate souls are reported to have chosen suicide."[75] Of course, the death of non-Nordic desperate souls remained undiscussed.[76]

Hitler's Janus face, which failed to conform to any of these hereditary axioms, be it in profile or *en face*, be it in terms of figure/gestalt or color, reflected this double bind. While Baldur von Schirach celebrated the great communal experience in *The Führer's Countenance*, the Georgian writer Grigol Robakidse rhapsodized about Hitler's "distant face":

I see him on the numerous images, but he looks different on every picture. You could think that his inner gaze escapes the lens: an unmistakable characteristic of the "distant face.". . .

From time to time I see him in the *Wochenschauen* [newsreels]. Here his face reveals itself more immediately and talkatively. The film of the wedding banquet of General Field Marshal Göring shows him almost like a symbol. Here he is close to everybody, especially to the celebrated couple—but still, he seems to be somewhere else at the same time, he is inapproachable. You feel as though a stranger had appeared at the festivities, who was nonetheless familiar to everyone immediately. His comrades-in-arms and friends who are close to him must, in their closeness to him, feel this "distance" most distinctly."[77]

There was little doubt about Hitler's double-, perhaps even "multi-facedness" (to which Speer testifies) even during his lifetime. Politically it asserted itself in his striking lack of character in word and deed, physiognomically as a mercurially changing play of expressions. André François-Poncet, the French ambassador between 1931 and 1938, writes in his memoirs:

Personally, I knew three faces [of Hitler], corresponding to three aspects of his nature: The first was of deep paleness and displayed indistinct features, a turbid color. Expressionless, somewhat protruding eyes looking lost in dreams, gave him something absent, distant: an impenetrable face, unsettling like that of a medium or a somnambulist.

The second [face] was excited, of lively coloration, passionately motive. The nostrils quivered, the eyes sent flashes, ferocity was in them, will to power, resistance against any constraint, hatred for his opponents, cynical temerity, wild energy, ready to overlook anything: a face marked by storm and stress, the face of a crazed man.

The third [face] was that of an everyday person, who is naïve, bucolic, coarse, common, easy to amuse, who breaks into loud laughter and slaps his thighs: a face you hit upon quite commonly, without a particular expression, one of those thousands of faces one can find in the wide world.

At times, in speaking to Hitler you could experience these three faces successively.[78]

The distant face, the close face, the average face: here we are not talking about facial expression, but rather about attitudes. These are no poses, rather figures of mentality. If one were to attempt a psychoanalytic interpretation, one might think of the notion of the split, or perhaps more accurately the classical model of the psychic apparatus as Freud described it: the ego, the id, and the superego alternately make their appearance. But is it really an appearance or a projection? Many eyewitnesses tell of two mentalities: the martial demeanor of the speaker for the masses, and the civilized demeanor of the musical, later perhaps also politically canny, man. Their triangulation is rare, however.

Where the point was not expressedly the transfixing gaze of the near-sighted photographic form, pictorial representation tended toward the "distant face." The films of Leni Riefenstahl as well as many Wochenschauen newsreels and the more official photos by Heinrich Hoffmann mostly show Hitler from below, with motionless features, apart from moments of oratory or when he posed for Hoffmann with a sharp line between his eyebrows or a glowing face-to-face stare. Once war began, and the more Hitler appeared in uniform, face and eyes disappeared more or less under his hat. No medium seemed capable of transmitting the flashing gaze, which must have appeared so charismatic in personal interaction. Even the much-praised and much-feared blueness of his eyes eluded black-and-white photography. Certainly he is often seen looking grim or exhausted. But only very few of the known photographs and film clips suggest a real, close mimic relationship with another person, not even with Geli Raubal, Hitler's niece, with whom he is believed to have had a sexual relationship. Very rarely a photograph with a smiling or laughing Hitler gained currency, and if it did it was more as a lapse, for example a photo of Hitler sitting next to Hindenburg in a motorcar, with a truly disgusting, feisty, wily grin[79] [Fig. 35]. More accurately, then, studies have spoken of a "sudden slip of expression and

Figure 35. In his 1932 collection *Hitler wie ihn keiner kennt* [Hitler as Nobody Knows Him] Heinrich Hoffmann compiled pictures of a relaxed Hitler. These showed him mostly either alone in nature or in the company of animals, children, or admirers. There doesn't seem to be one shot featuring friendly mimic qualities in a Hitler dealing with other persons. Here we see Hitler in May of 1933 sitting next to Hindenburg and wearing a feisty, devious grin. He has won the battle.

posture" in these pictures, not of mimic contact but of mimic lapse, the animated counterpart to mimic stasis.

All these findings rest on the known photographic material as well as select eyewitness accounts. How much more will be discovered in this area, and how much of it could serve to subvert our conclusions, remains to be seen. That Hitler for all intents and purposes was able to appear charming and relaxed is evident from accounts and private movies,[80] but as a statement it is as banal as the graphological attempts to diagnose Hitler's handwriting with a so-called thread connection, which is in turn adduced to prove his mendacity, or alternately with sudden shifts in his handwriting, which are then supposed to confirm that he was of violent temper.[81] The only connection between Hitler's handwriting and his gait that is really interesting physiognomically has never been studied, even though the early study by the graphologist Wenzel offers pointers in the right direction when it admonishes "the m's & n's, which are given highly unnatural corners."[82] In the movies and in the newsreels Hitler's gait appears unmistakably puppet-like, as energetic as it was inhibited, especially during representative functions and when climbing stairs. It was all there for Chaplin's imitation. But all this is irrelevant for the actions conceived and executed by this physiognomy. After all, other people too can write or walk tensely, without necessarily becoming mass murderers. Hitler's face expressed nothing special except brutality and fanaticism in some situations, indifference or absentmindedness in others, joy and triumph, or exhaustion and illness.

On the Self-Portrait

The fetishization of the (Nordic) shape/gestalt, reduced eventually to pure "hereditary information," negated not only the psychologically shamed, mimically interactive society of proximity. It also impaired the sense for proximity in art. No matter how artistic the technique of presenting figures against a background, for example in silhouettes, it is also inherently limited. It represses the possibility of the self-image/portrait *en face*. This is where the conception of art of the Nazi years has its blind spot. Among the six hundred objects in the *Degenerate Art* exhibition, there were only nine self-portraits. The reason for this is not that the exhibition's initiators were reluctant to display the ostracized artists prominently, as is evident from the fact that its rival, the *Great German Art Exhibition*, also featured only nine self-portraits. This is surprising especially in light of the prominence of the self-portrait in the dominant art movements of the time, above all expressionism. But why should a painter whose build might perhaps fall short of the Aryan standard present a self-portrait at all? In his 1924 book *Rasse und Stil* [Race and Style], Hans F. K. Günther had called for harmonization of the build of the artist and that of his figures; more than anyone Schultze-Naumburg demanded such conformity, even if, in *Kunst und Rasse* [Art and Race], he didn't show the bodies of the artists he criticized at all, but rather compared their paintings to photographs from medical physiognomy. Perhaps he was afraid that they might contradict his theory. The short circuit between racial portrait and self-portrait has ruined especially the latter for perpetuity. The thought that the artist should always be faced by his own race in his picture meant a disavowal of the tacit association implicit in the self-portrait with an existential self-interrogation.

Strangely, this disavowal fit rather well with the contemporary expansion of the new media of film and photography. Those too were not conducive to the self-portrait. Photographic self-portraits were an exception at the time,[83] and film is by its very mode of production incapable of self-portraiture. Directors work with actors and never with themselves alone. The same goes for the period's fashionable death mask pictures; here too the notion of the picture of/as another dominates the technology, for no one can take his or her own death mask. As though to compensate for his excursion into the realm of the absolute "non-self-portrait," in 1927 Ernst Benkard devoted himself to the study of the self-portrait before 1800, thus inspiring Fritz Ried's great study of 1931.

The transformation the self-portrait was undergoing at the hands of the NS poetics was moving became clear as early as 1937 in a poetic painting by Josef Weinheber, soi-disant "greatest lyric poet of the German language."[84] It only made sense that he would write a poem on Dürer's self-portrait in Munich's Alte Pinakothek museum: an icon of Christ transformed into the sum of racial clichés, into a ghostly figure: "As the valid form [gestalt] of my people I painted thee for all to see. Turned toward you is my face. Turn away from it and you will not be."[85]

Another party-line art theorist, Hans Wühr, in his 1939 work *The German Countenance in Art*, similarly exorcises the idea from the picture, in his case the self-portraits of Albrecht Altdorfer. The poetic self Altdorfer took recourse to seems to refer to the "immeasurable interior cosmos of the landscape"—a contradiction in itself, since landscape is by definition not immeasurable—and looks at the face as a landscape. "This is why one looks in vain for a clear, decisive self-portrait of the painter. His self-portrait is everywhere; in every face of the people abandoning themselves to the landscape in his pictures lies a feature of his countenance, playful, dreamy and in the vein of lyric allegory rather than literally. In keeping with his romantic nature, the German landscape painter is usually a poet, in particular Altdorfer, who like every poet mixes ipseity and landcape so inextricably that one feels one sees his self-portrait allegorically or literally in each of his landscapes." "Allegorically or literally"—Wühr is really talking about the latter, as becomes clearer a few lines on. For where landscape becomes the inner ambition of the self-portrait, the "second face" collapses into the first, physical face—a concept not very different from expressionism, but applied here to the German *Gau*: "The silent, thoughtful countenance of the pious wanderer and his mild inner dream-I [*Traumgesicht*] correspond so visibly and clearly that the viewer is struck by the original common meaning of 'face' as countenance and 'face' as vision."[86] This was perhaps meant as a response to Hubert Schrader, who had denied the identity of these two concepts just two years earlier.

Where the notion of self-portrait in NS aesthetics was heading emerges in the development of the periodical *The Art of the German Reich*, as it had been called since 1939. Essays and illustrations on the self-portraits of sculptors became frequent and gradually eclipsed the part played by the poetic self in self-design. Modeling oneself like a sculptor meant disciplining oneself (once again perfectly literally), taking "the

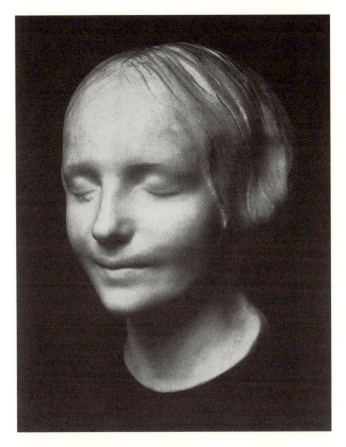

Figure 36. The mask of the Inconnue de la Seine, one of the most popular death masks around the turn of the century.

body as a guide" rather than entering into a potentially problematic conversation with oneself.

All three technologies—film, photography, and sculpture including the plaster mask, to say nothing of architecture—were much closer to NS aesthetics than traditional painting. For even if Ernst Benkard's gallery of dead faces creates a painterly impression, the plaster cast is an old instrument of anthropometrics now turned into an image through photography. Of course, one didn't put up photographic reproductions of death masks on the wall, but instead a replica of the mask itself. The cult around the beautiful Inconnue de la Seine [Fig. 36], the mask of a young woman who had supposedly thrown herself into the Seine, was not a photographic one, but a cult around a mask seemingly still imbued with the vitality of unhappy love. The raised perception of "figures" of/ as others thus didn't have an iconic counterpart in self-perception. The opposite was the case: the more the German face turned into a species face, the less it had any inkling of how terrifying it now looked [Fig. 38].

* * *

Hitler, painter manqué, left no known self-portrait besides a tiny, possibly apocryphal caricature [Fig. 37]. More than the pictures of himself he reportedly loved recordings of his voice—the very opposite of a conversation with oneself.[87] In 1939 in his exile in Paris, Heinrich Mann invented just this kind of self-conversation—one of the strangest satires on Hitler's physiognomy imaginable, a facial shock treatment, unearthed by Peter von Matt. It is entitled "The Speech":

"It must be a grandiose feeling when all the marching bands begin playing at eight in the morning just because I want to speak at one o'clock. Someone else might be confused, but not I. Because there is nothing to confuse. I simply make my Führer face; it is malevolent, but has something goofy as well, which disarms people. I flash evil eyes; naughty children will have to soil themselves of fright. Pallenberg could do that. By the way, I'll attach the raised nose in large format to my face, which [Pallenberg] wore as the good soldier Schweijk. I pull the corners of my mouth so far down that it makes a circle with my double chin. This creates an excessively large upper lip, which I fill with vegetation; it looks a bit like a mouse but doesn't move. It would be even more wonderful if it could be sometimes here sometimes there. Threatening expressions that are comical at the same time have the strange effect that I look as though I am afraid of myself. This is how I look into the world as my own hobgoblin, but the world only notices the hobgoblin. Furthermore, it is preoccupied with the aesthetic impact of my being. I pride myself on the arrangement of my hair, of a kind that only failed painters manage, loose strands around the forehead and a mass on the crown of my head. People of power who are nothing more than that are bald. I on the other hand am a genius.[88]

This wasn't Heinrich Mann's first satire on Hitler. Already in 1933, his pamphlet "Der Haß" (Hatred) presented its incendiary appeals against the new regime in sarcastic dialogues between Hindenburg and Hitler. In the later text, he changes strategies. He puts Hitler into the contemporary world of the media that is partly opposed, partly exploited by Hitler. Mann forces Hitler, who since 1936 really hasn't spoken to anyone but providence, into a revealing conversation with his environment. It consists for one thing of the Jewish actor Pallenberg, whose depiction of the soldier Schwejk* Hitler liked so much that he copied him. After all,

Good Soldier Schweik is a novel by the Czech writer Jaroslav Hašek (1883–1923), who drew on his own experiences in the army during World War I for the satire of an intransigent soldier who throws the army machine into disarray by following orders too exactly. Trans.

Figure 37. Henry Picker published this drawing ("Self-portrait as unsuccessful *Vabanque* Player") in his protocols of the "conversations by table" in the Führerhauptquartier of 1941–42. Karl Stauber's painting of the standard bearer shows the official version.

he is a good actor himself and the story Jaroslav Hašek tells of the soldier from the First World War is the very opposite of his own experiences, which makes it fun to imitate the small man "from below" who opposes the war.

Then there is the matter of the mouth, which is stretched into shape before a mirror: this refers to the famous scene from Fritz Lang's film about the murderer "M" of 1931. The actor playing the murderer Beckert, Peter Lorre, is a Jew; and in the scene in question he really performs an analysis in criminal physiognomy, bending the corners of his mouth simulating a particular shape of mouth that signifies a criminal or pathological predisposition. But the murderer Beckert manages to suppress such telltale signs; he looks just like everybody else and must be caught using different methods.

As for the matter of his hair—the good Aryan Hanns Johst, president of the Reichsschrifttumskammer, described it so wonderfully on Hitler's head, anticipating Stauber's painting of Hitler staring wildly ahead [Fig. 37]: "There is the hair. Neither picture nor sculpture has as yet managed to express its willfulness. Eichendorffian jollity strains against any doctrine. Neither steel helmet nor hat, neither comb nor brush managed to tame what obviously belonged to wind and weather. Like the clouds it at times throws shadows on his face, at others it opens up the face through its glow."[89] And lastly, *summa summarum*, there is the general conception of the artistic genius, which none other than Thomas Mann ascribed to Hitler in his essay "Brother Hitler" from the same year, 1939. Didn't Thomas Mann speak of Eichendorff's "good-for-nothing"* just like Johst? There must be something to this. [See Fig. 38.]

This is how one might read Heinrich Mann's text: As a derisive reply to his brother's essay, it collects the entirely contradictory ambitions of the small, antimilitarist soldier under Jewish direction, giving them alternately the face of the Führer and the face of the killer, keeping them close together, and all this in the—suppressed—name of Eichendorff. At an even deeper level, the portrait could of course be connected to the struggle between the brothers Mann, if one thought of Thomas's 1918 *Betrachtungen eines Unpolitischen* [Reflections of a Non-Political Man], which devotes an entire chapter to the good-for-nothing and declares German simplicity a national essence, for its "Gotteskindschaft" [divine progeny]. Much in this early text by Thomas Mann points to the juxtaposition of "degenerate" and "healthy" art in the spirit of Langbehn's "Rembrandt Germans." His brother Heinrich

---

(Leaves from the) Life of a Good-for-nothing is a novel by the romantic poet Joseph Freiherr von Eichendorff (1788–1857). The novel's hapless hero became a national German "type" invoked by Thomas Mann in his *Reflections of a Nonpolitical Man* as well as by the youth movement in the early twentieth century. Trans.

"HIMMEL! IS THAT ME?"

Figure 38. "Himmel! Is That Me?" A caricature by David Low, Hitler's sharpest critic with a drawing pen.

turns this into the false idol of an upstanding "little man," who is in league with the laws of nature, almost like the third and youngest brother of the fairy tale. A 1924 anthology by Josef Hofmiller, a highly esteemed essayist and connoisseur of literature, which gathered texts rather than images under the title *Das deutsche Angesicht* [The German Countenance], pays tribute to the spirit of the German fairy tale in just this tradition.

Heinrich Mann's satire opens the view on the flipside of the adulated German face and onto the dark underbelly of physiognomy. During the Hitler years, this aspect became more dramatic and uncanny to the same degree as the "German countenance" in its self-declarations attempted to become more beautiful. For not unlike Freud's conception of the psychic apparatus, physiognomic perception is divided into a day- and a night-side, into conscious and unconscious body images. The dream books of antiquity show body and face dis-figured beyond measure in dreams, in bits and pieces and fraught with portentous significance. This has been staged above all by Oscar Wilde in his novel *The Picture of Dorian Gray*; the beautiful face of daylight and life is secretly disfigured by evil wishes and deeds. It is the scene from Stevenson's *Dr. Jekyll and Mr. Hyde*—one of the most obtrusive parables of the Weimar years—in its film version by Robert Wiene. In his history of film and under the title *From Caligari to Hitler*, Siegfried Kracauer granted this scene a complete hermeneutic monopoly over the German mentality of those years, a tendency to split into a rational and an insane German persona according to the schema that Freud had proposed in his *Interpretation of Dreams* (1900) as a conflict between conscious and censored unconscious drives. The famous motto of the *Interpretation of Dreams*, "Flectere si nequeo superos, Acheronta movebo" (If I cannot master the above-world, then I will at least move the underworld), could just as well be the motto for those impotent depictions of the evil that many Germans and non-Germans recognized in Hitler. No matter how powerless their propaganda would remain, it was nonetheless quite telling.

Chapter 5

Shock Pictures 1939–1945

"Hitlerfresse": Caricature and Satire

The "face" that Hitler regained for Germany, both in the shape of territorial conquest and in terms of national self-image, between 1933 and 1938, he lost in the years after. The young lance corporal of 1919 had committed himself in incredible ideological fixation to a world war scenario, when he propagated the double fight against Bolshevism and capitalism, thereby speaking to the two main worries of the German elites. Bolshevism meant war against, or better, for, the East; capitalism meant war in the West, which was, however, dominated by the idea of revanche much more than by territorial visions. What held both targets of this aggression together, at least for the cursory observer, was the concept and the idea of the "Jew." The propaganda of Schönerer, Hitler's Austrian teacher, according to which the people had to be shown a clearly contoured enemy, not really an image of the enemy but a gestalt, recognizable in any variation, became terrifyingly real. Since 1933, Jews and Communists, as well as the scientific and artistic avant-garde, had fled Germany [Fig. 39]. The émigrés' resistance crystallized around the main places of exile, Paris, Prague, London, and the United States. By necessity it began as a symbolic resistance, in word and image.

Of course, satirical propaganda had its own laws. Turned against Hitler and his right-wing base, it began in 1923 and amplified in response to their electoral successes: In posters and newspapers, in particular those put out by the brothers Heartfield and Herzfelde, but also in *Simplicissimus* (somewhat later and somewhat less frequently), in the magazine *Pleite*, the *Arbeiter Illustrierte Zeitung*, the *Kladderadatsch*, the *Wahren Jakob*, and the *Fliegenden Blätter*, and many others. Many of these periodicals were "synchronized" after 1933, or did so voluntarily, for example *Simplicissimus*, which as early as 1932 featured an NS-compliant national portrait gallery commenting on the acquisition of an expensive van Gogh [Fig. 40]. How subtle a surrender the cartoon was becomes clear only on closer inspection. For none other than Max Liebermann had polemically censured the acquisition here ridiculed and had declared

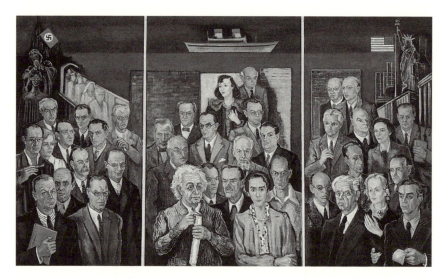

Figure 39. In his 1938 triptych, Arthur Kaufmann created a macabre Valhalla, a portrait gallery engineered by terror for men and women "of merit" on their way into exile. Between the swastika and the Statue of Liberty, half immured in a bunker, half gathered on a ship, the spiritual elite gathers, many with books or writings in hand.

Justi's acquisition policies insane.[1] Other periodicals relocated abroad and continued the fight from there, for example the *AIZ*. Prague became a center of this resistance. In 1934, it played host to an exhibition featuring works by Heartfield (thirty-five images just by him), Grosz, Thomas Theodor Heine, Erich Godel, and many others. But satire as a minority's weapon against the majority around its adored Führer remained toothless, certainly much more so than the systematic, centuries-old demonization of the Jewish physiognomy, since 1933 subject of the German Reich's official propaganda and the academicized racial dogmas in schools and universities.

When the head of the foreign press section of the Propaganda Ministry, Ernst Hanfstaengl, Hitler's longtime friend nicknamed Putzi, put out his two volumes of caricatures from around the world in 1933–34—*Tat gegen Tinte* [Deed against Ink]—the pictures bespoke their own political weakness: it was a Punch-and-Judy show rather than a political arsenal to be reckoned with [Fig. 41]. The book reflected the relative distance, even patronizing curiosity, the world outside Germany felt vis-à-vis the ridiculous figure of the Führer. Memoirs like those by Dorothy Thompson, Sinclair Lewis's wife, expressed what many felt and some also wrote. In her book *I Saw Hitler!* of 1932, which led to her expulsion

Figure 40. Just as macabre as Kaufmann's painting is this caricature of the idea of a national portrait gallery of the starving cultural elite, which appeared in the *Simplicissimus* of April 17, 1932. At the time, the painters who literally hang themselves here were defended by none other than Max Liebermann.

from Germany briefly after the Nazis' ascent to power, she describes an interview in the Kaiserhof Hotel: "When finally I walked into Adolph Hitler's salon in the Kaiserhof Hotel, I was convinced that I was meeting the future dictator of Germany. In something less than fifty seconds I was quite sure that I was not. It took just that time to measure the startling insignificance of this man who has set the whole world agog. [He is] formless, almost faceless, a man whose countenance is a caricature, a man whose framework seems cartilaginous, without bones. He is inconsequent and voluble, ill-poised, insecure. He is the very prototype of the Little Man."[2] Martha Dodd, daughter of the American ambassador, met Hitler at the Kaiserhof Hotel as well, and she did not seem repulsed in personal interaction, but instead seemed almost touched by his pale

Hitler

Figure 41. The caricatures gathered
here all come from Hanfstaengl's book
*Tat gegen Tinte: Hitler in der Karikatur der
Welt* [Deed against Ink: Hitler in the
Caricatures of the World] of 1933–34.
All of them seem somewhat harmless,
but they show that Hitler's face and
figure inspired satire all around.

Hitler

Adolf Hitler

M. Hitler

blue eyes and his awkward and yet strangely charming demeanor toward women.[3] William Shirer, the incorruptible American journalist, noted that he could not find anything exciting in Hitler's face and that he was glad that Hitler was not as given to theatrics as Mussolini with his stuck-out chin and thrown-back head, trying to give his eyes a glassy look. Nonetheless, Shirer wrote, "there *is* something glassy in his eyes, the strongest thing in his face."[4]

Not all Anglo-Saxons thought Hitler this harmless. The caricaturist David Low waged a veritable war with his drawings. But when Chaplin's film *The Great Dictator* was released, English and American men and women alike were once again struck merely by the resemblance between the appearances of the two men born in April of the same year. This resemblance seduced some into playing down Hitler. On the occasion of Hitler's fiftieth birthday, Harold Nicholson (who knew of Chaplin's project already) wrote that "no matter how different the rise of Hitler and of Chaplin and how different their reputation, they have one thing in common: their success rests on an understanding for the 'little man' of the lower middle class. . . ."[5] And a *Times* article on Hitler's fiftieth birthday gives a physical all-clear: "In the six years since his accession to power, Mr. Hitler has probably changed less than most men between their forty-fourth and fiftieth year. The lines in his face have deepened only slightly. He has gained perhaps twenty-five pounds and perhaps four inches in girth, but that is much less than some of his lieutenants." Even in 1943, on both men's fifty-fourth birthdays, the *New York Times* published an almost loving cartoon, which of course left no doubt about the highly different roles these two played in world history[6] [Fig. 42a].

Ernst Lubitsch's famous 1942 film, *To Be or Not to Be*, similarly borders on playing down Hitler. Unmasking by ridiculing was insufficient; if one takes into account that more than 150 anti-Nazi films were made in the United States alone, it was just one more attempt to work within the tradition of comedic satire instead of outright propaganda. It was in this latter tradition that the Walt Disney Corporation in 1942 conceived a

Figure 42a. As physiognomic fortune would have it, Hitler and Chaplin were not only born in the same month of the same year—April 1889—but both also played a role in world history. Even if it was claimed after 1945 that Hitler could not have acceded to power if people had seen more Chaplin films, in fact the two men's vague resemblance hurt more than it helped.

Figure 42b. Hitler was the undeserving object of somewhat affectionate and highly artistic satires. The photomontages of the French periodical *Marianne* miss their mark in this vein: They depict Hitler more as interesting than as dangerous.

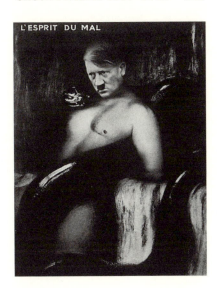

children's film entitled *Der Fuehrer's Face,* in which SS goons force Donald Duck to toil in a bomb factory. The title song, which contains the lyrics "in der fuehrer's face there is the master race," accompanies his work at the assembly line, where he is constantly forced to salute the Führer's portrait, until the huge explosion from which he wakes up as though from a nightmare, at last embracing the Statue of Liberty in tears.[7]

French Hitler satires had an almost gallant streak to them. Between 1932 and 1939 the illustrated weekly *Marianne* featured carefully thought-out photomontages playing on motifs of art history of uncertain number and origin. Obviously inspired by John Heartfield, the *Marianne* caricatures would, for instance, show Hitler around Wagner (Hitler and Winifred Wagner as Tristan and Isolde in 1933) or, toward the end of the 1930s, Hitler inserted into a painting such as *The Embodiment of Sin* by Franz Stuck, with Hitler lasciviously lounging like its model, a snake on his bare chest[8] [see Fig. 42b].

Inside Germany the satirical climate differed markedly. Almost everyone around him commented on Hitler's physical appearance, even if initially not as plastically as the historian Karl Alexander von Müller, who described him on trial in 1924. In time, a veritable tradition of verbal satire and a dramaturgy of facial shock developed, far exceeding the pictures in bite. Günther Scholdt combined such quotes into a sort of verbal "composite portrait":

A portrait composed of an "average" of the descriptions in question would give us a man looking as follows: a black kiss-curl falling onto his face, above it the hair, parted and pomaded, on an oh so backless head, and a bulging, plump, and even stupid ear, a revolting mouth with long pale lips and the little brush of his mustache—an invidious mustache running from his nose like dirt—an amorphous, hunched, fleshy, common, even obscene nose, and additionally shrunk little hands. Moreover mask-like, empty mouse-eyes, whose vaunted transfixing gaze turns out to be a mere dog's gaze from a pale, bloated visage.[9]

Invectives like these, like a majority of the anti-Semitic caricatures, draw heavily on the physiognomic obsession of the nineteenth century and its legacy. Each of the attributes compiled in Scholdt's collage could probably be found in the diaries of the Goncourt brothers, in the works of Balzac or Oscar Wilde, and the frequently spiteful journals of Virginia Woolf, but above all in the caricatures of the century: from heirs to Hogarth like Grandville all the way to Félicien Rops and Paul Weber. This was not because (or not simply because) European society of the nineteenth century was particularly sardonic, but because the caricature in word and image is the oldest playground of physiognomy and thus one of the main beneficiaries of its meteoric rise. In this spirit, Ernst Gombrich traced the history of caricature back all the way to the famous "[Study of Five] Grotesque Heads" of Leonardo da Vinci.

A society that makes selective breeding its program has to work with micro-didactics of expulsion, which puts every single one of its members under surveillance and approves or disapproves of its every innate physical trait. Arthur Schopenhauer formulated succinctly and guide-like the ideas of physiognomic breeding in currency at his time: a woman with a snub nose and a narrow pelvis has no opportunities for procreation. The real ancestry of this ideology was made explicit only in the Third Reich. Peter Weingart has made the connection to animal husbandry, which is in fact the origin of the so-called "doctrine of the exterior." In particular, horsebreeding in the English tradition sharpened the eye of the wealthy gentleman for physical shapeliness, and the cult of racing gave the concept of "race" a popular but in no way human content. As a science that speaks explicitly of naked bodies and is not a science of fashion, physiognomy's success since the end of the seventeenth century rests to a certain extent on that "doctrine of the exterior" dedicated to the appraisal of naked animal bodies.[10] Evaluating naked bodies on possible performance (or achievement) and character was something anyone looking to purchase an animal in the marketplace had to do, be it an individual animal or an entire herd.

This is why no physiognomic tradition is closer to caricature than that comparing humans with animals. The *Physiognomic Studies* of the Dane Sophus Schack became a best-seller toward the end of the nineteenth century,[11] supported and accompanied by Darwin's research that became the *Expression of Emotions in Humans and Animals*. This complex unfolded its demagogical potential in anti-Semitic caricatures, including the demonic image of the rats tunneling under the bourgeois floor, prevalent in the propaganda films of the Ufa.*

Reading the physical invectives against Hitler in context, it becomes clear that they connote more than simply visual aversion toward an ugly man. This aversion has from the beginning an admixture of disappointment: disappointment that here is someone who wants to be or has become a Führer without conforming to either the traditional "ruler image" or to the top of the newly established physical hierarchy. It was in this spirit that in 1931 Herbert Blank (really Weigand von Miltenberg) claims in his book *Adolf Hitler Wilhelm III*: "The features of his face, in the frightening center of which lies that black fly under his nose, are all soft and round. Often even good-natured and paternal. . . . Looking at him for just five minutes you are convinced that there is a long way to go to that Nordic master race that he wants to breed."[12] Klaus Mann experiences Hitler in 1932 eating a cake from close up, downright driven to despair over the contradictory physical messages of appearance and demeanor:

He stuffed himself with strawberry tartlets, which I am rather fond of myself but couldn't touch for months after having seen him swallowing three of them. I found him surprisingly ugly, much more vulgar than I had anticipated. There were only two things that puzzled me while I studied, with cold, disgusted curiosity, his unappetizing features: first, what was the secret of his fascination? Why and how did he manage to make people lose their minds? And second: Of whom did he remind me? He resembled someone whose picture I must have frequently seen. It was not Charlie Chaplin. Chaplin is engagingly attractive. No, the great comedian does not have Hitler's fleshy, nasty nose. Chaplin looks like an artist, whereas that gluttonous rat over there looked—like a gluttonous rat. He was flabby and foul and without any marks of greatness, a frustrated hysterical petty bourgeois.[13]

A few lines later, Mann decides that Hitler doesn't look like Chaplin, but rather like the child-killer Haarmann, the "homosexual bluebeard." This is one of the contemporary sources adduced for Hitler's alleged, albeit never proven, homosexuality. Klaus Mann's autobiography, *Der Wendepunkt* [The Turning Point] appeared in English in 1942 and in German only in 1952.

The eastern Prussian Junker Friedrich Reck-Mallezcewen would not even grant Hitler the negative comparison with a mass murderer. In his hate-filled diary he remarks:

August 11, 1936: I saw Hitler last in Seebruck, slowly gliding by in a car with armor-plated sides, while an armed bodyguard of motorcyclists rode in front as

---

*The Ufa (Universum-Film AG) was a German film production company founded in 1917 and responsible for many classic German films of the 1920s. Trans.

further protection: a jellylike, slag-gray face, a moonface into which two melan-
choly jet-black eyes had been set like raisins. So sad, so unutterably insignificant,
so basically misbegotten is this countenance that only thirty years ago, in the
darkest days of Wilhelmism, such a face on an official would have been impossible. Appearing in the chair of a minister, an apparition with a face like this
would have been disobeyed as soon as its mouth spoke an order—not merely by
the higher officials in the ministry: no, by the doorman, by the cleaning women!

September 9, 1937: Oh, it is the most shameful thing of all that this was not even
the physically beautiful and spiritually glittering antichrist of the legends, but
only a poor dung-face, in every aspect something akin to a *middle-class
antichrist . . .*

April 1939: The next day in front of the Reich Chancellery, packed into the
mob, deafened by the crash of drums, cymbals, and tubas of the marching
troops, I witnessed the festivities. I heard the clamor, saw the enraptured faces
of the women, saw, also, the object of this rapture. There he stood, the most
glorious of all, in his usual pose with hands clasped over his belly, looking with
his silver-decorated uniform and cap drawn far down over his forehead like a
streetcar conductor. I examined his face through my binoculars. The whole of
it waggled with unhealthy cushions of fat; it all hung, it was all slack and without
structure—slaggy, gelatinous, sick. There was no light in it, none of the simmer
and shining of a man sent by God. Instead, the face bore the sigma of sexual
inadequacy, of the rancor of a half-man who had turned his fury at his impotence into brutalizing others.[14]

"Not even the corporeally beautiful and intellectually sparkling Antichrist"—what is voiced here is the disappointment of an old aristocratic
perception always connected with breeding. But it is also the disappointment over the absence of Wallenstein's face, that icon of homofacial fascination with the leader-figure. Even Hitler's first biographer, Konrad
Heiden, was obsessed with this disappointment. In his grand portrait
from 1936, he writes:

There are no pictures of Hitler. No photography can capture his double existence, which flits constantly between its two poles. What we have are depictions
of the different states of the substance Hitler. He is never himself; he is in at any
minute a lie of himself; this is why every image is false. The photographic plate
lays hold only onto his external appearance, and this appearance is an inferior
shell. The face is an expressionless background, on which modest means have
plastered a mask. It is incontestable that of this mask the strand of hair and the
brush mustache are the most expressive features. The power of his eyes, praised
by his admirers, strikes sober observers as a greedy piercing without even a glim-
mer of grace, which would alone make his gaze compelling, a gaze that drives
you off more than that it binds you.[15]

Of course, the excessive fury of Hitler's contemporaries didn't restrict
itself to the surface, but dug deeper as well. One doesn't stay with the
face, but describes action: for example, Bertolt Brecht in his play *Arturo*

Ui; the other puts the dictator in his social context. Hitler is depicted as a warmonger [Fig. 43] even before, but certainly after, 1933 both inside and outside of Germany, for instance by John Heartfield in the famous montage of Franz Stuck's *War* of 1933, or in *The Nation* of April 5, 1933, which featured Hitler as the grim reaper. Truly political success was granted to the photomontage by Erwin Blumenfeld, who in his recollections about the "Hitlerfresse" [Fig. 44] reports that the picture was "dropped over Germany by the millions as an American pamphlet."[16] Here again, the spadework had been done by John Heartfield, who showed "the face of Fascism" in his cover design for *Italy in Chains* (1928): It shows Mussolini, half skinless skull, half corporeally recognizable. Later the American Secret Service produced a similar Hitler face as a death's head: the stamp with the barely readable inscription "Futsches Reich" [up-in-smoke empire] was smuggled into Germany in 1943 [Fig. 44].

The other front in the satirical onslaught devoted itself to the "great little man." Once again Heartfield provided one of the most brilliant versions with his photomontage "The Meaning of the *Hitlergruss*: A Small Man Asks for Great Gifts" (1932) with the caption "Millions Are Behind Me." Those who regarded Hitler as a great "little man" elevated themselves through this identification. More self-conscious observers such as Dorothy Thompson or hateful ones such as Heinrich and Klaus Mann found that the physical nobody falsified the expected greatness. George Orwell formulated this more cleverly but also more naïvely: "[Hitler] would be capable of killing a mouse and making us believe that he has slain a dragon."[17] This parody attained further truth if one took seriously the fairy-tale motif that it draws on. For in the fairy tale, the hero would conversely slay a dragon and speak of a mouse. Thus, the German self-image had long included the topos of the small man accomplishing great things—the topos of the youngest brother in the fairy tales, the topos of the blessed good-for-nothing, which Thomas Mann himself had introduced into the discussion over German nationhood in his 1918 *Reflections of a Nonpolitical Man*, with striking success. A related person of reference was the "Captain of Köpenick," the cobbler Wilhelm Voigt, whom Carl Zuckmayer made the hero of a successful 1930 play, after Fritz Kortner had given him the idea. The novelistic Voigt biography of 1930 by the right-wing author Wilhelm Schäfer also reached astonishing popularity. Was the reason the satire on the German devotion to the uniform or the paean of the successful good-for-nothing? Apparently it is uncertain whether Hitler knew the story of the captain, but it is highly probable. The answer the young lance corporal gave when he was supposed to be promoted to the rank of sergeant

Figure 43. Above, "Siegfried Hitler" by George Grosz in 1923; below, a caricature from *The Nation* of April 5, 1933.

Figure 44. In the end, only
the death's head was capable
of appropriately symbolizing
the driving motive of the
dictator. This one, "Hitler
fresse," was created by Erwin
Blumenfeld in 1933. The
postage stamp shown to the
right was smuggled into
Germany by the American
Secret Service (1943).

seems to point in this direction: "I would ask you to desist, I have more authority without stripes than with them."

Another relative of this great little man was the "the Good Soldier Schweijk,"* whom Heinrich Mann mentions in his satirical Hitler soliloquy as played by Max Pallenberg, the Jewish actor.[18] Heinrich Mann's satire had its own model. In 1934, the Austrian writer Anton Kuh had written an obituary on Max Pallenberg, who had died in an accident that same year. Kuh described the role of a lifetime the actor had missed— none other than Hitler:

A particularly Austrian obstinacy . . . drove him again and again to one particular object of portrayal: the small man. His small man, born in the Lueger years, later grown up, and finally turned megalomaniacal, never speaks pure German. He is, from his mask to his speech, copycat, blatherskite, omnium-gatherum. His nose looks as though adulterated with all the blood elements that ever formed an Austrian janitor into a German man. He has crawled from the files, and he speaks file paper. . . .

One evening he told us how he would play him, and he compacted his view of the role in one single sentence, heavy with significance: *He looks like a marriage swindler.* Only a genius of the masks could speak this sentence, only someone who couldn't put a mask before his face other than the one he just tore off someone else's face.[19]

In itself Kuh's satire is not exactly mind-boggling. But in the image of the marriage swindler it picks up the *cooperation* apparent to any suspicious observer between Hitler and the Germans, a captious love story. In 1946, Max Picard would cite the image of the marriage swindler in his great stock-taking account of "Hitler's face," only to reject it.[20] It was, like most of the caricatures, much too weak an image when compared to reality. Without a propagandistic apparatus as its vessel, satire was of limited effectiveness only.

The Voice of Evil: Charlie Chaplin and Theodor Haecker

The early 1930s provided another template for the topos of the great little man. In 1931, Charlie Chaplin visited Berlin—with staggering success. According to Chaplin's son, after 1933 all of Chaplin's movies were banned in Germany, not only because Chaplin was thought to be a Jew (which, according to Chaplin himself, he was not), but also because it was feared that Chaplin's mustache might incur a loss of face for Hitler. Reportedly, this prompted Chaplin's idea for a Hitler satire. *The Great*

Good Soldier Schweik is a novel by the Czech writer Jaroslav Hasek (1883–1923), who drew on his own experiences in the army during World War I for the satire of an intransigent soldier who throws the army machine into disarray by following orders too exactly. Trans.

Dictator was produced in 1938–39, but saw release only in 1940. Many Chaplin devotees were disappointed by the decision to split Hitler into the dictator Hynkel and the little Jewish barber. Rudolf Arnheim and Klaus Mann thought the film lacked all satirical bite; those who lauded the film, for example Eisenstein, perhaps wanted to console the director. Chaplin himself later remarked that he certainly would have made the film differently if he had been aware of what was known about the persecution of Jews even at the time. Remarkably, Siegfried Kracauer, in two works on film theory, doesn't mention *The Great Dictator* even once— and this although the theme of the schizophrenic split was to become central to Kracauer's film history *From Caligari to Hitler* (1947). The real filmic reply to Chaplin came in 1943 from the émigré Fritz Kortner. In *The Strange Death of Adolf Hitler* (the title itself is an allusion to Stevenson's *The Strange Case of Dr. Jekyll and Mr. Hyde*), a little Viennese municipal clerk one day imitates Hitler before friends and as punishment is whisked off by the Gestapo to a plastic surgeon. When he awakes, he has Hitler's face. He is told to act as Hitler's double. Things happen as they must: his own wife shoots him, and the plan to assassinate the dictator fails. Unlike in Chaplin's film it is not the great man, but the little man involuntarily formed in the great man's image who perishes. In other words, anyone empathizing with the little man in Hitler, even if only through his physical appearance, falls prey to a deadly error.

Besides the elegance and the heart-rending comedy of many scenes, besides even the visual satire, Chaplin's film offers another decisive and profound interpretation of Hitlerism. It is the interpretation via sound, via the voice. For Chaplin, *The Great Dictator* was the first sound film after his long refusal to work in the medium. For the Hitler speeches, Chaplin invented a language, an ugly gibberish, compared to which the regular language speech of the Jewish barber who later takes Hynkel's role is downright cathartic. The film charts this transition in three phases: first as silent play, then as disfigured speech, and last as real human speech, the normality of which is inseparable from its moral intent. In terms of technological development this sequence is of course chronological— first the silent movie, then sound; but physiognomically speaking, this is a reversal: Chaplin reverses the process of facialization that goes along with visualized racism by turning to spoken language. The people, spoken to *comprehensibly* by the benevolent dictator, are brought back to their senses; the facial nation reverts to a linguistic one. At least one German author had understood even then that the real point of attack for a physiognomic analysis was Hitler's voice rather than his appearance. But he was prohibited from speaking publicly—that author was Theodor Haecker.

* * *

Hitler's voice and rhetorical technique, the central and most efficient medium of agitation and seduction since 1919, didn't only inspire revulsion, but, like his appearance, from the very beginning exaltation as well. Until 1928, Hitler spoke without loudspeakers; only little by little, but with growing virtuosity, did he begin making use of radio technology. It gave him a new and invisible "mass" of listeners: on the one hand, the sick and the elderly, children and housewives; on the other hand, workers in factories and clerks in the administration, and finally crowds on streets and squares. Not everybody was pleased with this obstreperous production. The painter Paul Mathias Padua depicted the scene in 1937; the *Berliner Illustrierte* provided a more realistic corrective that same year: a scene of paralysis, which Karl Löwith would hearken back to fifty years later in his autobiography [Fig. 45].

After the seizure of power and with the skills that Goebbels brought to the job, the propaganda machine evolved rapidly. In 1935, it already looked to the radio as the "mental center of armament of the nation"; in 1940, it spoke simply of "radio as the will to power."[21] From 1938, the Greater German Radio Broadcast System was "restructured"; the news programs constantly increased in number, while the announcers and technicians were demoted or simply incorporated into the propaganda apparatus. In order to reach the populace as widely as possible, the price of the so-called Volksempfaenger radio was reduced by the factor of ten, with great success. Around 1933, there were five million radio listeners, in 1939 more than ten million, in 1943 sixteen million.

Conservative cultural critics loathed the radio. As early as 1929, Max Picard, in his successful book, *Das Menschengesicht* [The Human Face], gave a bleak prognosis, easily applicable to television today:

In radio, however, all we are left with is the inhuman apparatus, which simply strings everything together without connection. All that matters is *that* something is strung together; the *what* is of no concern. . . . Just like man today doesn't add, subtract, multiply, and so forth by himself, because he has a calculator to do this for him, just like that he has the radio as a machine for registering events; today man no longer needs to apperceive himself at all. Man seems to stand outside of the events and things, the radio carries them toward him and as though he were a god, his purview graciously scans the events that the radio parades on past him. . . . The radio doesn't merely report history, it appears to make history. The world appears to come out of the radio. Man certainly still sees things and events that happen, but the *happened* becomes real only when the radio has reported the event or the tabloid has provided pictures of it. . . . With this kind of apparatus Hitler had an easy time reshaping the existence of man in his—Hitler's—image.[22]

Of course, less critical listeners could be intoxicated by the radio and would adore Hitler's voice, for example the Georgian writer Robakidse

Figure 45. Since Hitler's true strength had always been oratory, pictures of Hitler speaking existed from the beginning. Here is a depiction by the painter Paul Mathias Padua from 1937. That same year, the *Berliner Illustrierte* published a photo report entitled "A People Listens to Its Führer." Karl Löwith reproduced the series in his memoirs, under the title "The Face of Germans During Führer Speeches": exhausted, in bad humor, or morose.

in 1939: "Behind the words of Adolf Hitler I always feel the reverbera-
tions of this voice. When he speaks, he is so seized by his words that from
time to time you lose the sense that this is the voice of an individual
human being at all. Truly, here appears the figure [gestalt] of the German self."[23] Kurt Tucholsky comments much more soberly to Walter
Hasenclever on March 4, 1933:

Yesterday we put in a radio and heard Adolf. My dear Max, what a strange experience. First Göring, an old, bloodthirsty shrew, screaming bloody murder. Very
disturbing and disgusting. Then Goebbels with his glowing eyes who spoke to
his people,* then *Heil* and roaring, commands and music, long pause, the Führer takes the rostrum. So at last, he was supposed to speak now, the one who . . .
I took a few steps back from the apparatus, and I confess I listened with my
entire body. And then something strange happened. Because then there was
really nothing. His voice isn't as unpleasant as one should think—it smells a bit
of trousers-seat, of man, a bit unappetizing, but other than that fine. Sometimes
he overdoes the screaming and vomits into the microphone. But other than
that: nothing, nothing, nothing. No tension, no climax, he doesn't grab me; I
am too much of an artist not to admire the artistry in this kind of guy—if there
were any artistry. Nothing. No humor, no warmth, no fire, nothing. He doesn't
say much more than the most stupid banalities, conclusions that are none—
nothing. *Ceterum Censeo*: I have nothing to do with this."[24]

Obviously, this would change soon. In November of 1933, Victor Klemperer heard the "mostly hoarse, strained, agitated voice, long passages in
the whining tone of a sectarian preacher";[25] and a few years later other
radio listeners too, for example the writer Theodor Haecker, heard
nothing in their Volksempfänger but "the horrible disease and the
depravity of the voices, their emptiness and their 'possession'—and that
is no contradiction—the spiritual stupidity and dumbness in the bellow-
ing mask."[26]

A native of pietist South Germany, Haecker had converted to Catholi-
cism in the early 1920s. As an essayist he had worked on Kierkegaard
and Cardinal Newman, had written cutting satires of war enthusiasm
during the First World War, but also against the Jewish press. A frequent
collaborator of conservative periodicals such as *Der Brenner* and *Hoch-
land*, in 1932 he wrote a study on Virgil, of which the new regime greatly
disapproved. Here he propagated the notion of an Occidental-Catholic
German Empire against the system of the "Third Reich." Although he
had been a member of the Reichskulturkammer [Chamber of Culture]
since 1934 as well as of the Reichsschrifttumskammer [Chamber of Lit-
erature] beginning two years later, the Bavarian political police imposed
on him a prohibition of public speech. In 1938, he was forbidden to

---

*Tucholsky is imitating the slightly Dutch tint of the dialect of Goebbels's native Rhine-
land: ". . . den löichtenden Augen, der zum Vollik sprach . . ." Trans.

write. Today Haecker is regarded as one of the spiritual fathers of the "White Rose"; since 1941 he had been a friend of the Scholl family.* He died in 1945. In his diaries between 1939 and 1945, and with growing horror, he recorded an acoustic portrait of hell:

[November 1939:] I have been horrified latterly at the capacity of the human voice, quite apart from what it says, simply in itself, to express the spiritual extinction of a whole people; and not merely individually, but to betray, to express and proclaim it typically, representatively. The voice of the *announcer*.

[November 1940:] "Three hundred thousand kilograms of bombs rained down on Birmingham today," Herr Goebbels announces through the voice of the German Radio Mission. But really, Ladies and Gentlemen, you ought to listen to the voice! But they have not got "second hearing," they hear and they do not hear. They have no conception of what is going on in Germany today, nor consequently of what will happen in Germany tomorrow. It is appalling to think that something so transitory as the human voice should have been chosen to reveal the depravity and the curse of a whole people, louder and more unmistakably even than its actions. How simple it looks: you have only to listen, and you will know everything! But the people listen, and when they listen they hear nothing but their own voice—praising and adoring them. . . .

1st January [1943:] Now you can already hear the howls and the whines of the demons more clearly in their dread-filled phrases. It is the last breathless gasp of the crazed man who runs amok, just before the end. An official, public call to hate![27]

What seems remarkable in these entries, although many entries could be cited in their stead, is the religious fury with which Haecker reacts not only to the Führer's voice but also to that of the announcer or any number of orators on the radio. He doesn't doubt that they are the "voices of evil," although an impartial modern-day hearer would probably find the announcements especially, which were spoken by select actors, sounding quite cultivated. Even the news of the time does not sound particularly shrill; certainly not in the recordings archived in the German Broadcast Archives in Frankfurt. If anything, only the reports of the Wochenschauen newsreels or from "Fox' Tönender Wochenschau" (which was broadcast until 1941) might have warranted Haecker's physical revulsion—but they are not commented on in his diary. Perhaps he had tuned his radio into a long-wave transmission, perhaps he simply owned a bad radio set. But Haecker wasn't attacking technological lacks: "Their voices, my God, their voices!" he noted on April 20, 1940. "I am overwhelmed anew by all that they betray. Their deadness is the most

*"White Rose" was the name of a student-led resistance group active in Munich in 1942 and 1943. Led by the siblings Hans and Sophie Scholl, the group mostly passed out pamphlets agitating against the Nazis. In 1943, the group was arrested and all its members executed. Trans.

frightful thing about them. The stinking corpse of a *vox humana*! Death, disease, and lies, and a solitude proud of being deserted by God."[28]

Presumably the Christian writer hated especially the notion of the so-called Deutsche Sendung with its double meaning, since he thought of "Sendung" (which in German can mean "broadcast" as well as missionary or prophetic receptivity) as a Christian notion desecrated by the Nazis. It is only consistent for him to demand a different tone of the preachers of the Holy Scriptures: "[April 1940:] What the preachers of Christ's words need is surely a new voice, and a different manner? . . . The style current now has surely become a quite shapeless, rusty old container[.] Both unnatural and contrary to nature, as well as unspiritual. A painful, false note, enough to make a man of the present day run away. Is there not a correlation between evil will, erroneous thought, and forced or false feeling (and what may it be?)."[29]

It is true that those responsible for NS broadcasts toyed with the double meaning of the word *Sendung* broadcast, mission. From the very beginning they delegated the vanishing grade of Christian religious consciousness to technology. One of Hitler's most fanatical devotees, Eugen Hadamovsky, *Reichssendeleiter* [chief of broadcasting] between 1933 and 1942, set the tone for this delegation: "What the edifice of the church is for religion, that is what the broadcast media will be for the cult of the state," he writes in 1934 and the religious allusion isn't intended merely as an aperçu: "I don't mean the broadcast system in the purely physical-technical sense, but ultimately in the spiritual sense of 'Sendung.' Everyone active in broadcasting is a carrier of the national socialist 'Sendung,' a propagandist and an apostle of the idea. . . ."[30]

That the exact opposite was true, that in reality the religious sense of "Sendung" had been displaced onto technology and that once again the principle of literalness in dealing with intellectual substance had won out—Haecker anticipated it, but he couldn't formulate it. Instead, he showed himself overjoyed in April of 1940 over the invention of the record, with the help of which one could capture the voice of evil, very much in the spirit of Cesare Lombroso and traditional criminology, which had up to then known visual methods of identification exclusively. Only in the 40s and towards the end of his life, Haecker finally abandoned the physiognomic dictate of the equation of genotype and phenotype. In his posthumous essay "Kierkegaards Buckel" (Kierkegaard's humpback), he showed that a small humpbacked man with a "thin voice" could nonetheless be an exceedingly rich intellect.

Faces Toward Death: Klaus Richter's Portrait of Hitler

With the invasion of Poland on September 1, 1939, Hitler entered the eastern territory that in the coming years was to fatally represent the "lost German face." The notion of repatriating Germans into the regions of Europe with the greatest concentration of Jews rested on concepts correlating race and space, body and nourishment. Even if, according to recent research by Götz Aly and Christopher Browning, the NS leadership conceived of the campaigns against the Jews as resettlement plans, either to Madagascar or simply further to the East,[31] the dehumanization of the victims took its course toward the literally final act. In a secret dossier from 1936, Hitler had blamed this on the Russians; Germany had to protect itself from them because "a victory of Bolshevism over Germany . . . [wouldn't] lead to another Versailles treaty, but the final destruction, even extinction of the German people."[32]

Between 1939 and 1945, the number of concentration and death camps rose from seven to twenty-two, with more than a thousand so-called *Aussenlagern* [subcamps]. We have evidence of industrialized murder in the camps from 1941 onward, preceded for years of course by the projects of eugenics and euthanasia. Films such as *Der ewige Jude* [The Eternal Jew] and *Ich klage an* [I Accuse], both from 1940 and premiering under Hitler's frenetic applause, provided the attendant propaganda for the "killing of unworthy life." In a highly symbolic gesture, the Germans had in the pogroms of November of 1938 smashed the shop windows, which could have offered the aggressors one last glimpse at self-recognition. The pensive self-image dispersed before the agitated and agitating racial image, and this new image called for an other, a negative "gestalt" or, better, "countertype," as the Leipzig psychologist Erich Jeansch had described it in 1938. As if the intention to kill had assumed a form and had suffocated any mimic empathy, the latter was displaced as a survival technique into the camps, into the everyday practice of destruction itself. Grete Salus reported from Auschwitz:

Their day began by scrutinizing the supervisor's face, trying to guess what kind of day it was. There were many shadings:

Uninterested—this meant a jackpot for us, we could try a few things and bring things along in our pockets.

Interested—that was unpleasant and brought surprises of all kinds.

Soldierly and breezy—this was bitter. We had to brace for frequent checks and penalties.

The worst—mild and gracious. Then all the sick were thrown from infirmaries, all mattresses tossed into the courtyard for reasons of public health, and other such humane motions.

We had already seen many faces, one uglier than the next, but the real grimace showed itself only under the SS cap and it drove us nearly insane with its grin. I envy those who have never seen all that can hide behind human faces.

A sweet, gentle woman's face—twisted into the enjoyment of the suffering of helpless people at her mercy.

The face of an even-tempered matron—torn open by the demoniacal lust for causing more pain.

A quiet, noble face—it turns stony, cruel, and cold at the first entreaties of tormented, badgered people.[33]

Satirizing and caricaturing the perpetrators had to fail when compared to experiences like this, as did even the silent film this report originally accompanied. And of course, there was a far greater number of "positive" images of the dictator in currency than of alarming ones. "To think that this face has managed to start this war, and we didn't wipe it out! And we are millions strong, and the earth teems with weapons, there is enough ammunition for three thousand years, but that face is still here, stretching wide high above us, the gargoyle of the Gorgon, and we have all turned to stone in murdering." Thus writes Elias Canetti in his diary in 1942.[34] Only the emblem of the Totenkopfverbaende [Death's Head Squads], the death's head itself, and the attendant bodily figure of the naked skeleton of the murdered could become the symbols of the camps—concentration camps as well as later the POW ones.

While the war took its course and while the camps put the principle of biologic "selection" into practice, Germans continued to be conditioned physiognomically—at first through film. The propaganda minister had built up the film industry parallel to the radio. Since 1939, he had not been working solely on ideological films, but also above all to find a coherent format for the Wochenschauen news reels. Beginning in 1939, theaters were obligated to show them before the feature presentation. The reels were stretched to forty minutes in length, were made more interesting and current, and thus inspired the population to head to the theaters even if the main feature was not really worth it. Between June of 1939 and June of 1940, theater attendance rose by almost 90 percent.[35] Hitler kept a close eye on the Wochenschauen, controlling both content and format. For good reason he didn't want to see his speeches reproduced in the original voice, but with a commentator; it is to be conjectured that he wanted to preserve the aura of his voice. Before the war he appeared in about every third Wochenschau, usually in the context of some festivity. But the handpicked cameramen were told to stick to certain shots and wide angles.[36] After 1941 he increasingly forbade filming him; the Wochenschau was told to focus on the soldiers to strengthen the troops. Hitler made his last appearance in the Wochenschau of April 4, 1945. It shows him at a reception for the Hitler Youth in the Reichskanzlei gardens.

But physiognomic conditioning continued in the old-fashioned sense as well, that is to say in the service of the national portrait gallery, which the people itself provided and which was created for them primarily by photographers. Some studied *The Language of the (German) Countenance* as such,[37] others rhapsodized over *The Countenance of the German*

Woman,[38] or tried to demonstrate "the overcoming of death through spirit" by depicting *Immortal Soldiers* in death masks.[39] At the same time, Goebbels suppressed Wochenschau sequences that showed *actual* German casualties or wounded. Instead, the audience was treated to extensive obsequies for fallen "comrades." It was only fitting that in 1940–41 alone three books appeared that dealt with Walter Flex, who had written after all, with "Wallenstein's Face," a cult classic of the Thanatos-inflected attachment to the face of a Führer.[40] A photo volume such as *The Mother's Countenance*[41] gave an idea of the origins of their heroic sons. *The German People's Face: Flanders and Norway*,[42] in contrast, promised more "ancestry" than ancestral pride or merit. While August Sander had long turned to landscapes, Willy Hellpach completed his *German Physiognomy* in 1942. Intended as a "Foundation [Grundlegung] for a Natural History of the Faces of the Nations," it was, in spite of its fashionable title, probably the only book that used these terms really purely in the sense of geographically variable facial landscape, looked at with Lavater in mind.

In natural science as well the positions calcified. In Königsberg, Konrad Lorenz pushed German biopsychology to its theoretical limits. His ambitious, supposedly Kant-inspired study on "the congenital form of a possible experience" was published, quite tellingly, in the *Journal of Animal Psychology*.[43] Quite possibly he wrote it during his military service in a military hospital in Poland as a biological version of Worringer's thesis on the sequentiality of "abstraction and empathy" in human and cultural history. Just like Worringer, Lorenz understood the phenomenon of mimic-physiognomic empathy, the childlike animation of the inanimate, as the sequel to abstraction, as a later stage of development. But even more important than this development was Spengler's thought that all empathy corresponds to a state of domestication, in its full sense of becoming a domestic animal, and thus to a weakening of what Lorenz called the "schemata." In this concept he totally naturalizes Worringer's "abstraction." It is not fear of the world around him that leads archaic man to develop mannerist forms for the mortification of space, but instead the other way around: the biological schema of good and evil, ugly and beautiful, the clarity of gestalt recognition, takes primitive man by the hand, as it were, and guides him safely through evolution. That we "so often react to an open brow, a glowing eye, or a good profile, although we know we have fallen for our congenital schemata [!] so frequently before,"[44] becomes for Lorenz a signal for nature's intent. Society has to respect this intent:

Since we recognize the functions of these congenital schemata as a last sheet anchor for the civilized peoples threatened by the destructive tendencies of civilization, the tolerable racial composition of a given people attains an entirely new significance in our eyes: It is after all one of the main preconditions for a normal functioning of the schemata. The "confusion of good and beautiful" that attaches to our reactions to our fellow human beings with the full stubbornness of the schema, gives ethical value to the aesthetic. [. . . We mustn't] ignore the deeply human reaction to aesthetic schemata, if we don't want to simultaneously hurt natural selection toward greater ethical value.[45]

Lorenz's essay found little mention after the war. It took more detailed scrutiny of his position in the NS state to actually expose him to public criticism[46]—perhaps for the first and the last time.

When the text appeared in 1943, "natural selection" had of course already cast its die: against the Germans. In January, the Sixth Army capitulated in Stalingrad—a defeat that triggered massive warmongering at the home front (Goebbels's famous Sportpalast speech) as well as merciless persecutions (mass deportation of Sinti and Roma, and of Dutch, Greek, and Macedonian Jews). In March, at Auschwitz the large crematoria with their gas chambers were completed; in June, the Allied air raids began.

*   *   *

In the years between 1941 and 1943, Hitler appeared less and less in the Wochenschauen reels—and the doctors among their viewership diagnosed a physical transformation when he did. Since 1941 his mimic expression appeared "stunted," the left arm increasingly stiff and often held at an angle, without actually bearing any weight. According to Ellen Gibbels, the Berlin neurologist de Crinis diagnosed Hitler with Parkinson's disease in 1941. One year later, Hitler's butler Linge states: "At the end of 1942, when the battle for Stalingrad entered its critical phase, his left hand began shaking. He had great trouble suppressing it or hiding it from visitors. The left hand pressed to his body—or held by the right—he attempted to hide his condition, which was very difficult especially since similar symptoms soon occurred in his left leg."[47]

In 1943, there was no more doubt. In 1944, the impairment of his movements—always also including mimic ones—became obvious. Hitler's personal physician, Morell, notes minor or major problems almost daily. Many visitors at the time described his outward appearance:

Leni Riefenstahl saw Hitler for the first time in three years on March 30, 1944: "I noticed his caved-in appearance [gestalt], his shaking hand and the unsteadiness of his eyes—Hitler had aged years since our last encounter." . . . Walter Schellenberg met Hitler for the first time in a while in the middle of 1944: "His back was very stooped and his movements were slow and cumbersome. His left arm shook so violently that he constantly had to hold it down using his right.

Only his voice remained strong and full." Goebbels gives us an idea of Hitler's physical decline in his diary entry of June 6: "From the distance you think you are looking at a deeply afflicted, bowed-down man, whose shoulders are threatening to give way under the burden of responsibility."[48]

As though this decline was more evident to an artist's gaze than to anyone else, there is a portrait of Hitler, painted by Klaus Richter, which deserves the moniker portrait more than any other. Apparently Richter did not oppose the regime very much initially. In 1933, a painting of Hitler from his hand adorned the cover of the periodical *Die Woche*. In the summer of 1941, Hermann Göring invited him to the Führerhauptquartier, Hitler's headquarters, in Rastenburg, in order to work on a portrait of him. Hitler was there for a meeting with Mussolini and so the painter had the opportunity to sketch Hitler directly. Immediately upon his return he set to work on the painting. Even the painting's title has a story behind it. First Richter titled it "Portrait/Adolf Hitler/1941" on the back of the painting. Then, worried that the painting might be discovered, he titled it "Portrait of a worker / of the J. P. Bemberg Corp. / who greatly resembles / Adolf Hitler." Finally, in 1945, he provided the painting with both the correct signature, "Klaus Richter 1941," on the bottom right and the title "Adolf Hitler 1941" on the upper left.[49]

The painting differs clearly from the other paintings created since 1933, especially for the grand German art exhibitions. Based on the models provided by Heinrich Hoffmann's photographs, most of them reproduced nebulously what George Orwell had described as "a pathetic dog-like face, the face of a man suffering under intolerable wrongs."[50] The paintings by Heinrich Knirr, Ernst Heilemann, and Hermann Jacobs, and to a certain extent the famous "Kragenbild" (the painting of Hitler with the upturned collar) by Willy Exner, give an idea of the excitement that surrounded this man at all times—usually through the literal excitement of his surroundings: the wild, cloudy sky in Knirr's painting, the unstable blue background in Jacobs's painting, the unquiet play of the light in Exner's, and the agitated blue in Heilemann's. At the same time, they unwittingly create the impression of a not entirely successful game of dress-up: For example, Heilemann presents Hitler in an oversized blue suit, and Hubert Lanziger depicts Hitler as a standard-bearer in an image that became a popular postcard [Fig. 46]. Hitler's favorite paintings, according to Henry Picker, were "in particular the one by Frank Triebsch (*Picture of the Führer*) and that by Professor Conrad Hommel (*The Führer on the Battlefield*)."[51]

It is impossible that Hitler saw Richter's portrait, but it was shown publicly on several occasions since 1945 and offered for sale in 1966. In 1977, it aroused the interest of museum director Eberhard Roters. The

Figure 46. A selection from the plethora of Hitler portraits based on photographs by Heinrich Hoffmann: Ernst Heilemann, Hitler in a blue suit; Hermann Jacobs, Hitler in brown-ochre representative uniform; Willy Exner, the "Kragenbild" (with the collar turned up).

fact that Berlin possesses two copies of the painting, one in the German Historical Museum and the other in the Municipal Museum, recently inspired Dominik Bartmann's report on the two versions, both of which are thought to be originals, and the painting's history in general.[52] That history is dominated by a legend. Supposedly, during his visit to the Wolfsschanze* Richter not only was able to observe Hitler in conversation from a hideout, but also witnessed Hitler flying into a fit of rage. Mussolini, the story goes, had mentioned the word "Jew." "Hitler hearing this word and arguing excitedly was the same thing. Post-haste Richter sketched the expression. It has been passed down to us in this painting from 1941."[53] This according to the reports of the antiques dealer Lüder H. Niemeyer, who offered the Hitler portrait for sale in 1966. Later reports (1970) from Hilde Richter-Laskawy, the painter's widow, do not mention this scene, which only Richter himself could have told her. Certainly, the painting shows a pale fellow with a slightly opened mouth. But does it really show the "insane demonical possession" of a man "whose psychosis clearly emerges here, at least indicating the criminal elements of the entire . . . National Socialist system"?[54] Others among Richter's portraits are characterized by a striking paleness, for example that of Göring, or that of Erwin Redslob of 1943. The question is whether, without the helpful commentary, one couldn't look at the Hitler portrait entirely differently [Fig. 47c].

By all accounts Klaus Richter, a student of Lovis Corinth and an academic, seems to have been quite in demand as a painter since the 1920s. A member of the Association of Artists in Berlin since 1929, he served as its chairman until 1933 and, after a brief break, again from 1937 until 1940. In that year Goebbels allegedly ejected him from his position. Whether he secretly was for or against the regime is not really of interest for the evaluation of the painting. Someone who doesn't know anything of Hitler's history won't find much more in the painting than the atmosphere of a pale man with a somewhat perplexed expression and an open mouth. This detail, the slightly opened mouth, indeed lends the face a central mimic quality. Together with the bourgeois correction of his coiffure—the famous strand has been combed out of the face—the mouth for the first time enters the picture as a real part of his body. It is larger than usual, because open, but not too large, well-proportioned, perhaps even embellished. That no other painters or sculptors hit upon this idea of depicting the world-famous demagogue literally as a "persona," as the appearance of a voice, the way Richter does here, shows

---

*"Wolfsschanze" was Hitler's code name for one of the headquarters of the German Wehrmacht, which became officially known as "Führerhauptquartier." Located in what is today Poland, it was the site of Claus Count Schenk von Stauffenberg's unsuccessful attempt on Hitler's life in 1944. Trans.

Figure 47a, b. Klaus Richter supposedly did the preliminary sketches for his portrait of Hitler in the summer of 1941 in Rastenburg (they are dated 1942 and 1943, however). Besides the painting, which survives in two versions, there are two remarkable sketches of the same date. All three pictures taken together mark the only serious attempt at a Hitler portrait of which we know. Figure 47d shows Hitler's head on a postcard of 1933 for comparison. Potentially the painting had another portrait as a model: the painting of Charles V by Christoph Amberger (1506), following Titian. Only here do we find a similar open mouth in the depiction of a ruler.

47a

47b

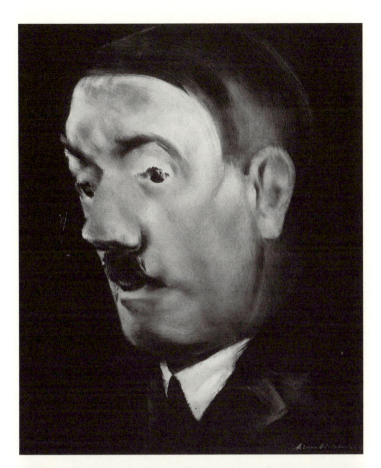

47c

47d

47e

47f

their general lack of ideas and false respect on the one hand, and Richter's inventiveness on the other. For the caricaturists had long taken advantage of this possibility, beginning with Heartfield, who depicted Hitler as a hyena with a wide-open muzzle running over fields strewn with corpses or, in his montage "Schluckt Gold und redet Blech" (also from 1932), Hitler with a wide-open mouth, all the way to Chaplin in whose Hitler movie the oral speech comes to destroy the very medium, the silent movie.

But were there models for Richter's oil painting? A postcard from 1933 could have been one relatively vulgar template: "The Chancellor at Lake Obersee near Berchtesgaden," resting after a hike and looking morosely to the right. The painter Richter gave his object a lower forehead, he set the chin back a little, pulled the gaze pensively to the ground, and of course moved the person into a dark room analogous to Hoffmann's early portraits. Only the misshapen, blunted nose might be perturbing if one thought of an Aryan ideal rather than an individual model. The facial expression doesn't bespeak the figure's insanity, if anything the painter's. He has made the Führer his own quite intimately. He has approached the topos of the "great little man" from the "little" side and portrayed a bourgeois, appearing almost anxious but dapperly attired.

One of Richter's contemporaries, Ulrich Gertz, reported in 1978 that the painter had sent photographs of his portraits of Göring and Hitler to his friends and acquaintances, "commenting on them in letters"[55]— probably in a caricaturist mode after all. Richter is universally described as an exceedingly educated man with great knowledge in the history of painting. Given that, it is imaginable that he did not restrict himself to depicting the "little" part of the "great little man," but that the painting's posture and expression are meant to travesty a "great" man as well. And this great man can be found. If we believe at least parts of the story told by the antiques dealer Niemeyer, then Richter did his session with Göring before he painted Hitler. Richter entertained Göring with anecdotes about "his colleagues Titian and Cranach on the one hand and the sitter Charles V on the other."[56] And in fact one could think of Titian's ruler portraits of Charles V or of its counterpart by Christoph Amberger from the Berlin Gemäldegallerie when looking at Richter's Hitler. The gaze is directed in the same direction (only laterally transposed), the mouth similarly half-open—a very unusual mimic quality in a ruler's portrait as such, not however in conjunction with the famous Hapsburg lip, and it was after all from the Hapsburg world that Hitler came.

Many years after the war Rudolf Kassner, who was fascinated by the ominous chin together with the smooth brow, described Amberger's painting: "Some may call his features uncreative. But that isn't it, rather it is as though the happy affiliation with a great dynasty, the imperial crown, the fact that one is the premier man in the world, itself already implied the solution to so and so many problems, of most terrestrial ones. Or as though the most complete relaxation would have to result when a world empire was put at one's feet like an unfurled world map."[57] Kassner couldn't have known Richter's painting of Hitler. He had long since moved to Switzerland. And yet he sees with uncanny accuracy the "great man" in Amberger's portrait as a counterimage to Richter's "little" one: both with their "world empire" put at their feet "like an unfurled world map." In just that July of 1941, when Richter was allowed to observe him from his hiding place and sketch him, Hitler was deciding with Göring and others on the conquest of Russia and the Großdeutsche Reich was within his reach.

Of course, the painter Richter gave his dictator a smooth brow as well, but it is clouded. Above all the man doesn't look in the same direction as the emperor. The head, originally looking to the right, is turned to the left, as though from east to west, into that direction in which Germany had lost its face in 1918 and in which it was at risk of losing it once more. Traces suggesting that it was painted over can still be found. It is the gaze to the left, as it were to the West—but what a repressed, fearful, expressively stunted gaze it is compared to the curious gaze Charles V casts toward the East. And what a production of the *typos* of the political salvation story, the opportunity of whose realization had been missed. "It isn't about being alone before God, but being it as an emperor," Kassner summarizes pithily in 1954.

"The Führer Has Become Very Stooped": Physiognomic Pathology

On July 20, 1944, Claus Count Schenk von Stauffenberg made an attempt on Hitler's life in Rastenburg, the Wolfsschanze in East Prussia, the very place where Klaus Richter had produced the last known live sketches of Hitler. The circumstances of the assassination attempt are as well known as the consequences. After denouncing the plot as the work of "a very small cabal of power-hungry, unscrupulous, and at the same time criminal, stupid officers," that very night Hitler swore bloody revenge over the airwaves.

Mass arrests ensued; some seven thousand perpetrators and suspects were rounded up and brought before the courts. Two hundred of them were condemned to death and executed. According to Albert Speer's testimony, which appears to have been reported incorrectly, Hitler had the films of their executions shown repeatedly for his pleasure.[58] What he saw here, as well as the executions that he had ordered since 1933 in league with his own "cabal of power-hungry, unscrupulous, and at the same time criminal" associates, seemed to pertain to nothing other than the establishment of a new leadership for the transition to surrender. Even if the resistance fighters were not really recognized after the war, as Joachim Fest wrote in 1994, even if they were regarded as adherents of the system in disguise both within and outside Germany,[59] and even if their death-defying assertions of social outrage, sense of justice, and familial pride were widely regarded as masks—the idea for which they eventually died or suffered remained untouched by it. The same went not only for aristocrats and officers, but, as detailed analyses of the resistance movements have since made clear, also for Communists, Social Democrats, no less than for Sinti and Roma and in general all who put up any kind of resistance against the regime. Since the real intellectual elite of Germany or the German-occupied territories had long since been driven out or murdered, the persecution and extermination of resistance movements created a new figuration of "merit and ancestral pride," as Ludwig Justi, director of the National Gallery and head of the National Collection of Images, had wanted to found for the emperor before the First World War: "The nation honors in gratefulness its great men and at the same time it erects a monument of its own age, its continuity, and its greatness." Were they "great" men and women? Until recently, detailed research has not been able to establish why this particular group expressed itself so secretly against the extermination of Jews. But it has nonetheless shown the phases of reflection, the desperate conspiracies, and the sense for civic and social responsibility. In any case, as though by some logic of media history, the men and women "of merit" after July 20, 1944 appeared in just that modern form that had disgusted Justi back before the First World War. "Just as the noble disposition of the ancien régime relates to the sober calculus of the present moment, thus relates the old princely gallery of honor to the modern state's delinquent album."

Another aspect of this development points back to the time before the war. Helmuth Plessner's subtle second-degree physiognomy, his laboriously deduced concept of the "inviolability of dignity," was central to the thought of the conspirators of the Kreisau circle; at least in its main figure, Helmuth von Moltke. It is probably from there that the concept, mediated by Carlo Schmid, made its way into the first article of the German Basic Law of 1949.[60]

From 1940 onward, as resistance in Germany was getting organized ever more urgently, the regime created its Valhalla around the secret center of the Führer's skull [Fig. 48]. The 1940 volume of *The Art of the German Empire*—opening with a coal drawing of Hitler by Otto von

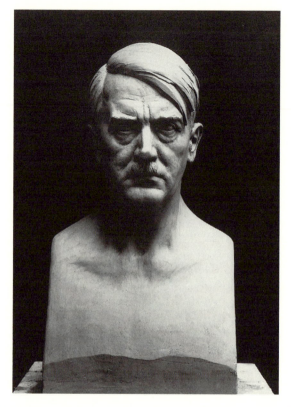

Figure 48. Hitler bust, probably by Josef Thorak, plaster, undated. The completely exhausted look is due to the lighting.

Kursell—is mostly devoted to German sculpture. It starts with the works of Arno Breker, then turns to the statues of the exhibition *1813–1815 Great German War of Liberation*—with its busts of the generals Scharnhorst, Schwarzenberg, Nollendorf, Yorck, Tauentzien, Radetzky, Wrede, and others—and finally presents its own gallery entitled "The Countenance of the Captain of Armies": il Duce by Josef Thorak, Moltke by Richard Knecht, Hindenburg by Arno Breker, Ludendorff by Fritz Klimsch, Brauchitsch by Hermann Joachim Pagels, Göring by Hans Haffenrichter, von Reichenau by Bernard Bleeker, and Keitel once again by Pagels. In its November issue the magazine presented its Valhalla of "Self-portraits of German Sculptors," with busts by Johann Heinrich Dannecker, Schadow, Rauch, Klimsch, Kolbe, Scheibe, Behn, Kölle—Breker was missing. The series continued with new depictions of Breker's works, then explicitly in 1943 with the two galleries "Depictions of German Musicians" (April) and "Poets of Our Time" (October). Among the musicians there were a fair number of names still well-known today, such as Furtwängler, Strauss, von Karajan, Backhaus, Pfitzner, and Knappertsbusch; among the poets most are forgotten today, for example Kolbenheyer, Seidel, Emil Strauss, Schäfer, and Miegel.

All in all, these galleries combined into a Valhalla of about forty-five heads other than those of the Führer and all those faces that only appeared in the retrospectives of individual sculptors: for example, those of Josef Thorak, Richard Scheibe, Georg Kolbe, Bertel Thorvaldsen, Ulfert Janssen, Fritz Klimsch and, again and again, Breker. All of them were set in scene in photographic reproductions and their perusal conceived as an intimate *en face* experience. Thus they finally rendered obsolete Ludwig Justi's objection from 1913 that sculptural monuments cannot really reach out because their face tend not to be very visible. Here, then, was a collection in the style of a family album of pompous body and phrenological architecture. One might have enjoyed them had not war and mass murder been their preconditions. No caricature touched on this sepulchral passion more than one drawn for the *Kladderadatsch* in 1933 [Fig. 49], for it intimated that the sculpture of this once again cruelly literalized "Bild-hauer" (sculptor, but literally "picture hitter") implied bloody sacrifices.

*   *   *

After the assassination attempt, Hitler's body went into steady decline. The medical diagnoses and eyewitness accounts from the time increasingly point toward Parkinson's disease. Ellen Gibbels reports minutely:

Goebbels's press secretary, von Oven, saw Hitler on August 5, 1944: "He has become an old man. He walks slowly and very stooped, as though under a heavy burden. . . . His hands are shaking, which he tries to conceal—in vain—by constantly burying [them] deep in his pockets." General Choltitz wrote after a meeting on August 7, 1944: "Then I stood before him and saw an old, stooped, bloated man with thin gray hair, a shaking, physically exhausted man." On August 11, 1944 General Kreipe had the impression that "the Führer has become very stooped. . . . He often shakes violently." General Warlimont says of August 1944: "Stooped and pulling his legs behind him he came into the situation room. . . . Bent down, his head deep in his shoulders, he crouched on the chair that had been provided for him. A quivering hand held on to the map table." . . . General von Manteuffel experienced Hitler on December 12, 1944 in the FHQ Ziegenberg: "A stooped figure, with a pale, bloated face, collapsed in his chair, his hands shaking, hiding as far as possible the left arm, which was violently shaking. . . . He walked dragging his leg."[61]

All of these descriptions, along with the doctors' diagnoses at the time, confirm what Gibbels identifies as a case of "idiopathological Parkin-

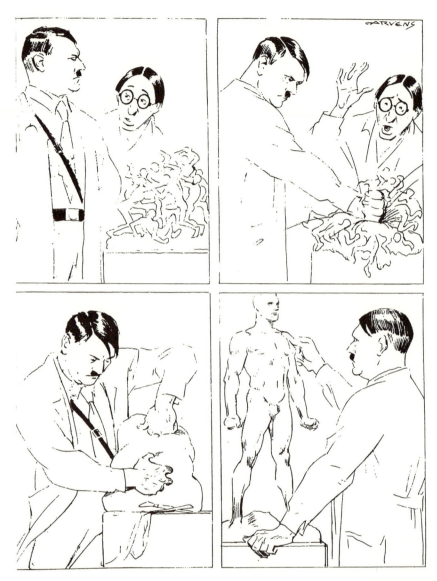

Figure 49. Hitler and his murderous fist literalized as "Bild-hauer" [in German, "sculptor," but literally "picture hitter/smasher"] of his "new man." A drawing from *Kladderadatsch* 86 (1933).

son's";[62] not however a "postencephalitic" one (actually the more frequent diagnosis), which would have already showed symptoms around Hitler's thirtieth year.

Nevertheless, Hitler apparently remained fully present intellectually. Not only was his voice still "clear and full," but also his memory was still functioning. His personal physician, Morell, who stayed with Hitler until April 21, 1945, testified to excellent memory for numbers, statistics, names, and spatial arrangements. Reports from briefings as well as Bormann's dictations confirm this. According to Percy Ernst Schramm, Hitler managed to baffle the general staff again and again with his memory, making his arguments hard to refute.[63] The clinical diagnosis seems clear. Up to the moment when Hitler put a pistol to his temple, he was in control of his own person and knew what he was doing. "Judging from the cited eyewitness statements as well as the confirmable reports of the last phase of Hitler's life, we can reasonably exclude the possibility of a decline in his intellectual abilities."[64]

Excursus on Speer's Last Führer Photograph

How thoroughly conditioned the facial attachment of Hitler's surroundings was in spite of his inexorable physical decline becomes clear in one of the most peculiar episodes from Albert Speer's *Erinnerungen*, which appeared in English as *Inside the Third Reich*. On March 18, 1945, Speer, in his capacity as secretary of armament [*Reichsrüstungsminister*], had sent Hitler a memorandum in which he declared that Germany was no longer able to pursue the war and that the final collapse of the German economy was imminent. Moreover, he wanted to inform Hitler of his rescission of Hitler's "scorched earth" order, which he had been subverting for a while already. The briefing was scheduled for the evening before his fortieth birthday. In this context he asked "Julius Schaub, Hitler's adjutant, to tell Hitler that I would like to have a photograph of him with a personal dedication for my impending fortieth birthday. I was the only close associate of Hitler's who had not asked him for such a photograph during the entire twelve years. Now, at the end of his rule and of our personal relationship, I wanted to let him know that although I was opposing him and had had to face up to the fact of defeat, I still revered him and valued the distinction of a dedicated photograph."[65] That same night Hitler gave him a photograph in a silver frame and a red leather case, apologizing for the slightly illegible dedication. The dedication, according to Speer, was nonetheless "unusually cordial." On May 1, when he had returned to Hamburg from his last visit with Hitler and heard of the latter's suicide, he remembered the picture: "When I unpacked my bag I found the red leather case containing Hitler's portrait. My secretary had included it in my luggage. My nerves had reached their limit. When I stood the photograph up, a fit of weeping overcame me. That was the end of my relationship with Hitler. Only now was the spell broken, the magic extinguished."[66]

Apparently Speer, whose relationship with Hitler reputedly had a homoerotic tinge to it, was able to transfer this closeness onto the distancing image only at the very end. What remains odd is that he was so certain of his own survival, for he requested the picture of a man he knew was about to die, not least perhaps because of the rescission of the so-called Nero order, which Speer, as Hitler's deputy, had himself effected. Whether Speer's were tears of relief or of loss, or perhaps both, is not clear from his account. After all, written down many years later, they come from a pensive distance. At the end of the book he cannot even remember that he had seen the picture before and even studied its dedication. Not only a student of literature might hear in this story a clear echo of "Wallenstein's Face," even if travestied. As though tailored by Walter Flex to fit the new situation, Speer is attached to his "Wallenstein" and his face, with the difference that here the leader/seducer dies and his vassal survives instead of sacrificing himself.[67]

In his memoirs, Speer made mention of several physiognomic episodes. They were all set in the sphere of the dialogical relationship of closeness and not in the realm of "figures." Perhaps, as an architect, he didn't need to convert living organisms into architecture. Not only did he notice Hitler's "many facedness" from the very beginning; even years later he never tired of relating the dictator's way of dealing with his face and eye. For example, he recalled that Hitler was in the habit of always giving the same picture of himself to his paladins, one designed by Gerdi Troost, but that Göring had had the photograph enlarged.[68] For example, he told Gitta Sereny of an episode in 1936, when Hitler forced him to engage in a staring contest at the dinner table. "It was he who looked away first. I had won."[69]

Nonetheless, or perhaps because of this, he sounds startled when he recounts a statement by an American historian who asked Speer about his attitude toward the forced laborers. In his capacity as secretary of armament, Speer had visited the Linz steel works in the summer of 1944

. . . where prisoners were moving freely among the other workers. . . . When I asked them, just to make conversation, whether they would prefer to return to the regular camp, they gave a start of fright. Their faces expressed purest horror. But I asked no further questions. Why should I have done so; their expressions told me everything. . . . An American historian has said of me that I loved machines more than people. He is not wrong. I realize that the sight of suffering people influenced only my emotions, but not my conduct. On the plane of feelings only sentimentality emerged; in the realm of decisions, on the other hand,

I continued to be ruled by the principles of utility. . . . What disturbs me more [than the Nuremberg indictment] is that I failed to read the physiognomy of the regime mirrored in the faces of those prisoners—the regime whose existence I was so obsessively trying to prolong during those weeks and months. I did not see any moral ground outside of the system where I should have taken my stand.[70]

The physiognomy of the regime, its "true face," the photographs of unspeakable terror and this terror itself became visible for Germans only after the opening and liberation of all the concentration camps and labor camps.

Chapter 6
Picturing Horror 1945–1949

In early January of 1945, the Soviet army captured Auschwitz and liberated the camp's few survivors—approximately eight thousand of once 1.5 million people. The remaining concentration camps were liberated in April and May—among them Buchenwald, Sachsenhausen, Flossenbürg, Dachau, Ravensbrück, Mauthausen, and finally on May 7, 1945 Theresienstadt. What the Allies saw and often recorded in photographs in these camps was to become an irreversible watershed in the history of moral as well as political consciousness. The "icons of annihilation,"[1] the images of piled bodies, of emaciated, brutalized, violated people not only confirmed the reports, but also triggered the shock that an irredeemable crime had been committed. The discussion that has circled around the inconceivable ever since has also been a discussion of the notion of the depiction and the concept of being an eyewitness of singular events. The role the physiognomic conditioning that had preceded it for decades played in the confrontation of the populace with the pictures has not been part of that discussion. Rather, all media historians work with or on photographs and films as techniques of mass-media education, which go along with the claim on documentary and evidentiary status and are accepted as such.

But the physiognomic prehistories of the kind of perception these media historians now called for, the subject of this study, cannot be set aside so easily. After all, the same media now called on had disseminated the regime's message between 1933 and 1945 and shaped the portrait of the Führer since 1923. The intricate link of the thinking in lines of ancestry (racism and the doctrine of hereditary racial characters) with the development of photography in science and society; the facial devotion to the "great man" in the hypnotic look on the Führer/seducer; the dehumanized counterimage of the Jewish or otherwise ethnic face; the stinging loss of face through the defeat of 1918; and the decisive role of the "vision" in the project of a German "re-erection"—this entire physiognomic field with its insistently established qualities had to collapse in 1945. Someone thus conditioned could no longer believe in any image, even those that wanted to demonstrate to Germans not only military defeat but also a moral loss of face of incalculable consequences. Almost automatically one took to coping mechanisms that had been effective after the First World War, in hopes that they might help even over this indescribable abyss. The very first publications after 1945, only marginally political, were at least in conflict with this seductive option. They were fragments of a grand confession and shards of a confession of megalomania, all scenes from the collapse. Erich Kästner for example tells of how he got a hold of a job as a screenwriter and of a shoot—one day before Hitler's last birthday—in Mayrhofen in Bavaria: "The camera whirred, the floodlights gleamed, the director gave his orders, the actors acted, the director of photography cavorted about, the stylist overdid the make-up and the village's youth observed us in amazement. How much greater would have been their amazement if they had known that the film cassette of the camera was empty! Reels are expensive, a bluff is enough. The title of the masterpiece, 'The Lost Face,' is even more profound than I thought."[2]

Johannes R. Becher, an expressionist poet and later secretary of culture in the GDR, a Communist and early emigrant to Moscow, steeps himself in the same face, writing a play entitled *Das Führerbild* [The Führer's Picture] even before the end of the war.[3] The text stages the story of the Third Reich as a physiognomic family drama. The father has had business dealings with Jews, whom he later betrays, the son is with the SS, the daughter loves a painter named Rocholl, who looks at society from without. Rocholl paints three paintings: one of the Führer, one of the father, and one of the soldiers at Stalingrad. All three paintings are conceived as "living images," not as depictions. Whether Becher has a particular painter in mind could not be established. What is clear however are Becher's epigonal verses, his socialist realism—"and when hunger calls out in the picture [. . .] / then the painted paints itself in us / and becomes the picture of our conscience"—and well-calculated physiognomic dramaturgy: "Mr. Rocholl, paint / this picture: the Führer stomping out the hell fire" of Communism after the burning of the Reichstag. But the painter has something different in mind. His Führer portrait shows an insurgent among a captive crowd, as even SS officer Leutwein notices: "The sketches of the Führer / on his sketchpad, I must say / if he were an enemy, I would not be surprised. / And on the last sheet he has / drawn, I see it clearly, the visage / clearly, the sailor's visage / perhaps this, perhaps this is then his Führer!"[4] The Jew Rosenzweig too recognizes the icon of the sailor Reichpietsch who incited the revolution in Kiel in 1917: "Stretched-out arms. Nothing but arms. / And only one face in the crowd, just a face . . . / as though HE was the Führer, that's / how this countenance strikes me."[5] The painting of the father renders him as a Dorian Gray; the old man suddenly recognizes something terrible in his image: "What kind of picture has that villain painted of me—such a naked, soulless knob—In my armchair before my desk, quite paternal . . . that's what the hoary old man looked like . . ."[6]

While Eva, the daughter, wants to avert her eyes and constantly covers her face with her hands, the painter Rocholl voyages to the front and meets the exhausted soldiers. They ask him for a final portrait. The painter becomes a front painter of an entirely different kind, an eyewitness to the "testament of horror" that the soldiers hope to bequeath on him. But while he paints, a voice comes from off-stage and demands that a sailor be included in the image: "Paint the one for all of them." More voices appear until the entire scene is drowned out by a choir. It is the choir of the reanimated: "Let us climb from our graves! Germany wants to be roused from the grave."[7] Even if Becher's turn toward the sound of the human voice is not really surprising for a former expressionist— what is remarkable for a physiognomist is that he outlines a return from the society of the face to that of language. The *Picture* shows the dying gathered; it was in sung, and especially spoken, language that the living came together.

Ernst Jünger was similarly thinking about survival in terms of physiognomy after 1945. In his small book *Sprache und Körperbau* [Language and Build][8] he reconstructs the bodily orientations of someone awakening from death or a deadly accident; what is the hand, what is right and left, head and toe, above and below, what are the five senses. Jünger concludes his book with this succinct formula for survival:

Let me say one last word on the occasion for this study. In the midst of the terrible misery and the moral and physical destruction that surrounds us, many may puzzle at someone who would occupy himself with these questions and may question it as luxury and excess. But it isn't simply Horatian equanimity in turbulent times that is evidenced here. It is at the same time also the following: after an accident, after a sudden fall we first inspect our own body. We check whether we have remained unharmed. It is the same here: the first labor after the catastrophe is this locus and origin of freedom, the image of divine power.[9]

What German other than Jünger would have thought of himself as an "image of divine power" at this historical moment? Or was Jünger's book a response to Max Picard, a devoted physiognomist, who had taken stock of the notion of *Hitler in uns selbst* (Hitler in Ourselves) in 1947? No better record for the obsession among physiognomists could be found than the pages upon pages of settling scores with "Hitler's face" in the book. Although Picard was an acrimonious enemy of psychoanalysis, he now stuck subconsciously to the script of "remembrance, repetition, working through," which were for Freud the hallmarks of a successful therapy. Picard didn't even stop at embarrassing simple-mindedness in deconstructing the ruler-image, in effecting the long overdue disenchantment of "Wallenstein's Face":

The Leader [*Führer*] of a people had until Hitler always had a face that was clearly shaped and impressed itself upon those led by him. It is therefore again surprising that Hitler could count as a leader. For he had a face [. . .] that was so totally nothing as everything in Hitler was "total." It wasn't explicit, it didn't impress the follower, unless you want to say that the nothing of the Führer had impressed itself upon the nothing of his followers.—So long as there is a history of man, never has such a nothing presented itself as a leader-face before a people. There were kings with the faces of murderers or criminals, there were rulers' faces showing the insanity that cowers in hiding behind them, there were rulers who were weak in spirit and body and whose faces clearly bespoke this weakness; you notice the defect,—but this is unprecedented, that a "Führer's face" doesn't even express weakness, and the amazing thing is that Hitler didn't stand apart or in the background of the people and of history, like those weak rulers, but that instead he stood at the very front, for all to see, so that at times it seemed as though there existed only he alone,—and what was so visible? Nothingness—pure nothingness. That too is unprecedented; that one who styled himself as world history itself looked not like a mask, not like a costume of world history, but instead like nothingness. . . .

If you see the face just as it appears: an empty zero, an empty white surface, which has two black dots where humans have their eyes, and with a black line there where the mouth should be, if you have it before you just like this, then it stands there like one of those white plates with black lines and dots, mounted on a pole by the side of the road to warn drivers of the abyss behind the bend of the road. . . ."[10]

Hitler's face mutated into a road sign: not a bad physiognomic idea, but nonetheless a somewhat weak one, perhaps pointing in the direction of Hannah Arendt's incendiary formulation on Eichmann.

* * *

Picard gave expression to a disappointment that had always lurked behind the cult of Hitler's face as a ruler-face. This disappointment was half existential, half literary, but it was not political in the least. For in those months the politicians still calculated with the survival of the "Führer face." As before in 1923, the question became "What does Hitler look like?"—and fearing he might escape, the Allies commissioned templates for warrants featuring his potential disguises only shortly after the landing in Normandy. Everything was considered variable except for the eyes, especially hair, beard, and glasses. Apparently, however, the only thing the artist couldn't imagine from the models provided for him was Hitler as a bloated, sick wreck of a man. Instead he embellished Hitler to the fullest extent of his talents in each of the seven pictures, imbuing him with the air of a revolutionary, the intellectual, the professor, and even the entrepreneur[11] [Fig. 50].

Other writers of the period finally demonstratively opposed the physiognomic conditioning of the pre-war years, attempting to deconstruct face and bodily gestalt as central organs of human dignity and soul. Theodor Haecker's *Kierkegaard's Humpback* appeared posthumously, a small work defending the ugly appearance of a great intellect. The Heidelberg psychiatrist Hans W. Gruhle, who had once written the commentary for the great photo volume with death masks by Richard Langer, in 1948 settled scores with all kinds of physiognomic speculation in one fell swoop. His *Interpretive Psychology* was meant to reconstruct the gesture of empathy—similar to a small book on the portrait: *Study on Empathy for Expression.*[12] In pursuing the study of expression Gruhle was in tune with the science of his time. In the 1950s and 1960s the Americans pursued the topic extensively. How backward the classical study of images had become in comparison becomes evident in the "handbook" of the "portrait as form" published around the same time by the archaeologist Ernst Buschor, in whose hands the picture shattered tortuously into many subcategories: the mirror portrait, fugitive portrait, core portrait, *in nuce* portrait, power portrait, rank portrait, mimetic portrait, portrait of appearance, portrait of essence, existential portrait, formative portrait, portrait of illumination, penetrating portrait, portrait by proxy, mentality portrait, exterior and interior portrait, model-based and imaginary portrait, and lastly as a concession to historical memory and to photography: the designative portrait. Buschor maintained the old perspective of typization and classification and nonetheless splintered his own object: the human face.[13]

One of the first books published by a German physician after the war on the topic of "facial expression" devoted itself just as tortuously to that topic which under the dictatorship of heredity had disappeared from psychology or had been pressed into the service of selection criteria. *Ausdruckssprache der Seele* [The Expressive Language of the Soul][14] performed pragmatically what Jünger had outlined aesthetically in his idea of "language and build": the reconstruction of a living, acting human being with facial expression, gestures, voice, and the feelings of anger, exultation, mournfulness, revulsion, haughtiness, and so on that go along with them. Nothing does more to betray the almost pathological search for a norm of a living human being than the genesis of this book, which aims to show in its 275 pictures what cannot be shown, at least not in the "still image." He regretfully noted that he hadn't collected enough photographic material to demonstrate every expression: "In particular I sought in vain the more flamboyant facial expressions such as rage or those not liable to appear before a camera, such as revul-

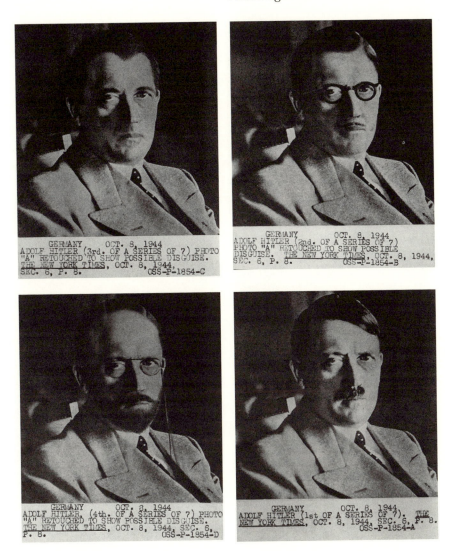

Figure 50. Hitler in the eyes of an American makeup artist after 1945. The U.S. Secret Service had these warrant cards created in case Hitler had not died but had instead managed to flee and change his appearance. It did not occur to the enemy artist that Hitler might end his life with a sick, bloated, palsied face. He shows Hitler as a mixture of entrepreneur and professor, agent and Russian intelligentsia.

GERMANY   OCT. 8, 1944
ADOLF HITLER (6th. OF A SERIES OF 7) PHOTO
"A" RETOUCHED TO SHOW POSSIBLE DISGUISE.
THE NEW YORK TIMES, OCT. 8, 1944, SEC. 6,
P. 8.   OSS-P-1854-F

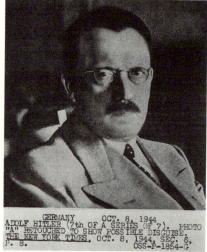

GERMANY   OCT. 8, 1944
ADOLF HITLER (7th OF A SERIES OF 7). PHOTO
"A" RETOUCHED TO SHOW POSSIBLE DISGUISE.
THE NEW YORK TIMES, OCT. 8, 1944, SEC. 6,
P. 8.   OSS-P-1854-G

GERMANY   OCT. 8, 1944
ADOLF HITLER (5th. OF A SERIES OF 7).
PHOTO "A" RETOUCHED TO SHOW POSSIBLE
DISGUISE. THE NEW YORK TIMES, OCT. 8,
1944, SEC. 6, P. 8.   OSS-P-1854-E

sion." But he did find a nurse: "She could reproduce almost every facial
expression I suggested with great empathy. I just had to name the content of the expression and to show what I myself thought the expression
should look like and almost without fail she recreated the desired
expression correctly." But the nurse didn't just imitate expressions,
above all she recreated gestures for the researcher: "I was forced to rely
on her collaboration entirely, for I had found no gestures in my case
histories."[15]

Lacking almost any scientific foundation, this book seems to have evolved in large parts from the wordless play between doctor and nurse, researcher and subject: the woman as pantomimic acrobat and mirror, following the scientist's clumsy mimic dictates in an unwitting Pygmalion parody. Even if the whole thing was probably rather comical, even if this researcher could complete his mimic palette—it was for good reason that this ambiguous play eschewed precisely that facial expression which, according to Darwin, really sets humans apart, and which would have been called for by the present historical moment: the expression of shame, of embarrassment—blushing. Only in the "Concluding Remark on the Reason for the Expressive Movements and Their Complementation by the Play of Pupils, Tears, and Blushing" does the author mention it, but then the book ends.

Remorseful self-indictments such as Albert Speer's, who puzzled at his own insensitivity vis-à-vis the suffering faces of the forced laborers in his conversation with an American historian, were relatively rare after the war. As yet there had been little information about events in the concentration camps, and the great trials in Frankfurt and Jerusalem still lay ahead. Thus it was possible for a number of publications to maintain the vision of the "great German in pictures" and thus the old project of the National Portrait Gallery of 1913. Paul Ortwin Rave, once assistant to Eberhard Hanfstaengl, and then director of the National Gallery in East Berlin, published at least one volume of what was supposed to be a three-volume project, *Das geistige Deutschland im Bildnis* [Intellectual Germany in Portraits], with an extensive account of the project's prehistory. Of the original plan to represent Dürer's, Goethes's, and Nietzsche's centuries, only Goethe's century materialized. The volume contained 338 portraits of famous men and women, "a band of highly gifted people, who created the splendor that illuminated their age from within."[16] As though nothing had happened, the author and longtime museum administrator laid out the conceptions of "physiognomy and artwork" that had motivated the project from its inception. To the book's reader and viewer he promised "a feeling of connection. So much lived life, so much affirmation of life seen face to face will also give wings to your will to life."[17]

At least Rave's gallery once again holds some Jewish faces: Moses and Dorothea Mendelssohn, Rahel Levin, Giacomo Meyerbeer, Henriette Herz, Heine, Börne, and Veit. Every face has a name and a short biography; all pictures are pictures of paintings or drawings or busts, none of them represents an actual photograph. The last portrait shows August Kopisch (1796–1853), the painter and writer who discovered the Blue Grotto at Capri and wrote the ballad, the "Leprechauns of Cologne."

Another essential building block for the reconstruction of the lost

German face was the rhapsodic commemorative volume by Robert Boehringer about Stefan George from 1951, which featured numerous photographs of the master, the "true face of secret Germany." But the way in which Boehringer leaned in over the "royalty" of the poet nonetheless bespoke the legacy of physiognomic conditioning and its mixture of geodesy and hope for greatness:

His picture around midlife: The profile of 1897 seems like a quattrocento bust. If you draw a straight line from the face by placing a sheet of paper behind it, left before the nose, then the modulation of the profile shows itself in the distances between this vertical and the [hair line], to the bulge of the brow above the eye, to the tip of the nose, to the upper and lower lip or to the chin. These distances vary greatly. The expression of great willpower in the chin is amplified by the lower jaw's ascending angle. The dark-skinned eye and the fleshless jowl give the head something unconditional, inescapable. Germans rarely looked so far from romantic, so unsentimental. Even the poet himself rarely shows himself in this remorseless nakedness. The photograph was made by Stoevig, a print of it hung in Lechter's study.[18]

Could someone conditioned by this tradition have devoted himself with the same exactitude and empathy to the images of horror that confronted Germans since 1945 in placards, tabloids, and educational pamphlets? The facial devotion of the "grandiose self" could function as a resistance mechanism on just that visual level at which the Allies presented their "shock photos." In the discourses of the Third Reich, physiognomic intuition was programmed to respond to power and innocence, greatness and figure, and not to powerlessness and guilt, gaze and countergaze. The documentary content of the early photographs, the reality principle, could thus be deflected by the concept of atrocity propaganda. This is how the article in the *Handbook of Newspaper Science* of 1940 had operated, anticipating all that was to come by attempting to debunk any German atrocities committed during World War I.[19] The face of the German people was to remain beautiful and clean, a landscape without guilt or shame.

In this spirit another photographic attempt at the project of "merit and ancestral pride" was made in 1952, this time not primarily concerned with dead Germans, but with the present elite—inspired by the right-wing photographer Erich Retzlaff. *The Intellectual Face of Germany*, conceived in 1944, was introduced by a long text by Hannes-Erich Haack, which dealt with the situation of the lost war and the terrible accusations of genocide. But it was precisely at this historical moment for Germany, the tenor of the piece went, that a reflective return to its own elite was more necessary than ever, since the masses needed the enlightened ones. The photographs were kept in the style of the 1930s: extreme close-ups and strong light in the eyes predominate. The volume

shows no Jewish faces, only church functionaries and philosophers, writers and politicians, scientists and engineers, musicians and painters,
totaling about ninety people.

Two years later, in 1954, a volume called *Das deutsche Antlitz in fünf
Jahrhunderten deutscher Malerei* [The German Countenance in Five Centuries of German Painting] was published—another proud line of ancestry
in the shape of a book, with an introduction by Rudolf Kassner. Here
too there were no Jewish portraits, but instead an angry taking to task of
the demystificatory pathos of psychoanalysis.

As early as October of 1945, the Allies began completely dismantling
the NSDAP, including its art possessions. All militarily or politically questionable objects were collected under the supervision of Captain Gor-
don W. Gilkey and brought to Washington, D.C., among them more
than eight thousand paintings, including the Hitler pictures and busts
thus far still in existence.[20]

That same year, George Grosz, in the United States since 1933, completed his large-scale oil painting *Cain or Hitler in Hell*. It was an attempt
at allegorizing "the 'apocalyptic beast' in human form, which sits there
in the hellish landscape designed by himself." The painting is of a giant
figure in the pose of the "little man," who sits down in exhaustion and
wipes the sweat off his brow. Grosz commented extensively: "Hatred is
what he sowed and hatred is what he reaped (both more or less symbolically): it is as if all those small human figures climb all around like hateful thoughts from the mud that was once a beautiful landscape, turned
into an infernal tumult in the wake of this monster. 'I bring pestilence
and the smell of death, I come from the ends of the earth, and where I
spit fire grows, death and slavery' (such are his thoughts). And as he sits
and looks sideways at the audience, there is hatred, fear, and distrust in
his gaze"[21] [Fig. 51].

* * *

Grosz's painting came too late to be a cenotaph. Motivationally as well
as technically it was the product of a bygone era. For what the prepara-
tions for the various trials now gathering steam—Nuremberg 1945–46,
Jerusalem 1961, Frankfurt 1963–65—and the trials themselves generated in terms of eyewitness accounts led to the complete disappearance
of the figure of the "great little man" as cause; or perhaps more accurately, they led to the figure's redistribution onto Hitler's executioners
and filled it with new contents. In printing *The Face of the Third Reich*,
Joachim Fest stated that as early as 1963 that Hannah Arendt's "ingenious formula" of the "banality of evil" did not apply solely to Adolf
Eichmann, for whom it was coined (incidentally also somewhat physiog-

Figure 51. George Grosz, *Kain oder Hitler in der Hölle* [Cain or Hitler in Hell], completed in his American exile.

nomically), but, "it describes at the same time the type which with very few exceptions, was prevalent in the innermost circle of the top [Nazi] leadership."[22]

The facialization of the Third Reich at Nurmeberg did not proceed from this somewhat jarring physiognomy of the perpetrators, but from the physiognomy of the victims, which, as Speer put it, "mirrored" the former. The strategy of the prosecution, which Cornelia Brink has traced, was largely founded on optical proofs in film and photography. Both, however, needed to be commented on by living eyewitnesses—and they were in the best cases—in order to become truly comprehensible. In his harrowing 1945 account of such a documentary film, Wilhelm E. Süskind wrote of the danger of aestheticizing even films like these in perception. "On the other hand: How else should we document these things? They can be fully documented only to those who have seen them immediately."[23] The confrontation of the evidence with the perpetrators became a physiognomic test in the second degree, itself a long-standing juridical tradition.[24] With the Nuremberg trials, Brink writes, a new photographic motif emerged: the image of the perpetrators on the dock.

The hope was that one would be able to read in the faces of the accused what their character, dispositions, and reactions were, in order to qualify the evidence as truly evident. "The perpetrators were arrested in the image; for the majority of the German population, this probably meant a lifting of their own guilt."[25]

These juridical proceedings too then did little to bring physiognomic thinking to an end. The psychology of expression was criticized,[26] but the academic field of expressive psychology achieved unimagined popularity in the United States in the 1960s. It is clear only today that it boiled down to a mechanic decipherment of facial expressions for industrial application or for the animation of robots.[27] The only real treatment the physiognomic received in the history of ideas, in which racism and "grandiose self"-portrait, thinking in expressions and figures, pictorial propaganda and facial devotion were understood as one lethal alloy, didn't come from science but from literature. None other than George Orwell, who had portrayed Hitler's "holy dog-face" so memorably in 1940, wrote immediately after the war the great dystopian novel *1984*, the story of how "Big Brother is watching you" (1949). It was a novel about the hellish conditions of a society that has put itself under televisual surveillance and can spot dissidents just from their facial expressions. It is a society that pictures its foes physically and cultivates its hatred in daily filmic rituals—the two minutes of hate against the Jew Goldstein. It is a society that is politically occupied with the fabrication of its own history, and otherwise degrades its people into a herd of ugly bugs. The motif of the "great little man" who overpowers everyone becomes evident in protagonist Winston's relationship with Big Brother—Thomas Mann had spoken of "Brother Hitler"—whose face pursues the spectator on countless posters all across the city. It is a face between Hitler and Stalin, closer perhaps to Stalin—the Wallenstein-motif in its most overpowering guise. The novel ends in a cruel historical punch line. The insubordinate Winston, who dares to love a woman, is harried and tortured almost to the point of physical annihilation. Finally he is made to sit at a table before a cage, which has a trap door in the shape of a face on the one side, behind it a hungry rat. During the interrogation he is forced to speak his answer through a mask—if he answers incorrectly, he is threatened with the release of the trap door. It was a kind of torture reported by the *Völkischer Beobachter* as an example of Bolshevik atrocities.[28] Whether it is true or pure propaganda: no historian and no psychoanalyst could have put the German panic, to which physiognomically speaking Hitler owed his breakthrough, more succinctly and more memorably. The subhuman, the rat, threatens *literally* to gnaw off the European man's face, and that such a thing is possible the psychotic German people believed they had learned from the East, from

Russia, from the direction of their hoped-for face. Orwell didn't expand on this context, perhaps he didn't even guess it. Instead he made his protagonist in a moment of devotion sink to his knees, a scene that Walter Flex had mapped out thirty years earlier in its basic features: "He gazed up at the enormous face. Forty years it had taken him to learn what kind of smile was hidden beneath the dark moustache. O cruel, needless misunderstanding! O stubborn, self-willed exile from the loving breast! Two gin-scented tears trickled down the sides of his nose. But it was all right, everything was all right, the struggle was finished. He had won the victory over himself. He loved Big Brother."[29]

Notes

Chapter 1

1. On the following cf. Brigitte Hamann 1999, pp. 395–98.
2. Hitler 1939, p. 165.
3. Hoffmann 1974, p. 33. Kershaw 1998, p. 633, n. 90, points to the role this picture played at the twentieth anniversary of the declaration of war in 1934.
4. Rave 1968, p. 74.
5. Justi 1936, p. 252.
6. Philipp 1991.
7. Justi 1936, p. 252.
8. Ibid., pp. 254–55.
9. Ibid., p. 264–65.
10. Rave 1968, p. 74.
11. Rave 1968.
12. Justi 1936, p. 255.
13. See Hüppauf, in Hirschfeld 1996, pp. 53–103.
14. Gantef+hrer 1997, pp. 433–46; see also Philipp 1991 and Brückle 2000.
15. Schoeppe 1937, p. 37.
16. Consider, for example, the works of Helmar Lerski and Erich Retzlaff.
17. Schoeppe 1937, p. 37.
18. In the novel *Malte Laurids Brigge.*
19. Rave 1967, p. 77.
20. Picker 1951, pp. 697–98.
21. Ibid., p. 714.
22. Hellpach 1942, p. 175.
23. Günther 1922; on his professional genesis and the scientific discussions on his teachings cf. Hoßfeld 2000, esp. p. 85.
24. Lavater 1775–78. Lavater research has seen a remarkable renaissance in recent years; cf. the bibliography in the catalogue by Gerda Mraz and Uwe Schögl 1999.
25. See Regener 1999.
26. Gall 1798 and Carus 1925 [1853].
27. Heinroth 1833.
28. Finkielkraut 1997.
29. On the following statements cf. the catalogue by Wilderotter and Pohl 1993.
30. Quidde 1977, pp. 19–20.
31. Quidde 1977, pp. 7–9. 1926 this study was reprinted, and Quidde wrote an *aide mémoire* mostly vindicating the emperor.
32. E. Müller 1914, p. 13.

33. E. Müller 1927, p. 76.
34. Klebinder 1913, p. 12.
35. See in the catalogue by Wilderotter and Pohl 1993, pp. 26–27.
36. I am indebted to Nicolaus Sombart for this information.
37. Grupp 1995, p. 210.
38. Kerr 1997, p. 252.
39. Op. cit. Picker 1951, p. 704.
40. Lavater 1777, vol. 3, pp. 222–23 [My translation. Trans.].
41. Goethe in conversation with J. D. Falk, summer 1794, in Goethe 1889–96, *Goethe Gespäche*, vol. 1, p. 150.
42. Carus 1925 [1853], p. 506.
43. Hofmannsthal 1956, p. 483.
44. Boehringer 1951.
45. Cf. Schmölders 1999.
46. S. Breuer 1995, p. 21.
47. Ibid., p. 75.
48. Haeckel 1914, p. 6.
49. On this topic cf. D. Breuer 1997.
50. Panizza 1923, pp. 214–15.
51. Before 1960, the book sold 120,000 copies; the *Wanderer between Two Worlds* sold more than a quarter million copies between 1916 and 1917, a success that was to repeat itself after 1945. Cf. Medicus 1999, pp. 98–99.
52. Picker 1951, p. 305.
53. Flex 1918, p. 42.
54. Ibid., p. 43.
55. Haeckel 1914, p. 4.
56. Ibid., p. 5.
57. Goebbels 1992, vol. 1, p. 95.
58. The Schiller citations follow the German Library edition (vol. 16), edited by Walter Hinderer. The passages are to be found at pp. 151, 199, and 134 respectively. [See Schiller 1991.]
59. Simmel 1968, pp. 484–85.
60. For example in the *Iconographie Nouvelle de la Salpêtrière* of Charcot.
61. Nietzsche 2000, p. 240 (Book 2, Nr. 40).
62. Timms 1986, pp. 37–39.
63. For example by Ferdinand Tönnies in the famous book of the same name (Tönnies 2001).
64. Storfer 1935, pp. 155–56.
65. Hitler 1939, p. 204.
66. Cf. Lethen 2002.
67. Kershaw 1998, pp. xxi–xxii.
68. Stierlin 1976.
69. Neckel 1991 does not touch on the national history of this shame.

Chapter 2

1. Kershaw 1998, p. 101.
2. Ibid., p. 110.
3. K. Müller 1954, p. 338.
4. Hitler 1939, p. 213.

5. Kubizek 1953, pp. 142–44. For a critique of Kubizek's account, see Kershaw 1998, p. 610, fn. 128.

6. B. Hamann 1999, p. 425, fn. 18.

7. Speer 1976, p. 308.

8. Hanfstaengl, 1970, p. 36. Hanfstaengl was also known as Hitler's "piano player" because he was asked to play Wagner for him over and over again.

9. Göttert 1998, p. 234: "When calm, the voice was a deep baritone, yet even in a high tenor pitch it managed without switching to falsetto, thus staying a strong voice coming from the chest. Hitler didn't just utilize its volume, without which a developed prosody is impossible, but he also used the seductively melodic figures in deeper ('warmer') registers. By and large we thus get a picture of total expressivity without monotony, the perfect mixture for suggestiveness."

10. Cf. Scholdt 1993, p. 209.

11. Fest 1974, p. 536.

12. Robakidse 1939, p. 10.

13. Hüppauf 1993, p. 56. I owe the following information to that study.

14. Hitler 1939, p. 167.

15. Kershaw 1998, p. 647, n. 31.

16. Mommsen 1996, p. 201.

17. Pessler, 1916, p. 100; cf. Brandt 1993, p. 290.

18. Pinthus 1994.

19. Ibid., pp. 27–28.

20. Boehringer 1911, p. 86.

21. Gundolf 1920, pp. 217–19.

22. Pinthus 1994, p. 272.

23. The book is by Fritz Klatt, a teacher of the Freie Volksgemeinde Wickersdorf; cf. Klatt 1921, p. 53.

24. The book is by Gustav Mensching, a theologian.

25. I am indebted to Hanns Zischler for pointing out the author Hans Kayser and his book.

26. Laid out by the Catholic philosopher Ferdinand Ebner; see Ebner 1919, p. 93.

27. Heidegger 1962, pp. 207–8.

28. Ibid., pp. 320–22.

29. Spengler 1932, p. 55.

30. Jünger 1932, p. 131.

31. Cf. Barry Eichengreen in *Die Welt,* October 26, 1999.

32. Heiden 1936, vol. 1, p. 134.

33. Fuchs 1902, addendum.

34. Hanfstaengl 1933 shows imitations of the Charivari caricature.

35. Herz 1994, p. 92.

36. Ibid., p. 93. The following exposition is also indebted to Herz.

37. Chamberlain 1928, letter of October 7, 1923.

38. Cf. Zelinsky 1976, p. 170.

39. Jaspers 1977, p. 101.

40. Kassner 1932, p. 67.

41. Hadamovsky 1936, p. 747.

42. Carus 1925, p. 397.

43. Brückner 1965 and 1978.

44. Cf., e.g., *Hände: Eine Sammlung von Handabbildungen großer Toter und Leb-*

ender (Hands: A collection of handprints of great living and dead men), published by Gebrüder Enoch Verlag in Hamburg in 1929.

45. Cf. below.
46. Transcribed from the typed original letter, archived at the Institut für Zeitgeschichte Munich, sign. MA 740.
47. Fest 1974, p. 540.
48. Turner 1987, pp. xi, 445.
49. Behrenbeck 1996.
50. Günther 1922, cited following the 1933 edition, p. 25.
51. Spengler 1932, p. 24.
52. Johst 1935, p. 206.
53. Fest 1973, p. 706.
54. Robakidse 1939, pp. 7–8.
55. R. Müller 1923, pp. 26–28.
56. Wolff 1989, p. 259.
57. Cf. Martin Blankenburg's broader bibliography on the "Sources of Physiognomics" in the Weimar Republic, in Schmölders and Gilman 2000.
58. On Kafka cf. esp. Peter von Matt 1983.
59. E.g., Jaensch 1930. Jaensch was a psychologist at the University of Leipzig.
60. In particular Lersch 1951.
61. The second volume appeared in 1922; a one-volume edition appeared in 1923.
62. Spengler 1928, p. 136.
63. Günther 1928, p. 21.
64. Cf. Chapter 5.
65. Lepenies 1976, p. 203.
66. Kershaw 1998, p. 248.
67. Spengler 1937, pp. 96–98.
68. Mendelssohn 1928.
69. Kershaw 1998, pp. 248–49.
70. Haffner 1989, p. 109.
71. Herland 1937.
72. A. Zweig 1928, pp. 172–73.
73. A. Zweig 2004, p. 2. Italics are the author's.
74. Matt 1983, p. 174. Von Matt analyzed the whole portrait.
75. Loesch 1935.
76. Brzsoka 1963.
77. Thiess 1923; second edition 1928.
78. Thiess 1931.
79. Mommsen 1989, p. 99.
80. Kessler 2000, p. 106.
81. Grupp 1995, p. 382, n. 14.
82. Ibid., p. 276.
83. Reck-Malleczewen 1970, pp. 49–50.
84. Klages 1971, pp. 603–8.
85. Schmölders 1999, pp. 403–22.

Chapter 3

1. Kershaw 1998, pp. 242–43.
2. Ibid., p. 240.

3. Cf. Köhler 2000, Klemperer 2000, and Schoeps and Schlör 1995.

4. Herz 1994, p. 100.

5. Ibid.

6. Ibid., p. 103.

7. Ibid., p. 111.

8. Loiperdinger 1995, p. 106, fig. 1.

9. Langer 1927.

10. E.g., Picard 1959 and Jaspers 1977.

11. Cf. the first chapter of this book.

12. Cf., in contrast, Schmölders and Gilman 2000 on the special role played by the famous Inconnue de la Seine in this dead men's society, 250–261. [The death mask of the "Inconnue de la Seine" was one of the most prevalent physiognomic images of the early twentieth century—sold widely as wall decoration and reproduced in countless photographs. According to its legend, the "unknown woman" was washed up by the Seine near the Isle de la Cité in Paris, and her death mask was taken from the famous Paris morgue by a medical assistant entranced by what became known as her "sublime" smile. Trans.]

13. On both books cf. Brückle 1997.

14. Brückle 1998.

15. Cf. Brandt 1993, p. 297–99.

16. Remark from a conversation with Alexander Kluge.

17. Herz 1994, p. 113.

18. *New English Weekly*, March 21, 1940.

19. Scholdt 1993, p. 81. The poem was written by Hermann Burte in 1931.

20. Scholdt ibid.

21. Eulenberg 1917. The book contains no pictures, but instead biographical portraits of "great Germans.".

22. Lübbe 1918, pp. 10 and 26.

23. Kassner 1910, p. 33.

24. Ibid.

25. Picard 1929, pp. 180–81.

26. Cf. Blankenburg 2000.

27. Benjamin 1999, vol. 2, p. 520.

28. Tucholsky 1972, p. 210.

29. Roth 1956, vol. 3, p. 689. Letter from the Harz Mountains to the *Frankfurter Zeitung* of December 14, 1930.

30. Tucholsky 1972, p. 10.

31. Steinert 1994, p. 142.

32. K. Müller 1966, p. 129.

33. Fest 1970, p. 31, following the protocol of the Hitler trial of 1924, Institut für Zeitgeschichte München.

34. Nissen 1928.

35. Herz 1994, p. 102.

36. Ibid., p. 163.

37. Ibid., p. 166.

38. Borrmann 1989, p. 26.

39. Herz 1994, p. 166.

40. On Goebbels cf. Moeller 2000, p. 380. The technique of mutually contradicting pictures was utilized again by the NS apparatus in 1940 when invading Alsace. In the brochure "All of our Hitler: How the Führer Has Been Portrayed to You and What He Is Really Like" (Berlin 1940), French caricatures are juxtaposed with Heinrich Hoffmann's photos.

41. Mayer 1999.
42. Ibid., p. 128 tells of Galton's "Life History Album."
43. Mürner 1997, p. 18.
44. Worringer 1997, p. x.
45. Worringer 1997, pp. 9–11.
46. Simmel 1901, p. 156.
47. S. Zweig 1930.
48. Kassner 1925, pp. 120–23.
49. Scholdt 1993, p. 49.
50. The poem cited is: Schumann, Heldische Feier, probably 1936. For citation and context see Scholdt 1993, p. 75.
51. Plessner 1999, p. 42.
52. Ibid., p. 68.
53. Ibid., p. 69–70.
54. Ibid., p. 77.
55. Ibid., p. 80.
56. Simmel 1902, p. 236.
57. Plessner 1999, p. 136.
58. Ibid., p. 122.
59. Ibid., p. 123.
60. Ibid., p. 115.
61. Ibid., p. 141–42.
62. Ibid., p. 194.
63. Friedell in Schaeffer 1929, pp. 9–10.
64. Rilke 1965, vol. 5, pp. 271–72.
65. Rilke 1966, vol. 6, p. 711.
66. Kassner 1932, p. 63.
67. Haffner 1979, pp. 42–44.
68. Herz 1994, p. 113.

Chapter 4

1. Speech of February 10, 1939, cited by Smelser et al. 1993, pp. 123–4.
2. Shirer 1941, pp. 421–22.
3. I. Müller 1991.
4. Hofer 1960, p. 36.
5. Cf. the reading provided by Köhler 2000, p. 196, who takes the figure in black armor next to Hitler to represent Barbarossa. Judging from the template, however, it simply represents the "leader" of the triumphal train from Ferdinand Keller's painting.
6. In Keller's painting, Wilhelm I parades in a quadriga pulled by white horses, followed by the crown prince on a black one, next to him Bismarck, and following him the generals Moltke and Roon.
7. A. Müller 1927, p. 22. Müller makes reference to Rathenau's book on the emperor from 1919 and suggests that its author may have been killed on account of this statement.
8. Hanfstaengl 1933, p. 15.
9. Fest 1970.
10. Arendt 1963, p. 51.
11. Wulf 1963, p. 199. Italics are the author's.

12. At the Kunsthaus Trittner. Thomae 1978, p. 163 thinks that it was probably the only one of its kind because this kind of exhibition was usually forbidden—for good reason.

13. But cf. Hoffmann's own recollections: here he dates a very similar photo of Hitler to 1922. Hoffmann 1974, pictures between pp. 63 and 65.

14. Hoffmann 1939, unpaginated.

15. Printed in the *Frankfurter Allgemeine Zeitung* of May 30, 1990 as a reaction to a report by Serge Klarsfeld.

16. Fest 1970, p. 100.

17. Meyer 1990, p. 374.

18. Jünger 1930, p. 11.

19. Jünger 1932, p. 122.

20. Ibid., pp. 42–43.

21. Jünger 1947, p. 254. Entry of May 4, 1943.

22. Jaensch 1930, pp. 113–14.

23. Schmölders 1994, pp. 242–59.

24. *Menschen der Zeit* [People of the Times] 1930, pp. 4–5.

25. Marcuse, 1975, pp. 145–46.

26. Schlichter and Jünger 1997, p. 497.

27. Schrade 1937, p. 4.

28. See also Brückle 1997.

29. On the omnipresence of the motif of the steel helmet in everyday life during World War I, cf. Hüppauf 1993, pp. 82–83.

30. Kroh 1934.

31. Lersch 1951; cf. Geuter 1984, p. 167.

32. Geuter 1984, p. 206.

33. Lange 1939, preface. Facial expression as muscle labor was studied in the nineteenth century by Duchenne in experiments.

34. K. Ganzer 1935, p. 238.

35. Engelhardt 1934, p. 5.

36. Brieger 1930.

37. Retzlaff 1930.

38. Lerski 1931.

39. Retzlaff 1930.

40. Lendvai-Dircksen 1942a. Cf. Brückle 1997, 1998

41. Hägele and König 1999, p. 69. Hans Retzlaff used the term "image" on an entire people, the so-called Siebenbürger Sachsen [Rumanian Germans]: "The Image of a German Peasant People," 1934 and 1936, and as late as 1959 under the title "Countenance of a German Peasant Tribe."

42. On the NS activities of the photographer cf. Philipp 1984.

43. Hellpach 1933.

44. Weingart 1985, p. 344.

45. Jünger 1932, p. 42.

46. Herz 1994, p. 53.

47. Ibid., p. 356, n. 58; Thomae 1978, p. 164 mentions the Berlin illustrator E. R. Vogenauer, who designed the postage stamps for Hitler's birthday in 1941 and 1942.

48. Picker 1951, p. 311.

49. Speer 1970, p. 87.

50. Herz 1994, p. 129.

51. Ibid., p. 136.

52. Ibid., pp. 134–35.
53. On the following cf. Loiperdinger 1995, pp. 79–81.
54. Moeller 2000.
55. Herz 1994, p. 356.
56. Kershaw 1998, p. 591.
57. Fallada 1932.
58. Most recently in *Der Spiegel* 43 (1999).
59. Kershaw 1998, pp. 529–31.
60. Koch-Hillebrecht 1999, chapter 2.
61. Riefenstahl 1993, p. 253.
62. Goebbels 1992, p. 1390. Koch-Hillebrecht (1999) looks to this as a key event in Hitler's love life. "Tamino sings that 'this portrait is bewitching' after being struck by the key excitation," he comments on Goebbels's entry. Cf. p. 115. However, the nonaggression treaty with Stalin, which presupposed this infatuation, had already been signed in August of 1939.
63. Herz 1994, p. 131.
64. Hentzen and Holst 1936.
65. Schrade 1937.
66. For the following cf. Schuster 1995, pp. 12–14.
67. Thomae 1978, p. 166 with very detailed information. For Richter's Hitler portrait of 1941, not mentioned here, cf. the following chapter.
68. All quotations that follow Boveri 1977, pp. 316–18.
69. Schuster 1987, pp. 12–14.
70. Wulf 1963 p. 393.
71. Frecot, Geist, and Kerbs 1972.
72. H.-D. Schäfer 1981.
73. Clauss 1941, pp. 46–48.
74. On Clauss cf. the monograph by Peter Weingart 1995.
75. Clauss 1941, p. 48.
76. Gereon Wolters recently distinguished "Race Clauss" from "Race Günther" [*Rassenclauss* and *Rassengünther* in German], and declared seeing in figures a version of intuition: an insufficient differentiation, for "figure" or "gestalt" also always refers to a certain consistency in the object, whereas facial expression always also refers to interaction. Wolters 1999, pp. 236–37.
77. Robakidse 1939, pp. 8–9.
78. De Boor 1985, pp. 321–22.
79. H.-D. Schäfer 1981, p. 200.
80. German public television channel ZDF recently showed film clips of Hitler's private pilot.
81. Cf. the study by Elizabeth Ullstein in the *New York Times Magazine* of June 13, 1943.
82. Cf. p. 00 in Chapter 2.
83. Cf. Brückle 1997, p. 12: "the retreat of the personal proceeds to the point of masquerade."
84. H.-D. Schäfer 1997, p. 217.
85. Ibid., p. 218.
86. All quotes follow Wühr 1939, vol. 1, p. 56.
87. According to rumors, Hitler occasionally listened to his own speeches as a relaxation method.
88. Cf. Matt 1983, p. 158.
89. Johst 1935, p. 205.

Chapter 5

1. See Schuster 1987, p. 24.
2. Cited in Sanders 1973, pp. 167–68.
3. Dodd 1939, pp. 64–65.
4. Shirer 1941, p. 17.
5. Nicholson 1939, p. 657.
6. *New York Times Magazine,* April 16, 1943.
7. Walt Disney Productions 1942. The film received the 1943 Academy Award for "Best Animated Feature."
8. Hägel 1995, pp. 47–60.
9. Scholdt 1993, pp. 199–200. I quote the text, which consists entirely of citations, without quotation marks for better readability.
10. Schmölders 1999.
11. Schack 1881.
12. Miltenberg 1930–31 and Herz 1994, p. 114.
13. K. Mann 1942, p. 236.
14. Reck-Malleczewen 1970, pp. 22–23, 49–50, and 75.
15. Herz 1994, p. 102.
16. Blumenfeld 1998, p. 265.
17. Orwell 1940.
18. W. Schäfer 1953. The Hitler quote [in the preceding paragraph] is reproduced in Matussek et al. 2000, p. 164.
19. Kuh 1934, p. 874.
20. Picard 1946, pp. 70–71.
21. Wessels 1985, p. 484.
22. Picard 1929, pp. 45–47.
23. Robakidse 1939, p. 11.
24. Scholdt 1993, p. 212.
25. Klemperer 1998, vol. 1, p. 39.
26. Haecker 1950, p. 44.
27. Ibid., pp. 2, 117, and 187.
28. Ibid., p. 42.
29. Ibid., pp. 45–46.
30. Wessels 1985, p. 121.
31. Aly 1995 and Browning 1985.
32. Hofer 1960, p. 85.
33. Salus 1981, p. 33.
34. Canetti 1978, p. 2.
35. Cf. Moeller 2000.
36. Ibid., p. 393.
37. Lang 1939.
38. Ganzer-Gottschweski 1939.
39. *Unsterbliche Soldaten* 1940.
40. The books were written by Johannes Banzhaf, Heinrich Lemke, and Emil Georg Zwahlen respectively.
41. Bäumer 1941.
42. Lendvai-Dircksen 1942b and 1942c.
43. Lorenz 1943.
44. Ibid., p. 313.
45. Ibid., p. 314.

46. Cf. Mehrtens and Richert 1980, pp. 189–91.

47. Gibbels 1994, p. 169.

48. Ibid., p. 175.

49. Bartmann 1999, pp. 306–7.

50. Based on Herz 1994, p. 125.

51. Picker 1951, p. 373, entry of May 5, 1942 from the Wolfsschanze.

52. Bartmann 1999, p. 303.

53. Ibid., pp. 307–8.

54. Thus writes Bartmann, ibid., p. 305.

55. Gertz 1978, p. 65.

56. Bartmann 1999, p. 307.

57. Kassner 1954, p. 7.

58. Speer later retracted his claim. In his 1969 memoirs he reports that he had seen "mostly lower ranking SS men" going to the showing of the films, but "not a single officer of the Wehrmacht attended" (Speer 1970, p. 395). Asked by Gitta Sereny about the film in 1995: "As far as I know Hitler never saw the film and I always said so. It wasn't his style to watch these things. I don't think he even looked at the photos, just like me" (Sereny 1995, pp. 526–27). Sereny also draws on the memoirs of Nicolaus von Below: "I eschewed looking at those pictures. Hitler too looked at them little, just like he didn't like to take note of the pictures of destroyed cities (ibid.). But cf. the contradictory account from Ursula von Kardorff of Pentecost Sunday 1945 in Kardorff 1992, p. 327, as well as that of Ruth Andreas-Friedrich of September of 1944, p. 170.

59. Fest 1996, pp. 324–69.

60. Moltke made Schmid's acquaintance on October 19 during a meeting of the Akademie für Deutsches Recht [academy of German law]. Schmid at the time was Privatdozent [adjunct professor] for State Law at Tübingen. He participated in at least three meetings of the Kreisau circle. Cf. Balfour 1972, pp. 163 and 243.

61. Gibbels 1994, p. 176.

62. Ibid., p. 188.

63. Ibid., p. 191.

64. Ibid., p. 195. The recently published study by Manfred Koch-Hillebrecht, *Homo Hitler*, 1999, contradicts these findings on account of most recent insights, which he however does not provide. See p. 85.

65. Speer 1970, p. 437. Friedländer 1982 is wrong on the origin of the picture; cf. ibid., p. 62.

66. Speer 1970, pp. 488–89. According to Joachim Fest, the photograph was taken away from Speer at his arrest, never to resurface.

67. Doubt has been cast on the entire episode on account of recent research. The historian Heinrich Schwendemann claims he found among the files a second memorandum dated the same day, which diametrically contradicts the first one and instead calls for the continuation of the war effort. This would explain why Hitler wrote such a cordial dedication on Speer's photograph. Cf. the report in the *Frankfurter Allgemeine Zeitung* of April 16, 2000, p. 52. According to Joachim Fest, however, Speer passed along his request for the photo with the first memorandum, as though to reassure Hitler of his undiminished loyalty. During the meeting on the eve of his birthday, he handed Hitler the second memorandum; if this is correct, Hitler's cordial personalization was written before it (conversation with Joachim Fest, July 28, 2000).

68. Speer 1970, p. 37.

69. Sereny 1995, p. 139.
70. Speer 1970, pp. 374–75.

Chapter 6

1. Brink 2000.
2. Kästner 1961, p. 96.
3. It was published several times in the Desch Verlag Munich, later under the title *Der Weg nach Füssen* [The Road to Füssen (1953)] as a text. In March of 1956 it had its premiere at the Gorki Theater (Berlin) with musical accompaniments by Paul Dessau, and was put on several more times until Becher's death in 1962. All citations follow Becher 1971.
4. Becher 1971, p. 747.
5. Ibid., p. 757.
6. Ibid., p. 785.
7. Ibid., p. 802.
8. Jünger 1947.
9. Ibid., p. 86.
10. Picard 1946, pp. 68–70.
11. Der Spiegel 19 (1998).
12. Gruhle 1948. Gruhle also published a separate book, *Über das Portrait* [On the Portrait].
13. Buschor 1961.
14. Leonhard 1949.
15. Ibid.
16. Rave 1999, p. xxii.
17. Ibid., p. xxx.
18. Boehringer 1951, p. 113.
19. See the entry "Greuelpropaganda" 1940, pp. 1372–88.
20. The remaining collections are today mostly under the administration of the German Historical Museum in Berlin.
21. Schuster 1995, pp. 378–79.
22. Fest 1970, p. 385, n. 43.
23. Brink 1998, p. 117.
24. Campe and Schneider 1996, pp. 153–82.
25. Brink 1998, pp. 118–19.
26. It was criticized by Alexander Mitscherlich; cf. ibid., p. 119.
27. Cf. the works from the school of Paul Ekman.
28. Kershaw 1998, p. 806, n. 108 references Nolte 1987, p. 115 and p. 564, n. 24.
29. Orwell 1954, p. 239.

Reference List

Catalogues and Collections

Film Museum, Potsdam, ed. 1998. *Leni Riefenstahl.* Berlin: Henschel Verlag.

Das Gesicht der Zeit. 1924. Exposition at the Kunsthalle in Mannheim.

Hanson, Patricia K., ed. 1999. *AFI—American Film Institute Catalogue of Motion Pictures: Feature Films 1941–1950.* New York: R. R. Bowker.

Honnef, Klaus, Rolf Sachse, and Karin Thomas, eds. 1997. *German Photography 1870–1970: Power of a Medium.* Cologne: DuMont.

The Jewish Museum, ed. 1995. *Die Macht der Bilder: Antisemitische Vorurteile und Mythen.* Vienna.

Mraz, Gerda, and Uwe Schlögl, eds. 1999. *Das Kunstkabinett des Johann Kaspar Lavater.* Vienna: Böhlau.

Pessler, W. 1916. Das Historische Museum und der Weltkrieg. *Museumskunde* 12, no. 3: 100.

Roters, Eberhard, ed. 1988. *Stationen der Moderne: Kataloge epochaler Kunstausstellungen in Deutschland 1910–1962.* Cologne: König.

Rochard, Particia, ed. 1989. *Der Traum von einer neuen Welt: Berlin 1910–1933.* Mainz: Verlag Hermann Schmidt.

Rother, Rainer, ed. 1994. *Die letzten Tage der Menschheit: Bilder des ersten Weltkrieges.* Berlin: Deutsches Historisches Museum (Ars Nicolai).

Velten, Andreas Michael, and Matthias Klein, eds. 1989. *Chaplin und Hitler.* Munich.

Volkmann, Barbara, ed. 1978. *Zwischen Widerstand und Anpassung: Kunst in Deutschland 1933–1945.* Berlin.

Kunstamt Kreuzberg, Berlin, and the Institute for Theater Studies at the University of Cologne, ed. 1977. *Weimarer Republik.* Hamburg: Elefanten Press.

Neue Gesellschaft für bildende Kunst. 1977. *Wem gehört die Welt: Kunst und Gesellschaft in der Weimarer Republik.* 4th rev. ed. Berlin.

Wilderotter, Hans, and Klaus-D. Pohl, eds. 1993. *Der letzte Kaiser: Wilhelm II im Exil.* Berlin: Deutsches Historisches Museum.

Primary Sources

Adler, H. G., ed. 1962. *Auschwitz: Zeugnisse und Berichte.* Frankfurt am Main: Europäische Verlagsanstalt.

Andreas-Friedrich, Ruth. 1947. *Berlin Underground, 1938–1945.* Trans. Barrows Mussey. New York: H. Holt & Co.

Arendt, Hannah. 1963. *Eichmann in Jerusalem: A Report on the Banality of Evil.* New York: Viking Press.

Balász, Béla. 1982. Der sichtbare Mensch. In *Kritiken und Aufsätze 1922–1926*. Munich.

Bauer, Karl. 1908. *Goethes Kopf und Gestalt*. Berlin.

Bäumer, Gertrud. 1941. *Das Antlitz der Mutter*. Berlin.

Becher, Johannes R. 1971. *Dramatische Dichtungen*. Berlin and Weimar: Aufbau.

Benjamin, Walter. 1999. Little History of Photography. Trans. Edward Jephcott and Kingsley Shorter. In *Selected Writings II*, Vol. 2. Cambridge, Mass.: Harvard University Press.

———. The Work of Art in the Age of Its Mechanical Reproduction. Trans. Edmund Jephcott and Kingsley Shorter. In *Selected Writings*. Vol. 3. Cambridge, Mass.: Harvard University Press.

Benkard, Ernst. 1926. *Das ewige Antlitz: Eine Sammlung von Totenmasken*. Berlin: H. Keller.

———. 1927. *Das Selbstbildnis vom 15. bis zum Beginn des 18. Jahrhunderts*. Berlin: H. Keller.

Blei, Franz. 1940. *Zeitgenössische Bildnisse*. Amsterdam: Allert de Lange.

Blumenfeld, Erwin. 1998. *Einbildungsroman*. Franfurt: Eichborn.

Boehringer, Robert. 1911. Über Hersagen von Gedichten. In *Jahrbuch für die geistige Bewegung*.

———. 1951. *Mein Bild von Stefan George*. Munich: Bondi.

Boveri, Margaret. 1977. *Verzweigungen: Eine Autobiographie*. Munich and Zurich: Piper.

Brieger, Lothar. 1930. *Das Frauengesicht der Gegenwart*. Stuttgart.

Buschor, Ernst. 1961. *Das Gesicht*. 2d rev. ed. Munich. Original edition, *Bildnisstufen*, Munich, 1947.

Canetti, Elias. 1978. *The Human Province*. Trans. Joachim Neugroschel. New York: Seabury Press.

Carus, Carl Gustav. 1925. *Symbolik der menschlichen Gestalt: Handbuch zur Menschenkenntnis*. 3d ed. Celle. Original edition, Leipzig: Brockhaus, 1853.

Cassirer, Ernst. 1953. *The Philosophy of Symbolic Forms*. Trans. Ralf Manheim. New Haven, Conn.: Yale University Press.

Chamberlain, Houston Stewart. 1928. *Briefe 1882–1924*. 2 vols. Munich: F. Bruckmann.

Christiansen, Broder. 1930. *Das Gesicht unserer Zeit*. Buchenbach in Baden: Felsen.

Clauss, Ludwig Ferdinand. 1941. *Rasse und Seele: Eine Einführung in den Sinn der leiblichen Gestalt*. 17th ed. Berlin.

Darwin, Charles. 1872. *The Expression of Emotions in Man and Animals*. London: John Murray.

Das geistige Gesicht Deutschlands. 1952. Stuttgart: Union Deutsche Verlagsanstalt.

Dodd, Martha. 1939. *Through Embassy Eyes*. New York: Harcourt Brace.

Dovifat, Emil. 1937. *Rede und Redner: Ihr Wesen und ihre politische Macht*. Leipzig.

Ebner, Ferdinand. 1919. *Das Wort und die geistigen Realitäten*. Innsbruck: Brenner.

Engelhardt, Victor. 1934. *Das Heilige Deutsche Antlitz*. Berlin: Greif-Bücherei.

Eulenberg, Herbert. 1917. *Das deutsche Angesicht: Eine Auswahl fürs Feld*. Berlin: B. Cassirer.

Fallada, Hans. 1932. *Kleiner Mann—Was nun?* Berlin: Rowohlt.

Flex, Walter. 1918. *Wallensteins Antlitz: Gesichte und Geschichten vom 30jährigen Kriege*. Munich. [Also in *Gesammelte Werke: Erster Band* (Munich: C. H. Beck, 1925).

Friedrich, Ernst. 1924. *Krieg dem Kriege*. Berlin: Freie Tugend.

Frobenius, Leo. 1923. *Vom Kulturreich des Festlandes: Dokumente zur Kulturphysiognomik.* Berlin: Volksverband der Bücherfreunde, Wegweiser-Verlag.

Fuchs, Eduard. 1902. *Die Karikatur der europäischen Völker vom Altertum bis zur Neuzeit.* Berlin.

Fülöp-Miller, René. 1926. *Geist und Gesicht des Bolschewismus: Darstellung und Kritik des kulturellen Lebens in Sowjet-Rußland.* Zurich.

Gall, F. J. 1798. Des Herrn Dr. F. J. Gall Schreiben . . . über die Verrichtungen des Gehirns der Menschen und der Thiere. *Der Neue Teutsche Merkur* (December): 312–23.

Ganzer, Karl Richard. 1935. *Das deutsche Führergesicht: 200 Bildnisse deutscher Kämpfer und Wegsucher aus 2 Jahrtausenden.* Munich.

Ganzer-Gottschewski, Lydia. 1939. *Das deutsche Frauenantlitz: Bildnisse aus allen Jahrhunderten deutschen Lebens.* Munich.

Gleichen-Rußwurm, Alexander von. 1919. *Das wahre Gesicht: Weltgeschichte des sozialistischen Gedankens.* Darmstadt.

Goebbels, Joseph. 1992. *The Goebbels Diaries, 1939–1941.* Trans. Fred Taylor. New York: Putnam.

Goebbels, Joseph. 1992. *Tagebücher 1924–1945.* Ed. Ralf Georg Reuth. 5 vols. Munich: Piper.

Goethe, Johann Wolfgang von. *Goethes Gespräche.* Ed. Woldemar Freiherr von Biedermann. 10 vols. Leipzig: 1889–96.

Grosz, George. 1921. *Das Gesicht der herrschenden Klasse.* Berlin: Malik.

"Greuelpropaganda." 1940. In *Handbuch der Zeitungswissenschaft,* 1372–88. Leipzig.

Gruhle, Hans W. 1948. *Verstehende Psychologie: Ein Lehrbuch.* Stuttgart: Thieme.

Gundolf, Friedrich. 1920. *George.* Berlin: Bondi.

Günther, Hans F. K. 1922. *Rassenkunde des Deutschen Volkes.* Munich: J. F. Lehman.

Hadamovsky, Eugen. 1936. Die Hände des Führers. *Die neue Literatur* (December 1936).

Haeckel, Walther, ed. 1914. *Ernst Haeckel im Bilde: Eine physiognomische Studie zu seinem 80. Geburtstage.* Berlin.

Haecker, Theodor. 1948. *Kierkegaard the Cripple.* Trans. C. Van O. Bruyn. London: Harvill Press.

———. 1950. *Journal in the Night.* New York: Pantheon Books.

Hamann, Richard, ed. 1922. *Deutsche Köpfe des Mittelalters.* Marburg an der Lahn: Seminar.

Hanfstaengl, Ernst. 1933. *Hitler in der Karikatur der Welt: Tat gegen Tinte: Ein Bildsammelwerk.* Berlin: Braune Bücher, Carl Rentsch.

———. 1970. *Zwischen Weissem und Braunem Haus: Memoiren eines politischen Aussenseiters.* Munich: R. Piper.

Hansen, Heinrich. 1938. *Das Antlitz der deutschen Frau.* Dortmund: Westfalen Verlag.

Hausenstein, Wilhelm. 1933. Das deutsche Antlitz. *Velhagen und Klasings Monatshefte* 47: 1–11.

Heidegger, Martin. 1962. *Being and Time.* Trans. John Macquarrie and Edward Robinson. New York: Harper.

Heiden, Konrad. 1936. *Adolf Hitler: Eine Biographie.* 2 vols. Zurich: Europa Verlag.

Heinroth, Johann Christian. 1833. *Grundzüge der Criminal-Psychologie.* Berlin.

Hellpach, Willy. 1933. Der völkische Aufbau des Antlitzes. *Die Medizinische Welt* 7.

———. 1942. *Deutsche Physiognomik: Grundlegung einer Naturgeschichte der Nationalgesichter.* Berlin: de Gruyter.

Hentzen, Alfred, and Nils von Holst, ed. 1936. *Die großen Deutschen im Bild.* Berlin: Propyläen.

Herland, Leo. 1937. *Gesicht und Charakter: Handbuch der praktischen Charakterdeutung.* Zurich: Rascher.

Hitler, Adolf. 1939. *Mein Kampf.* New York: Stackpole & Sons.

Hoffmann, Heinrich. 1939. *Das Antlitz des Führers.* Berlin.

———. 1974. *Hitler, wie ich ihn sah: Aufzeichnungen seines Leibfotografen.* Munich: Herbig.

Hofmannsthal, Hugo von. 1956. *Briefe des Zurückgekehrten.* In *Werke,* vol. 2, *Erzählungen und Aufsätze.* Frankfurt am Main: S. Fischer.

Hofmiller, Josef, ed. 1926. *Das deutsche Antlitz: Ein Lesebuch.* Munich.

Jaensch, Erich. 1923. *Über den Aufbau der Wahrnehmungswelt und ihre Struktur im Jugendalter.* Leipzig.

———. 1930. *Eidetic Imagery and Typological Methods of Investigation: Their Importance for the Psychology of Childhood, the Theory of Education, General Psychology, and the Psychophysiology of Human Personality.* Trans. Oscar Oeser. New York: Harcourt, Brace.

Jaspers, Karl. 1977. *Philosophische Autobiographie.* Munich: Piper.

Johst, Hanns. 1935. *Maske und Gesicht, Reise eines Nationalsozialisten von Deutschland nach Deutschland.* Munich: Albert Langen/Georg Müller.

Jünger, Ernst, ed. 1930. *Das Antlitz des Weltkrieges.* Berlin: Neufeld & Henius.

———. 1932. *Der Arbeiter: Herrschaft und Gestalt.* Hamburg: Hanseatische Verlagsanstalt.

———. 1942. *In Stahlgewittern.* Berlin: Mittler.

———. 1947. *Sprache und Körperbau.* Zürich: Verlag der Arche.

———. 1955. *Strahlungen.* Tübingen: Heliopolis.

Justi, Ludwig. 1936. *Aufgabe und Umfang der deutschen Bildnissammlung.* In *Im Dienste der Kunst* ed. A. Herzen, and P. O. Rave. Breslau: W. K. Korn.

Kafka, Franz. 1948–49. *The Diaries of Franz Kafka.* Trans. Joseph Kresh. New York: Schocken Books.

Kardorff, Ursula von. 1992. *Berliner Aufzeichnungen.* Munich: Biederstein Verlag.

Kassner, Rudolf. 1910. *Von den Elementen der menschlichen Größe.* Leipzig: Insel.

———. 1925. *Die Verwandlung: Physiognomische Studien.* Leipzig: Insel-Verlag.

———. 1930. *Das physiognomische Weltbild.* Munich: Delphin Verlag.

———. 1932. *Physiognomik.* Leipzig: Insel-Verlag.

———. 1954. *Das deutsche Antlitz in fünf Jahrhunderten deutscher Malerei.* Zurich: Atlantis Verlag.

———. 1979. *Zahl und Gesicht.* Frankfurt am Main: Suhrkamp.

Kästner, Erich. 1961. *Notabene 45: Ein Tagebuch.* Berlin: C. Dressler.

Kempowski, Walter. 1999. *Haben Sie Hitler gesehen? Deutsche Antworten.* Munich: Goldmann.

Kerr, Alfred. 1997. *Wo liegt Berlin? Briefe aus der Reichshauptstadt 1895–1900.* Berlin: Aufbau-Verlag.

Kessler, Harry Graf. 2000. *Berlin in Lights: The Diaries of Count Harry Kessler, 1918–1937.* Trans. Charles Kessler. New York: Grove Press.

Klages, Ludwig. 1932. *The Science of Character.* Trans. W. H. Johnston. Cambridge, Mass.: Science-Art Publishers.

———. 1971. *Gesammelte Werke.* Bonn: Bouvier.

Klatt, Fritz. 1921. *Die schöpferische Pause.* Jena: Diederichs.

Klebinder, Paul. 1913. *Der Deutsche Kaiser im Film.* Berlin: Paul Klebinder.

Klemperer, Victor. 1998. *I Will Bear Witness: A Diary of the Nazi Years.* Trans. Martin Chalmers. New York: Random House.

————. 2000. *The Language of the Third Reich—LTI, Lingua Tertii Imperii: A Philologist's Notebook*. Trans. Martin Brady. London, New Brunswick, N.J.: Athlone Press.

Kretschmer, Ernst. 1936. *Physique and Character: An Investigation of the Nature of Constitution and of the Theory of Temperaments*. Trans. W. J. H. Sprott. London: K. Paul, Trench, Trubner & Co.

Kroh, Oswald. 1934. Das physiognomische Verstehen in seiner allgemeinen psychologischen Bedeutung. *Neue psychologische Studen* 12.

Kubizek, August. 1953. *Adolf Hitler, Mein Jugendfreund*. Graz: L. Stocker.

Kuh, Anton. 1934. Pallenberg über Hitler. *Die neue Weltbühne* 27.

Kupfer, Amandus. 1948. *Menschenkenntnis: Carl Huters Psycho-Physiognomik*. Winterthur-Seen: Schwaig.

Lange, Fritz. 1939. *Die Sprache des menschlichen Antlitzes: Eine wissenschaftliche Physiognomik und ihre praktische Verwertung im Leben und in der Kunst*. Munich: Lehmann.

Lang, Jochen von, ed. 1968. *Adolf Hitler: Gesichter eines Diktators*. Hamburg: C. Wegner.

Langer, Richard. 1927. *Totenmasken*. Leipzig: Thieme.

Lavater, Johann Caspar. 1775–78. *Physiognomische Fragmente zur Beförderung der Menschenkenntniß und der Menschenliebe*. 4 vols. Winterthur.

Lendvai-Dircksen, Erna. 1937. *Das Gesicht des deutschen Ostens*. Berlin: Zeitgeschichte Verlag und Vertriebs-Gesellschaft.

————. 1942a. *Das deutsche Volksgesicht*. Bayreuth: Gau-Verlag.

————. 1942b. *Das Germanische Volksgesicht: Flandern*. Bayreuth: Gau-Verlag.

————. 1942c. *Das Germanische Volksgesicht: Norwegen*. Bayreuth: Gau-Verlag.

Leonhard, Karl. 1949. *Ausdruckssprache der Seele: Darstellung der Mimik, Gestik und Phonik des Menschen*. Berlin.

Lersch, Philipp. 1951. *Gesicht und Seele: Grundlinien einer mimischen Diagnostik*. Munich: Reinhardt.

Lerski, Helmar. 1931. *Köpfe des Alltags*. Berlin: Verlag Hermann Rockendorf.

Levinas, Emmanuel. 1975. "Max Picard and the Face." In *Proper Names,* 94–98. Stanford, Calif.: Stanford University Press.

Loesch, Karl Christian von. 1935. *Deutsche Züge im Antlitz der Erde*. Munich: Bruckmann.

Lorenz, Konrad. 1943. "Die Angeborenen Formen Möglicher Erfahrung." *Zeitschrift für Tierpsychologie* 5: 235–409.

Lübbe, Axel. 1918. *Deutsches Antlitz: Gedichte zu Bildnissen Dürers*. Leipzig.

Mann, Heinrich. 1991. *Mut: Essays*. Frankfurt am Main: Fischer.

Mann, Klaus. 1942. *The Turning Point: Thirty-five Years in This Century*. New York: L. B. Fischer.

Marcuse, Ludwig. 1975. *Mein zwanzigstes Jahrhundert*. Zurich: Diogenes.

Maser, Werner, ed. 1975. *Mein Schüler Hitler: Das Tagebuch seines Lehrers Paul Devrient*. Pfaffenhofen/Ilm: Ilmgau Verlag.

Mendelssohn, Georg, and Anja. 1928. *Der Mensch in der Handschrift*. Leipzig: E. A. Seeman.

Miltenberg Weigand von, [Herbert Blank]. 1930–31. *Adolf Hitler: Wilhelm III*. Berlin: Rowon.

Mühsam, Erich. 1994. *Tagebücher*. Munich: Deutscher Taschenbuch Verlag.

Müller, Ernst. 1914. *Cäsarenporträts: Teil I*. Bonn: Webers Verlag.

————. 1924. *Cäsarenporträts: Teil II*. Berlin: Walter de Gruyter.

————. 1927. *Cäsarenporträts: Teil III*. Bonn: Webers Verlag.

Müller, Karl Alexander von. 1954. *Mars und Venus: Erinnerungen, 1914–1919.* Stuttgart: G. Kilpper.

———. 1966. *Im Wandel einer Welt: Erinnerungen, 1919–1932.* Munich: Süddeutscher Verlag.

Nicholson, Harold. 1939. *The Spectator* (April).

Nietzsche, Friedrich. 2000. *Basic Writings.* Trans. Walther Kaufmann. New York: Modern Library Classics.

Nikl, Peter [Johannes Wüsten]. 1936. *Gesichter des Dritten Reiches: Karikaturen.* Prague.

Nissen, Momme. 1928. *Dürer als Führer: Vom Rembrandtdeutschen und seinem Gehilfen.* Munich: Josef Müller.

Orwell, George. 1940. Review of *Mein Kampf,* by Adolf Hitler. *New English Weekly,* March 21.

———. 1954. *Nineteen Eighty-Four.* London: Penguin.

Panizza, Oskar. 1923. Der operierte Jud. In *Visionen der Daemmerung.* Munich: G. Müller.

Peiner, Werner. 1937. *Das gesicht Ostafrikas, eine Reise in 300 Bildern.* Frankfurt am Main: Schirmer & Mahlau.

Picard, Max. *Das Menschengesicht.* Munich: Delphin.

———. 1937. *Die Grenzen der Physiognomik.* Erlenbach b. Zurich: E. Rentsch: Leipzig: E. Rentsch.

———. 1946. *Hitler in Our Selves.* Trans. Heinrich Hauser. Hinsdale, Ill.: H. Regenry.

———. 1959. *Das letzte Antlitz: Totenmasken von Shakespeare bis Nietzsche.* Munich: Ahrbeck, Knorr & Hirth Verlag.

Picker, Henry. 1951. *Hitlers Tischgespräche im Führerhauptquartier.* Bonn: Athenäum.

Pinthus, Kurt, ed. 1994. *Menschheitsdämmerung: Dawn of Humanity.* Trans. Joanna M. Ratych, R. Ley, and C. Conard. Columbia, S.C.: Camden House.

Plessner, Helmuth. 1999. *The Limits of Community: A Critique of Social Radicalism.* Trans. Andrew Wallace. Amherst, N.Y.: Humanity Books.

Quidde, Ludwig. 1977. *Caligula: Schriften über Militarismus und Pazifismus.* Reprint, Frankfurt am Main: Syndicat.

Rave, Paul Ortwin. 1999. *Das Jahrhundert Goethes, in 338 Porträts berühmter Frauen und Männer.* Cologne: Parkland. Original edition, Berlin: Berlin, Verlag des Druckhauses Tempelhof, 1949.

Reck-Malleczewen, Friedrich P. 1970. *Diary of a Man in Despair.* Trans. Paul Rubens, London: Macmillan.

Reinhold, Kurt. 1932. Das Unwiderstehliche. In *Das Tage-Buch.*

Retzlaff, Erich. 1930. *Antlitz des Alters: Photographische Bildnisse.* Düsseldorf: Pädagogischer Verlag.

———. 1944. *Antlitz des Geistes.* Stuttgart.

Ried, Fritz. 1930. *Das Selbstbildnis.* Berlin: Die Buchgemeinde.

Riefenstahl, Leni. 1993. *Leni Riefenstahl: A Memoir.* New York: St. Martin's Press.

Rilke, Rainer M. 1965–66. *Gesammelte Werke.* Frankfurt am Main: Suhrkamp.

———. 1930. *The Notebook of Malte Laurids Brigge.* Trans. John Linton. London: Hogarth Press.

———. 1973. *Tagebücher aus der Frühzeit.* Frankfurt am Main: Insel Verlag.

Robakidse, Grigol. 1939. *Adolf Hitler, von einem fremden Dichter gesehen.* Jena: Eugen Diederichs.

Rogers, Malcolm. 1990. *Camera Portraits: Photographs from the National Portrait Gallery, London 1839–1989.* New York: Oxford University Press.

Rollet, Hermann. 1883. *Die Goethe-Bildnisse, biographisch-kunstgeschichtlich darges-tellt*. . . . Vienna: Braumüller.

Roth, Joseph. 1956. *Gesammelte Werke in Drei Bänden*. Vol. 3. Cologne: Kiepen-heuer & Witsch.

Salus, Grete. 1981. *Niemand, Nichts—ein Jude: Theresienstadt, Auschwitz, Oederan*. Damstadt: Verlag Darmstädter Blätter.

Sander, August. 1929. *Antlitz der Zeit*. Munich: K. Wolff.

———. 1986. *Citizens of the Twentieth Century: Portrait Photographs, 1892–1952*. Trans. Linda Keller. Cambridge, Mass.: MIT Press.

Schack, Sophus. 1881. *Physiognomische Studien*. Trans. Eugen Liebich. Jena: Her-mann Costenoble.

Schaeffer, Emil, ed. 1914. *Goethes äußere Erscheinung: Literarische Dokumente seiner Zeitgenossen*. Leipzig: Insel.

———, ed. 1929. *Das letzte Gesicht: 76 Bilder*. Zurich: Orell Füssli.

Schäfer, Wilhelm. 1953. *Der Hauptmann von Köpenick*. Munich: P. List.

Schamoni, Wilhelm. 1938. *Das wahre Gesicht der Heiligen*. Leipzig: Verlag Jakob Hegner.

Schiller, Friedrich. 1991. *Schiller II (German Library)*. Ed. Walter Hinderer. New York: Continuum.

Schoeppe, Wilhelm, ed. 1937. *Meister der Kamera erzählen*. Halle a. d. Saale: Knapp.

Schlichter, Rudolf and Ernst Jünger. 1997. "Briefwechsel." *Sinn und Form* 49.

Scholdt, Günther. 1993. *Autoren über Hitler: Deutschsprachige Schriftsteller 1919–1945 und ihr Bild vom "Führer."* Bonn: Bouvier.

Schrade, Hubert. 1937. *Das deutsche Gesicht: In Bildern aus acht Jahrhunderten deut-scher Kunst*. Munich: Albert Langen / Georg Müller Verlag.

Schultz, Edmund, ed. 1931. *Das Gesicht der Demokratie: Ein Bilderwerk zur Geschichte der deutschen Nachkriegszeit*. Leipzig: Breitkopf & Härtel.

Schultze-Naumburg, Paul. 1928. *Kunst und Rasse*. Munich: J.F. Lehmanns Verlag.

Shirer, William. 1941. *Berlin Diary*. New York: Alfred A. Knopf.

Simmel, Georg. 1901. Die ästhetische Bedeutung des Gesichts. In *Der Lotse I*.

———. 1902. Rodins Plastik und die Geistesrichtungen der Gegenwart. In *Der Zeitgeist: Inlay* for the "Berliner Tageblatts" (September 29).

———. 1968. *Soziologie: Untersuchung über die Formen der Vergesellschaftung*. 5th ed. Berlin: Duncker & Humbolt.

Speer, Albert. 1970. *Inside the Third Reich: Memoirs*. Trans. Richard and Clara Win-ston. New York: Macmillan.

———. 1976. *Spandau: The Secret Diaries*. Trans. Richard and Clara Winston. New York: Macmillan.

Spengler, Oswald. 1928. *The Decline of the West*. Trans. Charles Francis Atkinson. New York: Alfred A. Knopf.

———. 1932. *Man and Technics: A Contribution to a Philosophy of Life*. Trans. Charles Francis Atkinson. New York: Alfred A. Knopf.

———. 1937. *Reden und Aufsätze*. Munich: Beck.

Staatliche Museen—Nationalgalerie, ed. 1936. *Große Deutsche in Bildnissen ihrer Zeit: Ausstellung aus Anlaß der XI. Olympischen Spiele August–September 1936 Ber-lin, im ehemaligen Kronprinzenpalais*.

Stahl, Fritz. 1904. *Wie sah Goethe aus?* Berlin: Reimer.

Stepun, Fedor. 1961. *Das Antlitz Rußlands und das Gesicht der Revolution*. Munich: Kösel.

Storfer, A. J. 1935. *Wörter und ihre Schicksale*. Berlin: Atlantis.

Thiess, Frank. 1923. *Das Gesicht des Jahrhunderts.* Stuttgart: J. Engelhorn.
———. ed. 1931. *Die Wiedergeburt der Liebe: Essays.* Berlin: Zsolnay.
Thompson, Dorothy. 1932. *I Saw Hitler!* New York: Farrar & Rinehart.
Tönnies, Ferdinand. 2001. *Community and Civil Society.* Trans. Jose Harris and Margaret Hollis. New York: Cambridge University Press.
Tucholsky, Kurt. 1972. *Deutschland, Deutschland über alles: A Picture-Book by Kurt Tucholsky.* Photos assembled by John Heartfield. Trans. Anne Halley. Amherst: University of Massachusetts Press.
Turner, H. G., ed. 1987. *Hitler aus nächster Nähe: Aufzeichnungen eines Vertrauten 1929–1932.* Kiel, Arndt.
Unsterbliche Soldaten: Von der Überwindung des Todes durch den Geist. 1940. Berlin.
Waetzold, Wilhelm. 1908. *Die Kunst des Porträts.* Leipzig.
Wahl, Hans, ed. 1930. *Goethe im Bildnis.* Leipzig: Insel.
Waldeck, Heinrich Suso [Augustin Popp]. 1930. *Die Antlitzgedichte.* 3d ed. Vienna: Verlagsanstalt Tyrolia.
Wolff, Theodor. 1989. *Die Wilhelminische Epoche.* Frankfurt am Main: Athenäum.
Worringer, Wilhelm. 1997. *Abstraction and Empathy: A Contribution to the Psychology of Style.* Trans. Michael Bullock. Chicago: Ivan R. Dee.
Wühr, Hans. Das deutsche Antlitz in der Kunst: Selbstbildnisse Albrecht Altdorfers. *Kunst im Dritten Reich 1* (1939).
Zarncke, Friedrich. 1988. *Kurzgefasstes Verzeichnis der Originalaufnahmen von Goethes Bildnis.* Leipzig.
Zweig, Arnold. 1928. *The Case of Sergeant Grischa.* Trans. Eric Sutton. New York: Viking Press.
———. 2004. *The Face of East European Jewry.* Trans. Noah Isenberg. Berkeley: University of California Press.
Zweig, Stefan. 1930. *Three Masters: Balzac, Dickens, Dostoesky.* Trans. Eden and Cedar Paul. New York: Viking Press.

Secondary Sources

Aly, Götz. 1995. *"Endlösung": Völkerverschiebung und der Mord an den europaeischen Juden.* Frankfurt am Main: Suhrkamp.
Arnheim, Rudolf. 1997. Antifaschistische Satire. In *Film Essays and Criticism.* Trans. Brenda Benthien. Madison: University of Wisconsin Press.
Balfour, Michael, ed. 2001. *Theatre and War 1933–1945: Performance in Extremis.* New York: Berghahn Books.
Balfour, Michael, et al. 1972. *Helmuth von Moltke: A Leader Against Hitler.* London: Macmillan.
Barbian, Jan-Pieter. 1998. Politik und Film in der Weimarer Republik: Ein Beitrag zur Kulturpolitik der Jahre 1918 bis 1933. *Archiv für Kulturgeschichte* 80: 213–45.
Barkhausen, Hans. 1970. Die NSDAP als Filmproduzent. In *Zeitgeschichte in Film—Und Tondokument,* ed. Günter Moltmann et al. Göttingen: Musterschmidt Verlag.
Bartmann, Dominik. 1999. Der gedoppelte Hitler. Beitrag zur Lösung eines Verwirrspiels um zwei Gemälde von Klaus Richter. In *Jahrbuch 1997.* Berlin: Stiftung Stadtmuseum Berlin.
Behrenbeck, Sabine. 1996. "Der Führer": Die Einführung eines politischen Markenartikels. In *Propaganda in Deutschland: Zur Geschichte der politischen Mas-*

senbeeinflussung im 20. Jahrhundert, ed. Gerald Diesener and Rainer Gries. Darmstadt: Primus.

Benz, Wolfgang, and Hermann Graml, eds. 1988. *Biographisches Lexikon zur Weimarer Republik.* Munich: C. H. Beck.

Benz, Wolfgang, Herman Graml, et al, eds. 1997. *Enzyklopädie des Nationalsozialismus.* Stuttgart: Klett-Cotta.

Bessel, Richard. 1993. Die Heimkehr der Soldaten: Das Bild der Frontsoldaten in der Öffentlichkeit der Weimarer Republik. In *"Keiner fuehlt sich hier mehr als Mensch . . . ,"* ed. Gerhard Hirschfeld. Frankfurt am Main: Klartext.

Blankenburg, Martin. 2000. Der Seele auf den Leib gerückt: Physiognomik im Streit der Fakultäten. In *Gesichter der Weimarer Republik,* ed. Claudia Schmölders and Sander L. Gilman. Cologne: Dumont.

Borrmann, Norbert. 1989. *Paul Schulze-Naumburg, 1869–1949.* Essen: Richard Bacht.

Brandt, Susanne. 1993. Kriegssammlungen im Ersten Weltkrieg: Denkmaeler oder Laboratoires d'histoire? In *"Keiner fuehlt sich hier mehr als Mensch . . . ,"* ed. Gerhard Hirschfeld. Frankfurt am Main: Klartext.

Breuer, Dieter et al., eds. 1997. *Moderne und Nationalsozialismus im Rheinland.* Paderborn.

Breuer, Stefan. 1995. *Ästhetischer Fundamentalismus: Stefan George und der deutsche Antimodernismus.* Darmstadt: Wissenschaftliche Buchgesellschaft.

Brink, Cornelia. 2000. *"Auschwitz in der Paulskirche": Erinnerungspolitik in Fotoausstellungen der sechziger Jahre.* Marburg: Jonas Verlag.

Browning, Christopher R. 1985. *Fateful Months: Essays on the Emergence of the Final Solution, 1941–42.* New York: Holmes & Meier.

Brückle, Wolfgang. 1997. Politisierung des Angesichts: Zur Semantik des fotografischen Portraits in der Weimarer Republik. *Fotogeschichte* 65: 3–24.

———. 1998. Wege zum Volksgesicht: Imagebildung für das Kollektiv im fotografischen Porträt des Nachexpressionismus. In *Bildnis und Image,* ed. Andreas Köstler and Ernst Seidl. Cologne: Böhlau.

———. 2000. "Kein Portrait Mehr? Physiognomik in der Deutschen Bildnisphotographie um 1930." In Schmölders and Gilman 2000, pp. 131–55.

Brzsoka, Emil. 1963. *Das deutsche Antlitz Oberschlesiens.* Bonn.

Bucher, Peter. 1984. *Wochenschauen und Dokumentarfilme im Bundesarchiv-Filmarchiv.* (Findbuecher zu den Bestaenden des Bundesarchivs, vol. 8). Koblenz: Bundesarchir.

Campe, Rüdiger, and Manfred Schneider, eds. 1996. *Geschichten der Physiognomik: Text, Bild, Wissen.* Freiburg im Breisgau: Rombach.

De Boor, Wolfgang. 1985. *Hitler: Mensch. Übermensch, Untermensch: Eine kriminalpsychologische Studie.* Frankfurt am Main: Fischer.

Eskildsen, Ute, and Jan-Christopher Horak. 1982. *Film und Foto der zwanziger Jahre: Eine Betrachtung der Internationalen Werkbundausstellung "Film und Foto" 1929.* Stuttgart: Württembergischer Kunstverein.

Fest, Joachim. 1970. *The Face of the Third Reich: Portraits of the Nazi Leadership.* Trans. Michael Bullock. New York: Pantheon Books.

———. 1974. *Hitler.* Trans. Richard and Clara Winston. New York: Harcourt Brace.

———. 1996. *Plotting Hitler's Death: The Story of the German Resistance 1933–1945.* Trans. Bruce Little. New York: Henry Holt.

———. 2001. *Speer: The Final Verdict.* Trans. Ewald Osers and Alexandra Dring. London: Weidenfeld & Nicolson.

Finkielkraut, Alain. 1997. *The Wisdom of Love.* Trans. Kevin O'Neill and David Suchoff. Lincoln: University of Nebraska Press.

Frecot, Janos, Johann Friedrich Geist, and Diethart Kerbs. 1972. *Fidus, 1968–1948: Zur ästhetischen Praxis Bürgerlicher Fluchtbewegungen.* Munich: Rogner & Bernhard.

Frei, Norbert, and Johannes Schmitz, eds. 1989. *Journalismus im Dritten Reich.* Munich: Beck.

Friedländer, Saul. 1984. *Reflections of Nazism: An Essay on Kitsch and Death.* Trans. Thomas Weyr. New York: Harper & Row.

Gander, Gero, ed. 1993. *Der Film der Weimarer Republik.* Berlin.

Ganteführer, Anne. 1997. Der Photograph August Sander und sein künstlerisches Umfeld im Rheinland. In *Moderne und Nationalsozialismus im Rheinland,* ed. Dieter Breuer et al., Paderborn.

Gersch, Wolfgang. 1988. *Chaplin in Berlin.* Berlin: Henschelverlag.

Gertz, Ulrich. 1978. Der Verein Berliner Künstler e.V. In *Zwischen Widerstand und Anpassung: Kunst in Deutschland zwischen 1933–1945,* ed. Barbara Volkmann. Berlin: Akademie der Künste.

Geuter, Ulfried. 1984. *Die Professionalisierung der Deutschen Psychologie im Nationalisierung der Deutschen Psychologie im Nationalsozialismus.* Frankfurt am Main: Suhrkamp.

Gibbels, Ellen. 1994. Hitlers Nervenkrankheit: Eine neurologisch-psychiatrische Studie. *Vierteljahresschrift für Zeitgeschichte* 42: 155–220.

Gilman, Sander L. 1978. Zur Physiognomie des Geisteskranken in Geschichte und Praxi 1800–1900. *Sudhoffs Archiv* 62: 209–34.

———. 1991. *The Jew's Body.* New York: Routledge.

Göttert, Karl-Heinz. 1998. *Geschichte der Stimme.* Munich: Wilhelm Fink.

Gray, Richard T. 2004. *About Face: German Physiognomic Thought from Lavater to Auschwitz.* Detroit: Wayne State University Press.

Grupp, Peter. 1995. *Harry Graf Kessler 1868–1937: Eine Biographie.* Munich: Beck.

Haarmann, Herman. 1999. *Pleite glotzt euch an—Restlos: Satire in der Publizistik der Weimarer Republik—ein Handbuch.* Opladen: Westdeutscher Verlag.

Haffner, Sebastian. 1979. *The Meaning of Hitler.* Trans. Ewald Osers. London: Weidenfeld & Nicolson.

———. 1989. *The Ailing Empire: Germany from Bismarck to Hitler.* Trans. Jean Steinberg. New York: Fromm International.

Hägel, Ulrich. 1995. Wenn Hitler Anstreicher geblieben ware . . . Fotomontagen gegen Krieg und Faschismus in der französischen Wochenzeitung "Marianne." *Fotogeschichte* 55: 47–59.

Hägele, Ulrich, and Gudrun M. König, ed. 1999. *Volkskundliche Dokumente: Hans Retzlaffs Fotografien 1930 bis 1945.* Marburg.

Hagner, Michael, ed. 1999. *Ecce Cortex: Beiträge zur Geschichte des modernen Gehirns.* Göttingen: Wallstein.

Hamann, Brigitte. 1999. *Hitler's Vienna: A Dictator's Apprenticeship.* Trans. Thomas Thornton. New York: Oxford University Press.

Herz, Rudolf. 1994. *Hoffman and Hitler: Fotografie als Medium des Führer-Mythos.* Fotomuseum im Münchener Stadtmuseum. Munich: Klinkhardt & Biermann.

Hirschfeld, Gerhard, ed. 1993. *"Keiner fuehlt sich hier mehr als Mensch . . ." Erlebnis und Wirkung des Ersten Weltkrieges.* Frankfurt am Main: Klartext.

Hofer, Walther, ed. 1960. *Der Nationalsozialismus: Dokumente 1933 bis 1945.* Frankfurt am Main: Fischer Taschenbuch Verlag.

Hoßfeld, Uwe, et al. 2000. *Evolutionsbiologie von Darwin bis Heute.* Berlin: VWB.

Hüppauf, Bernd. 1993. Schlachtenmythen und die Konstruktion des "Neuen Menschen." In *"Keiner fuehlt sich hier mehr als Mensch . . . ,"* ed. Gerhard Hirschfeld.

Keller, Ulrich. 1977. Die deutsche Porträtfotografie von 1918 bis 1933. *Kritische Berichte* 5.

Kempowski, Walter. 1999. *Haben Sie Hitler Gesehen? Deutschen Antworten.* Munich: Goldmann.

Kershaw, Ian. 1987. *The "Hitler Myth": Image and Reality in the Third Reich.* New York: Oxford University Press.

———. 1998. *Hitler, 1889–1936: Hubris.* New York: W. W. Norton.

Klönne, Arno. 1999. *Jugend im Dritten Reich: Die Hitler-Jugend und ihre Gegner.* Munich: Piper.

Klöss, Erhard. 1967. *Reden des Führers: Politik und Propaganda Adolf Hitlers 1922–1945.* Munich: Deutscher Taschenbuch Verlag.

Koch-Hillebrecht, Manfred. 1999. *Homo Hitler: Psychogramm des deutschen Diktators.* Munich: Siedler.

Köhler, Joachim. 2000. *Wagner's Hitler: The Prophet and His Disciple.* Trans. Ronald Taylor. Malden, Mass.: Blackwell Publishers.

Köstler, Andreas, and Ernst Seidl, eds. 1998. *Bildnis und Image: Das Porträt zwischen Intention und Rezeption.* Cologne: Böhlau.

Lehmann, Hans-Thies. 1991. *Das Welttheater der Scham. Merkur* 45: 824–39.

Lepenies, Wolf. 1976. *Das Ende der Naturgeschichte: Wandel kultureller Selbstverständlichkeiten in den Wissenschaften des 18. und 19. Jahrhunderts.* Munich: Hanser.

Lethen, Helmut. 1997. Neusachliche Physiognomik. Der Deutschunterricht 40, no. 2: 6–19.

———. 2002. *Cool Conduct: The Culture of Distance in Weimar Germany.* Trans. Don Reneau. Berkeley: University of California Press.

Ley, Michael, and Julius H. Schoeps. 1997. *Der Nationalsozialismus als politische Religion.* Bodenheim b. Mainz: Philo. Verlagsgesellschaft.

Loiperdinger, Martin. 1987. *Rituale der Mobilmachung: Der Parteitagsfilm "Triumph des Willens" von Leni Riefenstahl.* Opladen: Leske und Budrich Verlag.

———. 1995. *Führerbilder: Hitler, Mussolini, Roosevelt, Stalin in Fotografie und Film.* Munich: Piper.

Matt, Peter von. 1983. *. . . . Fertig ist das Angesicht: Zur Literaturgeschichte des menschlichen Gesichts.* Munich: Hanser.

Matussek, Paul, and Peter Matussek, et al. 2000. *Hitler: Karriere eines Wahns.* Munich: Herbig.

Mayer, Andreas. 1999. "Von Galtons Mischphotographien zu Freuds Traumfiguren." In Hagner 1999, pp. 110–44.

Medicus, Thomas. 1999. Jugend in Uniform: Walter Flex und die deutsche Generation von 1914. In *Willensmenschen: Über deutsche Offiziere,* ed. Ursula Breymayer et al. Frankfurt am Main: Fischer Taschenbuch Verlag.

Mehrtens, H., and S. Richert, eds. 1980. *Naturwissenschaft, Technik, und NS-Ideologie.* Frankfurt am Main: Suhrkamp.

Merseburger, Peter. 1998. *Mythos Weimar: Zwischen Geist und Macht.* Stuttgart: Deutsche Verlags-Anstalt.

Meyer, Martin. 1990. *Ernst Jünger.* Munich: Hanser.

Meyer-Büser, Susanne, ed. 1994. *Das schönste deutsche Frauengesicht: Tendenzen der Bildnismalerei in der Weimarer Republik.* Berlin: Reimer.

Mitscherlich, Alexander, and Margarete Mitscherlich. 1975. *The Inability to Mourn: Principles of Collective Behavior.* Trans. Beverly R. Placzek. New York: Grove Press.

218   Reference List

Moeller, Felix. 2000. *The Film Minister: Goebbels and the Cinema in the Third Reich.* Trans. Michael Robinson. Stuttgart: Edition Axel Menges.

Moltmann, Günter, et al., eds. 1970. *Zeitgeschichte in Film: Und Tondokument.* Göttingen: Musterschmidt Verlag.

Mommsen, Hans. 1989. *Aufstieg und Untergang der Republik von Weimar 1918–1933.* Berlin.

Müller, Ingo. 1991. *Hitler's Justice: The Courts of the Third Reich.* Trans. Deborah Lucas Schneider. Cambridge, Mass.: Harvard University Press.

Müller, Robert. 1923. *Rassen, Städte, Physiognomien: Kulturhistorische Aspekte.* Berlin: Erich Reiss Verlag.

Mürner, Christian. 1997. *Gebrandmarkte Gesichter.* Herzogenrath: Murken-Altrogge.

Neckel, Sighard. 1991. *Status und Scham: Zur symbolischen Reproduktion sozialer Ungleichheit.* Frankfurt and New York: Campus.

Nolte, Ernst. 1987. *Der Europäische Bürgerkrieg 1917–1945.* Berlin: Propyläen.

Paul, Gerhard. 1990. *Aufstand der Bilder: Die NS-Propaganda vor 1933.* Bonn: Dietz.

Paul, Jürgen. 1999. Der Rembrandtdeutsche in Dresden. *Dresdner Hefte* 57: 4–13.

Philipp, Claudia Gabriele. 1984. Erna Lendvai-Dircksen: Repraesentantin einer weiblichen Kunsttradition oder Propagandistin des Nationalsozialismus? In *Frauen Kunst Geschichte,* ed. Cordula Bischoff. Gießen.

———. 1991. *Portraitfotographie in Deutschland 1850–1918.* Hamburg.

Pohl, Klaus-D. 1993. Der Kaiser im Zeitalter seiner Technischen Reproduzierbarkeit: Wilhelm II in Fotografie und Film. In *Der letzte Kaiser: Wilhelm II im Exil,* ed. Hans Wilderotter and Klaus-D. Pohl. Berlin: Deutsches Historisches Museum.

Rave, Paul Ortwin. 1968. *Die Geschichte der Nationalgalerie Berlin.* Berlin.

Regener, Susanne. 1999. *Fotografische Erfassung: Zur Geschichte medialer Konstruktionen des Kriminellen.* Munich: W. Fink.

Röhl, John C. G. 1998. *Young Wilhelm: The Kaiser's Early Life, 1859–1888.* Trans. Jeremy Gaines and Rebecca Wallach. Cambridge and New York: Cambridge University Press.

Rothermund, Erwin. 1999. Denkarbeit und physiognomische Erkenntnis: Zu Joachim Günthers Publizistik im "Dritten Riech." *Zeitschrift für Germanistik* NF 2: 329–43.

Rüther, Günther, ed. 1997. *Literatur in der Diktatur: Schreiben im Nationalsozialismus und DDR-Sozialismus.* Paderborn: Schöningh.

Sanders, Marion K. 1973. *Dorothy Thompson: A Legend in Her Time.* Boston: Houghton Mifflin.

Schäfer, Hans-Dieter. 1981. *Das gespaltene Bewusstsein: Ueber deutsche Kultur und Lebenswirklichkeit 1933–1945.* Munich.

———. 1997. Kultur als Simulation: Das Dritte Reich und die Postmoderne. In *Literatur in der Diktatur,* ed. Günther Rüther. Paderborn: Schöningh.

Schenck, Ernst Günther. 1989. *Patient Hitler: Eine medizinische Biographie.* Düsseldorf: Droste.

Schmölders, Claudia. 1994. Das Profil im Schatten: Zu einem physiognomischen "Ganzen" im 18. Jahrhundert. In *Der ganze Mensch: Anthropologie und Literatur im 18. Jahrhundert,* ed. H.-J. Schings. Stuttgart: Metzler.

———. 1995. *Das Vorurteil im Leibe: Eine Einführung in die Physiognomik.* Berlin. Akademie Verlag.

———. 1997. "Die Stimme des Bösen:" Zur Klanggestalt des Dritten Reiches. *Merkur* 581: 681–93.

———. 1998. Der Charakter des Pferdes: Zur Physiognomik der Veterinäre um 1800. In *Evidenze e ambiguitá della fisionomia umana: Studi sul XVIII.eXIX. Secolo,* ed. Elena Agazzi and Manfred Beller. Viareggio.

———. 1999. Physiognomik des Sohnes: Rudolf Kassner eher psychologisch betrachtet. In *Rudolf Kassner: Physiognomik als Wissensform,* ed. Gerhard Neumann and Ulrich Ott. Freiburg: Rombach Verlag.

———, ed. 1997. *Der exzentrische Blick: Gespräch über Physiognomik.* Berlin: Akademie Verlag.

Schmölders, Claudia, and Sander L. Gilman, eds. 2000. *Gesichter der Weimarer Republik: Eine physiognomische Kulturgeschichte.* Cologne: DuMont.

Schoeps, Julius H., and Joachim Schlör, eds. 1995. *Antisemitismus: Vorurteile und Mythen.* Munich: Piper.

Scholdt, Günther. 1993. *Autoren über Hitler: Deutschsprachige Schriftsteller 1919– 1945 und ihr Bild vom "Führer."* Bonn: Bouvier.

Schulte, Christoph. 1997. *Psychopathologie des Fin de siècle: Der Kulturkritiker, Arzt, und Zionist Max Nordau.* Frankfurt am Main: Fischer Taschenbuch Verlag.

Schuster, Peter-Klaus, ed. 1995. *George Grosz, Berlin/New York.* Berlin: Ars Nocolai.

———, ed. 1987. Nationalsozialismus und "Entartete Kunst." Munich: Prestel.

Sereny, Gitta. 1995. *Albert Speer: His Battle with Truth.* New York: Alfred A. Knopf.

Sloterdijk, Peter. 1995. Weltanschauungsessayistik und Zeitdiognostik. In *Literatur der Weimarer Republik 1918 bis 1933,* ed. Bernhard Weyergraf. Munich: C. Hanser.

Smelser, Ronald, and Rainer Zitelmann. 1993. *The Nazi Elite.* New York: New York University Press. Trans. Mary Fisher.

Steinert, Marlies. 1994. *Hitler.* Munich: C. H. Beck.

Stierlin, Helm. 1976. *Adolf Hitler: A Family Perspective.* New York: Psychohistory Press.

Strasser, Peter. 1984. *Verbrechermenschen: Zur kriminalwissenschaftlichen Erzeugung des Bösen.* Frankfurt: Campus Verlag.

Thomae, Otto. 1978. *Die Propaganda-Maschinerie: Bildende Kunst und Oeffentlichkeitsarbeit im Dritten Reich.* Berlin: Gebr. Mann.

Timms, Edward. 1986. *Karl Kraus, Apocalyptic Satirist: Culture and Catastrophe in Habsburg Vienna.* New Haven, Conn.: Yale University Press.

Ullrich, Wolfgang. 1998. *Uta von Naumburg: Eine deutsche Ikone.* Berlin: Klaus Wagenbach Verlag.

Velten, Andreas-Michael, and Matthias Klein, eds. 1989. *Chaplin und Hitler.* Munich.

Warnke, Martin. 1982. Politische Ikonographie. In *Die Lesbarkeit der Kunst: Zur Geistes-Gegenwart der Ikonologie,* ed. Andreas Beyer. Berlin.

Weingart, Peter. 1985. Eugenik: Eine Angewandte Wissenschaft. Utopien der Menschenzüchtung zwischen Wissenschaftsentwicklung und Politik. In *Wissenschaft im Dritten Reich,* ed. Peter Lundgreen. Frankfurt am Main: Suhrkamp.

———. 1995. *Doppel-Leben: Ludwig Ferdinand Clauss zwischen Rassenforschung und Widerstand.* Frankfurt am Main: Campus Verlag.

Wessels, Wolfram. 1985. *Hörspiele im Dritten Reich: Zur Institutionen-, Theorie-, und Literaturgeschichte.* Bonn: Bouvier.

Weyergraf, Bernhard, ed. 1995. *Literatur der Weimarer Republik 1918 bis 1933.* Munich: C. Hanser.

Wolters, Gereon. 1999. Der "Führer" und seine Denker. *Deutsche Zeitschrift für Philosophie* 47: 223–51.

Wulf, Josef. 1963. *Die bildenden Künste im Dritten Reich: Eine Dokumentation.* Gütersloh: S. Mohn.

Wurmser, Leon. 1981. *The Mask of Shame.* Baltimore: Johns Hopkins University Press.

Zelinsky, Hartmut. 1976. *Richard Wagner: Ein Deutsches Thema.* Frankfurt am Main: Zweitausendeins.

Index

Acknowledgments

I would like to acknowledge two particularly astute readers of the manuscript or chapters thereof, Frank-Lothar Kroll and Karl Schlögel, but above all the two Hitler biographers Joachim Fest and Ian Kershaw. This study owes important perspectives to their work.

Further, I would like to thank the Warburg-Haus in Hamburg, the people at the German Historical Museum in Berlin, Monika Flacke and Wilfried Rogasch, Angelika Wesenberg from the Nationalgalerie as well as the Zentrum für Antisemitismusforschung, both also in Berlin. Moreover, the Institut für Zeitgeschichte and the collector Karl Stehle in Munich. And finally the Bayerisches Hauptstaatsarchiv, Munich, and the Bayerisches Armeemuseum, Ingolstadt, for help with images.

For conversations and pointers I would further like to thank Martin Blankenburg, Gustav Seibt, Michael Hagner, Peter Heyl, Marie-Luise Janssen-Jurreit, Anton Kaes, Peter von Matt, Peter Merseburger, Alan Posener, Nicolaus Sombart, and Bernhard Weyergraf.

Without the friendly encouragement of Jürgen Kocka and the assistance of the Wissenschaftskolleg Berlin this book would not have been possible.